Social Studies

Resource Guide

with

Core Curriculum

THE UNIVERSITY OF THE STATE OF NEW YORK · THE STATE EDUCATION DEPARTMENT

http://www.nysed.gov

ACKNOWLEDGMENTS

Many State Education Department staff members have made significant contributions to the *Social Studies Resource Guide With Core Curriculum*. *Edward Lalor and Roseanne DeFabio* originated the concept of the resource guides and served as primary motivating forces in its development. *George Gregory, JoAnn Larson, and Gary Warren,* in collaboration with the entire Social Studies group, directed this curriculum development project, reviewed and selected materials for inclusion in the document, and offered their subject area expertise to the overall document. *Anne Schiano, Jeanette Canaday, and Virginia Hammer* developed and coordinated the process used to request and review the sample learning experiences from teachers across the State that appear in this publication. *John Maryanopolis, Jan Christman, Major Capers, and Patricia Mulligan* contributed their creative and technical capabilities to the overall design. *Edith Toohey, Patricia Webster, and Judith Golombiski* served as coordinating editors.

The State Education Department acknowledges the assistance of teachers and school administrators from across New York State, as well as resources from other states and countries, in the development of the Social Studies Core Curriculum. Local and State social studies professional associations gave invaluable support and publicity to the request for learning experiences. Special thanks to *Cathie Fish Peterson* who served as the Social Studies consultant/coach for the learning experiences project.

FOREWORD

New York State is engaged in a serious effort to raise standards for students. The strategy for raising standards, as clearly articulated by Commissioner Richard Mills, includes three elements:

1. Setting clear, high expectations/standards for *all* students and developing an effective means of assessing student progress in meeting the standards;

2. Building the local capacity of schools/districts to enable *all* students to meet standards; and

3. Making public the results of the assessment of student progress through school reports.

The learning standards approved by the Board of Regents reflect the intensive, collaborative work conducted over the past few years by the State Education Department and by national groups, such as the National Center for Restructuring Education, Schools and Teaching (NCREST), the Council of Chief State School Officers, and the New Standards Project.

Learning standards have two primary dimensions. **Content standards** describe what students should know, understand, and be able to do. **Performance standards** define levels of student achievement pertaining to content. However, the teaching and learning which takes place in between is the heart of the matter. This addresses **opportunity to learn standards** and is, perhaps, the most crucial element of the entire process.

Classroom teachers have a tremendous challenge. They must bring reality to the **teaching and learning** process in order to assure that *all* of their students will perform at higher levels. They also have a wonderful opportunity for both professional and personal growth. Numberless occasions are available for teachers to really examine their instructional practice, to share what it is they do each day with their students, to work in collaboration with other teachers and students and, thereby, to grow in their understanding of the craft of teaching. In his book, *Teaching: Making Sense of an Uncertain Craft* (Teacher's College Press, 1992), Joseph McDonald states that:

> "Real teaching. . .happens inside a wild triangle of relations—among teachers, students, subject—and all points of the triangle shift continuously."

This Resource Guide with Core Curriculum has been developed to get inside this triangle and provide some clarity, to demonstrate concretely how colleagues across the State are tackling the job of standards-based teaching and learning, and to offer examples of resource/research materials which can serve to inform local curriculum development. The standards define the points of the triangle; they are the starting point. Assessments are simultaneously ends and beginnings; they serve both as benchmarks to ascertain what and how well students are learning and as springboards for further teaching and learning. Real teaching shifts continuously in response to the needs of students as they strive to understand the content and to demonstrate their understanding in a variety of assessment contexts.

The Board of Regents recognizes the diversity of students in New York State, including students with disabilities, students with limited English proficiency, gifted students, and educationally disadvantaged students, and has made a strong commitment to integrating the education of all students into the total school program. The standards in the framework apply to all students, regardless of their experiential background, capabilities, developmental and learning differences, interests, or ambitions. A classroom typically includes students with a wide range of abilities who may pursue multiple pathways to learn effectively, participate meaningfully, and work toward attaining the curricular standards. Students with diverse learning needs may need accommodations or adaptations of instructional strategies and materials to enhance their learning and/or adjust for their learning capabilities.

The *Social Studies Resource Guide with Core Curriculum* has been conceptualized using these philosophical bases. The content has been selected to address important aspects of the teaching and learning process. It is our hope that all the partners in all learning communities in New York State will find the document useful, practical, and informative.

CONTENTS

Social Studies

Overview

Why Study Social Studies?

In social studies classes students confront questions about the wonder and excitement of humankind in the world. How have humans defined themselves and made meaning of the world? How are we connected to and different from those who have come before us? What does all of humankind have in common? Who are we as a nation and what are our values and traditions? How did we get to be the way we are? How have we found unity in the midst of our diversity? Which individuals and groups contributed to our development? What are our great achievements as a nation? Where have we failed and what do we need to change? What are our responsibilities to ourselves and to society at large? What will we be like in the future? What is our place in the world? In short, social studies classes help students understand their roots, see their connections to the past, comprehend their context, recognize the commonality of people across time, appreciate the delicate balance of rights and responsibilities in an open society, and develop the habits of thoughtful analysis and reflective thinking.

In helping students answer these questions, social studies courses engage students in the study of history, geography, economics, government, and civics. Instruction draws on other disciplines such as anthropology, sociology, political science, psychology, religion, law, archaeology, philosophy, art, literature, other humanities subjects and the sciences.

Courses of study should give students the knowledge, intellectual skills, civic understandings, and dispositions toward democratic values that are necessary to function effectively in American society. Ultimately, social studies instruction should help students assume their role as responsible citizens in America's constitutional democracy and as active contributors to a society that is increasingly diverse and interdependent with other nations of the world. For example, students should be able to use the knowledge and skills acquired through social studies courses to solve problems and make reasoned decisions in their daily lives. Social studies courses should provide students with the background to conduct research in order to cast informed votes, with the skills to place conflicting ideas in context, and with the wisdom to make good judgments in dealing with the tensions inherent in society such as the enduring struggle to find the proper balance between protecting the rights of the individual and promoting the common good.

Dimensions of Teaching and Learning

As a prelude to stating the standards which define the overriding goals of social studies, it is important to define critical dimensions of teaching and learning that should be used to develop curriculum and instruction based on the standards. These dimensions can be used to establish criteria for selecting the historic, social, cultural, geographic, economic, and political understandings that students might investigate. The first two dimensions are the most critical because they define, more explicitly than the standards, the intellectual skills that students must develop.

The dimensions challenge what we teach, how we teach, and how we assess student learning. To ensure rich, engaging, and meaningful social studies programs, they should be an integral part of all social studies curriculum and instruction. The eight dimensions are:

- intellectual skills

- multidisciplinary approaches

- depth and breadth

- unity and diversity
- multiculturalism and multiple perspectives
- patterns to organize data
- multiple learning environments and resources
- student-centered teaching, learning, and assessment

1. Intellectual Skills

The development of students' intellectual skills and their ability to think reasonably, rationally, logically, and reflectively is central to each of the standards for social studies in the State of New York. Giving students a sound knowledge base goes hand in hand with expanding their intellectual skills and their ability to engage in analytical thinking. Instruction based on these standards should require social studies students at all levels to use a variety of intellectual skills to master content, probe ideas and assumptions, ask and answer analytical questions, take a skeptical attitude toward questionable arguments, acquire and organize information, evaluate data, draw conclusions, and view the human condition from a variety of perspectives.

In developing thinking skills in social studies, students should combine the disciplinary methods and processes of history, geography, economics, government, and civics with interdisciplinary approaches as they examine the past, study the present, and speculate about the future. They should learn to consult and interpret databases and a wide variety of primary sources, such as original documents, speeches, cartoons, artifacts, photos, art, music, architecture, literature, drama, dance, popular culture, biographies, journals, folklore, historic places, and oral histories.

Drawing on a variety of sources, students should take and defend positions on past and contemporary issues and controversial events by evaluating evidence and formulating rational conclusions. Furthermore, social studies classes should offer many opportunities for research activities. Students should conduct research by posing questions, identifying problems, collecting evidence, developing generalizations, presenting interpretations, and defending conclusions.

2. Multidisciplinary Approaches

Social studies courses must help students understand both the specialized processes and approaches of certain academic disciplines and the connection of ideas, information, issues, and perspectives across the disciplines. In drawing on history, the social sciences—particularly geography, economics, government, and civics—the humanities, and, to a lesser degree, the sciences, social studies provides a perfect opportunity for curriculum integration. But too often instruction presents people and events in isolation, without context.

The standards in this framework have a discipline focus combining content and process, but in each standard and its performance indicators there is provision for synthesis and connecting ideas and knowledge from one discipline to another. These synthesis statements should lead to instruction that provides a rich context of the subject and increasing intellectual proficiency.

3. Depth and Breadth

The broad scope of subject matter and the amount of material that could be included in social studies is a serious concern for social studies educators. All agree that selection of what to study is a major issue in planning instruction. The challenge for social studies curriculum developers and teachers is to design instruction that "emphasizes depth of development of important ideas within appropriate breadth of topic coverage." (Taken from "A Vision of Powerful Teaching and Learning in the Social Studies: Building Social Understanding and Civic Efficacy," *Social Education*, September 1993, p. 216). The content selected should represent worthwhile, "important ideas for understanding, appreciation, and life application." (ibid, p. 216). Finding a justifiable balance of depth and breadth is a great challenge. The standards and sample performance indicators establish broad goals. However, the K-12 scope and sequence that follows specifies concepts and content in more detail. This scope and sequence will be used to develop State social studies examinations. Curriculum needs to reflect the reality that some events are more important than others, that some have had more influence than others, that some beliefs and practices, are more defensible than others, and that knowledge and scholarship need to be reflected in the curriculum.

4. Unity and Diversity

Social studies classes that focus on local, state, and national subject matter should examine the concepts of unity and diversity in American society. Students should see how most inhabitants of the United States are united by certain shared values, practices, traditions, needs, and interests, some of which have evolved over centuries. They should understand how the nation's political institutions developed and created many of these traditions. Students should examine democratic ideals such as the dignity of humanity, the value of diversity, limited government, equity, freedom of speech, freedom of religion, freedom to pursue economic opportunity, government by consent of the governed, rule of law, and popular sovereignty. They should also understand America's political institutions including the independent judicial system, political parties, and governmental mechanisms by which to redress grievances. The changing nature of these institutions should be studied and analyzed by focusing on the interactions among individuals, groups, and society at large.

Students should also understand diversity and the multicultural context of American society. This includes the study of the various immigrations which have created the diverse nature of American people from the earliest Native American groups to the landing of the first European settlers to the forced migration of enslaved Africans to the waves of immigrants from all regions of the world, many of whom came seeking the "American Dream" of economic opportunity, political freedom, and religious toleration. Migrants from Asia, Europe, Africa, and the Americas brought with them rich strands of racial, religious, ethnic, and linguistic traditions that created and continue to influence American society. These people have made the United States one of the most diverse nations on Earth.

Study of the interactions of these diverse peoples over time provides students with a context for understanding how such diverse peoples have been able to create a strong and united nation. The development of common democratic values, institutions, and traditions, evolving through struggle, has created a people committed to a united, national identity while preserving many of their individual cultural traditions.

5. Multiculturalism and Multiple Perspectives

Contemporary multicultural issues, while linked to earlier movements for ethnic studies (1970s) and improving intergroup relations (1950s), differ from them in important ways. With respect to social studies, the primary issue is the nature and extent of inclusion of the histories and cultures, experiences, and perspectives of the diverse groups that constitute what is now the United States. "Multicultural education needs to be more broadly defined and understood so that teachers from a wide range of disciplines can respond to it in appropriate ways." (James Banks, "The Dimensions of Multicultural Education," *Multicultural Leader*, Vol. 3, 1990, p. 1). Implementation of the standards should go beyond the addition of long lists of ethnic groups, heroes, and contributions to the infusion of various perspectives, frames of reference, and content from various groups. As a result, students better understand the nature, complexity, and development of United States society as well as societies in other nations throughout the world. Effective multicultural approaches look beyond ethnic particularism, examine differences in light of universal human characteristics, focus on multiple perspectives, and attend to the mutual influences among groups within and across national boundaries. (Adapted from: James Banks, "Approaches to Multicultural Curriculum Reform," *Multicultural Leader*, Vol. 1, 1988, p. 2).

In examining different perspectives about events and issues and how ethnic, racial, gender, religious, and socio-economic background can influence opinion, students should understand that all members of a given group will not necessarily share the same view. Recognizing diversity within groups and multiple group memberships is necessary to avoid stereotyping.

Social studies classes should also help students acquire knowledge that will lead to greater tolerance and empathy for people who hold varying viewpoints on social, political, or economic issues. Students "will respect and practice basic civic values," including respect for self and others (Regents Goal 5). But accomplishing this goal is not simple. Throughout history there have been events inconsistent with basic American values. Tolerance for practices such as the Nazi Holocaust, totalitarianism, chattel slavery, the subjugation of peoples, and the infringement of human rights are not acceptable. They must be studied in historical context, but evaluated within a values perspective.

6. Patterns to Organize Information

Social studies courses should help students identify patterns for organizing data. One approach is to look for systems. A system describes how any group of facts, ideas, principles, or concepts are arranged or classified to explain the functioning of a logical or constructed whole. For example, political systems can be defined and classified as totalitarian, democratic, authoritarian, parliamentary, and so forth. Economic systems can be traditional, command, market, or combinations of these types. Social systems describe what is meant by human society, explaining the roles of men and women across time and place, the status and characteristics of various groups and classes, and "how economic, religious, cultural, and political changes have affected social life." (Taken from: *Lessons From History, The National Center for History in the Schools*, 1992, p. 25).

Another approach to patterning is to use a few broad concepts such as continuity and change, cause and effect, and interdependence, to help students make meaning out of unfamiliar people, events, and cultures. Using such concepts gives students a frame of reference for analyzing the human condition past and present.

For example, the concepts of continuity and change and interdependence can provide an interesting context for studying the impact, costs, and benefits of scientific and technological developments over eras or time periods. Focusing on interdependence can illuminate and give new meaning to breakthroughs in transportation and communication that have brought communities and nations closer together. Understanding interdependence helps students have a broader context for dealing with the phenomenon that what happens today in one part of our world can have important implications for others in distant places.

7. Multiple Learning Environments and Resources

Using local resources and different learning sites can be an effective way to let students experience firsthand how scholars conduct their work and how communities function and use the intellectual skills learned in social studies. Classes might be held, for example, in conjunction with a higher education (college/university) class, in the community at social service, government, and health agencies; at community-based organizations; in libraries and other cultural institutions; and in factories, business, or other work sites. By working and studying at these alternative learning sites, students gather information from a wide range of resources, learn how scholars contribute to their fields and how various organizations provide services.

With increased access to more advanced technologies, schools now can expand their learning environments to include databases, information-retrieval systems, and other library and museum resources throughout the world. Through Internet, electronic study groups, and international education networks, teachers can plan class-to-class long-distance learning activities. Students retrieve, process, and organize information gathered from libraries, cultural institutions, museums, archives, and government document repositories. They can share this information using computer links with other students studying similar topics, issues, and problems. The challenge is twofold: 1) to learn how to use these resources, and 2) to encourage schools and communities to expand instruction beyond the walls of the schools.

8. Student-Centered Teaching, Learning, and Assessment

In an effort to engage students more effectively in the learning process and to provide real opportunities for the application of intellectual skills, many educators have called for linking teaching, learning, and assessment to the world of the student. For this to happen, students need to participate in many different kinds of activities to gain a broad knowledge base, develop thinking skills, and take responsibility for their own learning. In addition to the more traditional learning tasks, activities should include independent reading on and investigation of topics identified by the teacher and by the student, performances that require in-depth understanding, complex questioning and thinking, and opportunities to present conclusions in new ways. Many assessment tasks should be embedded in learning activities to mesh instruction and monitoring students' progress toward the attainment of learning goals. (Grant Wiggins, "Assessment to Improve Performance, Not Just Monitor It: Assessment Reform in the Social Sciences," *Social Science Record*, Vol. 30, No. 2, Fall 1993, p. 10.) Using this approach at all levels is supported by recent studies showing that students can conceptualize and employ complex thinking skills at a very young age.

Concepts and Themes for Social Studies

Concepts and themes serve as content organizers for the vast amounts of information people encounter every day. Concepts represent mental images, constructs, or word pictures that help people to arrange and classify fragmented and isolated facts and information.

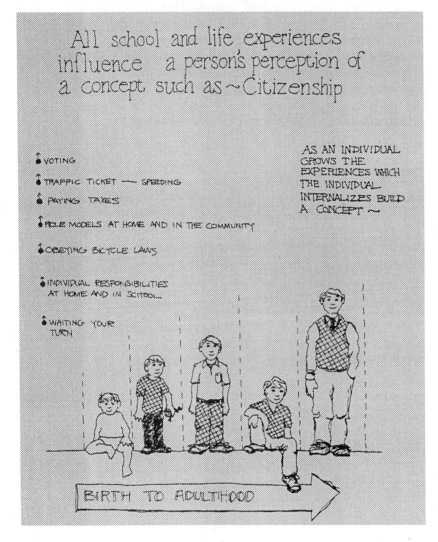

All school and life experiences influence a person's perception of a concept such as ~ Citizenship

- VOTING
- TRAFFIC TICKET —— SPEEDING
- PAYING TAXES
- ROLE MODELS AT HOME AND IN THE COMMUNITY
- OBEYING BICYCLE LAWS
- INDIVIDUAL RESPONSIBILITIES AT HOME AND IN SCHOOL
- WAITING YOUR TURN

AS AN INDIVIDUAL GROWS THE EXPERIENCES WHICH THE INDIVIDUAL INTERNALIZES BUILD A CONCEPT ~

BIRTH TO ADULTHOOD

A concept is

■ usually abstract, as opposed to concrete

■ a product of the analysis and synthesis of facts and experiences rather than a definition to be learned

■ constantly subject to change and expansion of meaning and delineation of detail, as different experiences provide settings and different relationships in new contexts.

Students construct concepts and themes as they interact with their environments. This process of concept formation is ongoing, stimulated by active, meaningful involvement, and developmental in nature. To demonstrate the developmental nature of concept learning, the concepts and themes of the K-12 social studies program are listed on each page of the scope and sequence.

Illustrated graphically, students grow to incorporate new experiences into their existing conceptual frameworks and at the same time modify that mental framework, constantly changing and expanding it.

The key concepts of the K-12 social studies program are:

History

Belief Systems means an established orderly way that groups or individuals look at religious faith or philosophical tenets.

Change involves the basic alterations in things, events, and ideas.

Conflict is a clash of ideas, interests, or wills that result from incompatable opposing forces.

Choice means the right or power to select from a range of alternatives.

Culture means the patterns of human behavior that includes ideas, beliefs, values, artifacts, and ways of making a living which any society transmits to succeeding generations to meet its fundamental needs.

Diversity means understanding and respecting others and oneself including similarities and differences in language, gender, socioeconomic class, religion, and other human characteristics and traits.

Empathy means the ability to understand others through being able to identify in one's self responses similar to the experiences, behaviors, and responses of others.

Identity means awareness of one's own values, attitudes, and capabilities as an individual and as a member of different groups.

Interdependence means reliance upon others in mutually beneficial interactions and exchanges.

Imperialism means the domination by one country of the political and/or economic life of another country or region.

Movement of People and Goods refers to the constant exchange of people, ideas, products, technologies, and institutions from one region or civilization to another that has existed throughout history.

Nationalism means the feeling of pride in and devotion to one's country or the desire of a people to control their own government, free from foreign interference or rule.

Urbanization means movement of people from rural to urban areas.

Geography

The six essential elements of geography:*

The World in Spatial Terms—Geography studies the relationships between people, places, and environments by mapping information about them into a spatial context.

Places and Regions—The identities and lives of individuals and peoples are rooted in particular places and in those human constructs called regions.

Physical Systems—Physical processes shape Earth's surface and interact with plant and animal life to create, sustain, and modify ecosystems.

Human Systems—People are central to geography in that human activities help shape Earth's surface, human settlements and structures are part of Earth's surface, and humans compete for control of Earth's surface.

Environment and Society—The physical environment is modified by human activities, largely as a consequence of the ways in which human societies value and use Earth's natural resources, and human activities are also influenced by Earth's physical features and processes.

The Uses of Geography—Knowledge of geography enables people to develop an understanding of the relationships between people, places, and environments over time—that is, of Earth as it was, is, and might be.
(*Taken from: *Geography for Life: National Geography Standards*, 1994, pp. 34-35. Permission applied for.)

Environment means the surroundings, including natural elements and elements created by humans.

Economics

Needs and Wants refer to those goods and services that are essential such as food, clothing, and shelter (needs), and those good and services that people would like to have to improve the quality of their lives, (i.e., wants—education, security, health care, entertainment).

Economic Systems include traditional, command, market, and mixed systems. Each must answer the three basic economic questions: What goods and services shall be produced and in what quantities? How shall these goods and services be produced? For whom shall goods and services be produced?

Factors of Production are human, natural, and capital resources which when combined become various goods and services (e.g., How land, labor, and capital inputs are used to produce food.).

Scarcity means the conflict between unlimited needs and wants and limited natural and human resources.

Science and technology means the tools and methods used by people to get what they need and want.

Civics, Citizenship, and Government

Justice means the fair, equal, proportional, or appropriate treatment rendered to individuals in interpersonal, societal, or government interactions.

Nation-state means a geographic/political organization uniting people by a common government.

Citizenship means membership in a community (neighborhood, school, region, state, nation, world) with its accompanying rights, responsibilities, and dispositions.

Political Systems such as monarchies, dictatorships, and democracies address certain basic questions of government such as: What should a government have the power to do? What should a government not have the power to do? A political system also provides for ways that parts of that system interrelate and combine to perform specific functions of government.

Power refers to the ability of people to compel or influence the actions of others. "Legitimate power is called authority."

Government means the
> *"formal institutions and processes of a politically organized society with authority to make, enforce, and interpret laws and other binding rules about matters of common interest and concern. Government also refers to the group of people, acting in formal political institutions at national, state, and local levels, who exercise decision making power or enforce laws and regulations."*

(Taken from: *Civics Framework for the 1998 National Assessment of Educational Progress*, NAEP Civics Consensus Project, The National Assessment Governing Board, United States Department of Education, p. 19).

Decision Making means the processes used to
> *"monitor and influence public and civic life by working with others, clearly articulating ideals and interests, building coalitions, seeking consensus, negotiating compromise, and managing conflict."*

(Taken from: *Civics Framework*, p. 18).

Civic Values refer to those important principles that serve as the foundation for our democratic form of government. These values include justice, honesty, self-discipline, due process, equality, majority rule with respect for minority rights, and respect for self, others, and property.

Human Rights are those basic political, economic, and social rights that all human beings are entitled to, such as *the right to life, liberty, and the security of person*, and *a standard of living adequate for the health and well-being of himself and of his family*. Human rights are inalienable and expressed by various United Nations Documents including the *United Nations Charter* and *Universal Declaration of Human Rights*.

Social Studies Skills

Content, concepts, and skills form the basis for the learning standards and goals for the State social studies curriculum. Social studies skills are not learned in isolation but rather in context as students gather, organize, use, and present information. These skills are introduced, applied, reinforced, and remediated within the framework of the K-12 social studies program. Students understand the importance of social studies skills as they use them to interpret, analyze, and evaluate social science concepts and understandings. Students aim for mastery of skill objectives at the same time that they pursue the other cognitive and affective objectives of the social studies program.

Learning, practicing, applying, extending, and remediating social studies skills is a developmental process. Just as students who lack social studies facts and generalizations have difficulty in applying information to new situations and analyzing new issues and historical problems, students with limited understanding of social studies skills have great difficulty in processing information, reaching higher cognitive levels, and learning independently. The teaching of social studies skills needs to be built into every classroom activity so that students engage in a systematic and developmental approach to learning how to process information.

Social studies skills can be classified into thinking skills and thinking strategies. (See: Barry K. Beyer, *Developing A Thinking Skills Program*, Boston: Allyn and Bacon, 1988). Thinking skills include the ability to gather, interpret, organize, analyze, evaluate, and synthesize information. Thinking strategies involve processing information as students engage in problem-solving, decision-making, inquiry, and conceptualizing. The following skills charts provide examples of how thinking skills and strategies can be organized throughout the social studies curriculum, K-12. The social studies standards, performance indicators, and core curriculum provide additional examples of skill development strategies.

Source: *Incorporating Skills Into Social Studies Programs K-12*. The New York State Education Department, Albany, NY.

Chart A: Social Studies Skills

I. GETTING INFORMATION

Students shall be able to:

identify a variety of sources of information:
- multiple sources of the same types of information
- varying approaches, viewpoints, interpretations
- reference works, newspapers, magazines, primary and secondary sources
- tables, graphs, charts, diagrams
- maps, globes, atlases, vocabulary
- visuals, field trips, artifacts
- listening
- observing

recognize advantages and limitations of various sources

locate sources of print and nonprint information:
- libraries (card catalogs, indices, library guides such *as Readers' Guide to Periodical Literature*)
- tables of contents, appendices, glossaries, bibliographies, and indices
- museums, galleries, public and private collections, motion pictures, television, radio, recordings, conversations, interviews

identify the types and kinds of information needed:
- recognition of information that is relevant as differentiated from information that is irrelevant
- use of subquestions and/or predicted consequences
- understanding of purposes for which information is to be used

locate information in print and nonprint sources:
- main elements
- main ideas
- supportive elements

organize collected information:
- orderly, precise, summarized notes
- cited sources

II. USING INFORMATION

Students shall be able to:

classify and/or categorize data by:
- selecting appropriate headings for data
- distinguishing between relevant and irrelevant information and events placing ideas in order, chronological and other
- developing tables, charts, maps, and graphs to clarify data and ideas
- identifying differences and similarities in data

evaluate data by:
- differentiating fact from opinion
- identifying frames of reference
- identifying value-laden words
- detecting evidence of propaganda
- evaluating author's or person's qualifications

draw inferences from data by:
- identifying relationships among the parts
- detecting inconsistencies
- weighing conflicting facts and statements

check on completeness of data and question hypotheses based on sufficiency of evidence by:
- using simple mathematical and statistical devices to analyze data
- testing, refining, and eliminating hypotheses and working out new ones where necessary
- drawing conclusions

generalize from data by:
- applying previously learned concepts and generalizations to the data or situation
- checking reasoning against basic principles of logic and looking for inconsistencies, limitations of data, and irrelevancies
- creating a broad statement which encompasses findings

scrutinize possible consequences of alternative courses of action by evaluating them in light of basic values, listing arguments for and against such proposals, and selecting courses of action most likely to achieve goals

revise generalizations in the light of new data

Chart A: Social Studies Skills

III. PRESENTING INFORMATION	IV. PARTICIPATING IN INTERPERSONAL AND GROUP RELATIONS

Students shall be able to:

speak in an effective way by:
- spending sufficient time in planning and preparing, whether it be for an individual oral report or as a member of a panel, debate, forum, etc.
  - talking in complete sentences
  - keeping to the topic
  - using appropriate visuals
  - learning and developing the skills of being a discussion leader or participant

use media and various visuals for communicating ideas by:
- previewing such media and visuals
- preparing appropriate commentary
- using a variety of media forms: films, film-strips, photographic essays, etc.
- constructing and using appropriate tables, charts, graphs, cartoons, etc.

write in an expository way by:
- thinking logically
- communicating ideas coherently
- forming generalizations based on appropriate data
- supporting such generalizations through the use of relevant factual information
- using different forms of written exposition: investigative, informative, interpretive, argumentative
- following an acceptable format that includes an introductory element, a body containing the basis of the exposition, a conclusion

recognize and use nonverbal means of communication by:
- understanding the variety of kinds of nonverbal communication: gestures, touching, eye language, etc.
- appreciating that the amount and kind of nonverbal communication varies from culture to culture

Students shall be able to:

incorporate a set of positive learning attitudes by:
- recognizing that others may have a different point of view
- observing the action of others
- being attentive to situational as well as personal causes of conflict
- listening to reason
- recognizing and avoiding stereotypes
- withholding judgment until the facts are known
- objectively assessing the reactions of other people to one's own behavior

participate in group planning and discussion by:
- following democratic procedures in helping to make group decisions
- initiating ideas
- giving constructive criticism
- suggesting means of group evaluation
- suggesting ways of resolving group differences
- anticipating consequences of group action

assume responsibility for carrying out tasks:
- individual
- group

be alert to incongruities and recognize problems

define basic issues by:
- defining terms
- identifying basic assumption
- identifying value conflicts

set up hypotheses and/or alternative courses of action

Chart B: Problem-Finding/Solving Skills

Developing skills in dealing with conflicts, incongruities, and problems facing individuals and societies has been recognized for a number of years as a major skills area. By learning to resolve problems in a classroom or a school setting, students are given practice in approaching problem tasks in a rational manner. It is hoped that by making this practice a continuing one, K-12, the process can be transferred by the students to their outside encounters. Pupils need practice in rational approaches to working out conflicts and problems. The steps in this process generally consist of having students:

1. define or identify a problem
2. hypothesize and investigate data
3. make a decision based upon step #2
4. recognize value conflicts
5. redefine the decision in attempting to accommodate any conflicts in values.

Students should be helped to realize that while one problem may be resolved by taking one action or another, the solution may well raise new problems. This realization should encourage students to weigh alternative solutions carefully.

Each person or group determines which solution to apply by a combination of rational thinking and subjective judgments which may be intuitive, value-laden, or emotional. The process of problem-solving is developmental in nature; the solution of a problem or the changing of the decision gives the student the skills needed to approach another problem. If we conceptualize the basic steps in problem-solving, we can see how attempting to solve one problem will provide the student with the experiences and skills needed to solve another problem.

Chart B applies the skills found in Chart A in an attempt to specifically apply that material to social studies content: problem-solving, conflict resolving, and decision-making. The format is that of objectives which when followed would enable students to proceed through the process. People do not necessarily proceed step-by-step through the process, but may omit steps because of previous knowledge or intuitive reaction. Students without these advantages for whatever the reason should be given many opportunities for application and practice.

Each of the steps in this process, as in the continuum, can be assessed, taught/learned, practiced, and used outside the problem context. But the student learns best when the skill is learned and practiced in the context of real or vicarious experiences requiring resolution of some kind.

Objective I:

The student will be able to find problems.

The student will:

- raise questions related to a problem
  - question beyond the who, what, when, where and include the how and why
  - generate ideas and questions which show originality, flexibility, and inventiveness

- recognize that a problem exists
  - identify several aspects of a problem area identify gaps or missing links in the events and ideas
  - recognize conflicts in data
  - point out relationships between conceptual areas not usually related

- use higher level thinking skills of comprehension, analysis, synthesis, and evaluation
  - establish a network of related facts and concepts
  - organize and bring structure to ideas, events, and things
  - reach some tentative conclusions or hypotheses
  - define basic issues, terms, assumptions, value conflicts

The student will be able to solve problems which are either presented by the teacher or which are identified by the student.

The student will:

- write a sentence or paragraph which states the problem
  - include a clear identification of the problem
- write a series of questions using stems which indicate increasing levels of complexity, for use as a guide for problem-solving
- develop a plan for problem-solving
  - include use of time, location, and date of completion
  - include appropriate age level, the objective, and available resources
  - include alternative courses of action
  - assume responsibility for carrying out individual and group tasks
- obtain information from a variety of sources by
  - using libraries (card catalogs, indices, library guides such as *Reader's Guide to Periodical Literature*)
  - using reference works, newspapers, magazines, primary and secondary sources
  - using tables of contents, appendices, glossaries, bibliographies, and indices
  - identifying main ideas and supportive elements
  - using maps, globes, atlases, visuals, field trips, artifacts, tables, graphs, charts, diagrams, people, museums, galleries, public and private collections, motion pictures, television, radio, recordings, conversations, and interviews
- evaluate the sources of information by
  - using multiple sources of the same types of information
  - varying approaches, viewpoints, interpretations
  - checking on completeness of data

- recognizing advantages and limitations of various sources
- testing, refining, and eliminating questions and working out new ones where necessary
- understanding purposes for which information was provided
- differentiating fact from opinion
- identifying frames of reference and value-laden words
- detecting evidence of propaganda
- evaluating author's or person's qualifications
- recognizing information likely to be relevant as differentiated from information likely to be irrelevant
- organize and use data by
  - categorizing data
  - selecting appropriate headings for data
  - distinguishing between relevant and irrelevant information and events
  - placing ideas in order, chronological and other
  - developing tables, charts, maps, and graphs to clarify data and ideas
  - identifying differences and similarities in data
  - drawing inferences from data
  - seeing relationships among the parts
  - recognizing inconsistencies
  - identifying conflicting views and statements
  - checking on completeness of data and questioning hypotheses based on sufficiency of evidence
  - using simple mathematical and statistical devices to analyze data
  - drawing conclusions
  - generalizing from data

- drawing on previously learned concepts and generalizations
- checking reasoning against basic principles of logic and looking for inconsistencies, limitations of data, and irrelevancies
- scrutinizing possible consequences of alternative courses of action, by evaluating them in light of basic values, listing arguments for and against such proposals, and selecting courses of action most likely to achieve goals
- when necessary, redefine the original problem or identify "new" problems by
  - arranging and recombining data to create new structures for looking at the problem
  - thinking of new ways to use old or standard ideas and things
  - thinking of novel, unique, or unusual possibilities
  - thinking of different kinds of possibilities by manipulating, adapting, and modifying ideas
  - embellishing the possibilities
- develop a product or conclusion which summarizes the information and can be shared
  - orally: mini-lecture or debate tapes of interviews or discussions, records
  - visually: chalkboard maps, diagrams, charts photographs, collages models
  - by demonstration
  - in writing
    report   letter
    article   poem
    mock diary   story
    drama

Chart B: Problem-Finding/Solving Skills

Objective III:

The student will be able to work with others engaged in problem-finding/solving skills.

The student will:

- participate in group planning and discussion by
  - following democratic procedures in helping to make group decisions
  - initiating ideas
  - giving constructive criticism
  - suggesting means of group evaluation
  - suggesting ways of resolving group differences

- incorporate a set of positive learning attitudes by
  - recognizing that others may have a different point of view
  - observing the actions of others
  - being attentive to situational as well as personal causes of conflict
  - listening to reason
  - recognizing and avoiding stereotypes
  - withholding judgment until the facts are known
  - assessing the reactions of other people to one's own behavior

- recognize and use nonverbal means of communication by
  - understanding the various kinds of nonverbal communication: gestures, touching, eye language, etc.
  - appreciating that the amount and kind of nonverbal communications varies from culture to culture.

Objective IV:

The student will be able to communicate orally, visually, and/or in writing the results of the problem-finding/solving effort.

The student will:

- speak in an effective way by
  - spending sufficient time in planning and preparing whether it be for an individual oral report or as a member of a panel, debate, forum, etc.
  - talking in complete sentences
  - keeping to the topic
  - using appropriate visuals/gestures, etc.
  - learning and developing the skills of being a discussion leader or participant

- use media and various visuals for communicating ideas by previewing such media and visuals
  - preparing appropriate commentary
  - using a variety of media forms: films, filmstrips, photographic essays, etc.
  - constructing and using appropriate tables, charts, graphs, cartoons, etc.

- use different forms of written expression: investigative/informative, interpretive, argumentative, narrative, and descriptive by
  - following an acceptable format that includes an introductory element, a body containing the basis of the work, and a conclusion
  - thinking creatively
  - thinking logically
  - communicating ideas coherently
  - forming generalizations based on appropriate data
  - supporting such generalizations through the use of relevant factual information

SKILL DEVELOPMENT PROCEDURES

The following diagram suggests a systematic procedure for skill development in the social studies. Teachers should determine at the beginning of each year the proficiency level of students in the various skill areas.

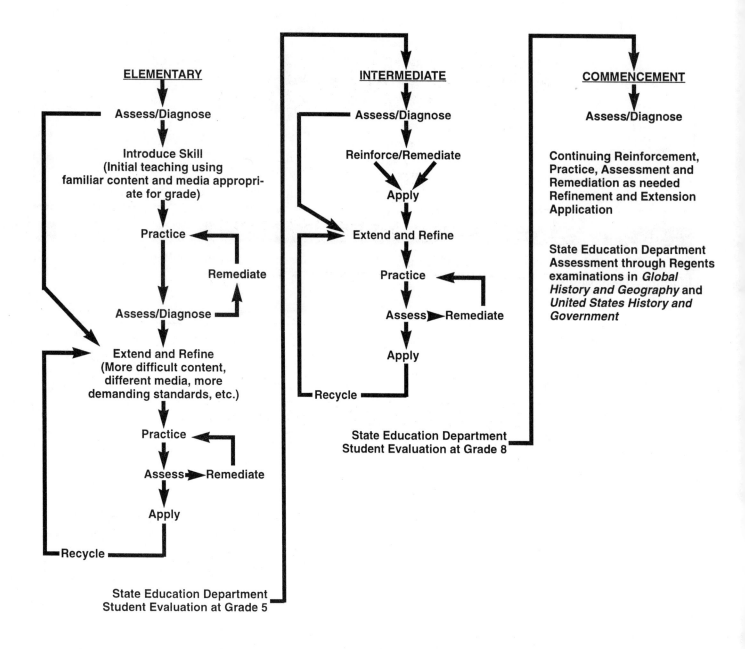

Source: *Social Studies 11: United States History and Government.* The New York State Education Department, Albany, NY.

Social Studies

Core Curriculum

Level K: Self and Others

The social studies program at the kindergarten level focuses on helping students develop awareness of themselves as growing individuals. Children's unique qualities as well as similarities to others are stressed. Children learn about values, ideas, customs, and traditions through folktales, legends, music, and oral histories. In addition, children's relationships with others in the classroom and the school become sources for social studies learning. Social interaction skills are integral to the kindergarten program. Emphasis is placed on using content that is relevant and personally meaningful. A wide range of interdisciplinary activities can help children grow and develop and gain knowledge and skills. Children also begin to learn about their role as citizens by accepting rights and responsibilities in the classroom and by learning about rules and laws.

Level K—Content Understandings	Concepts/Themes
Myself and others	
My physical self includes gender, ethnicity, and languages.	Identity
Each person has needs, wants, talents, and abilities.	
Each person has likes and dislikes.	
Each person is unique and important.	
People are alike and different in many ways.	
All people need others.	
All people need to learn and learn in different ways.	Change
People change over time.	
People use folktales, legends, music, and oral histories to teach values, ideas, and traditions.	Culture
My family and other families	
My family and other families are alike and different.	Identity
My school and school community	
What is a school?	
My neighborhood	
My neighborhood can be located on a map.	Places and Regions
Different people live in my neighborhood.	
Location of home, school, neighborhood, and community on maps and globes	Places and Regions
Land and water masses can be located on maps and a globe.	
The United States can be located on a map and a globe.	
Basic human needs and wants	
People define basic human needs and wants.	Needs and Wants
Families have needs and wants.	

People helping one another to meet needs and wants (e.g., recycling and conservation projects) People rely on each other for goods and services in families, schools, and the neighborhood. People make economic decisions and choices.	Interdependence
Symbols of citizenship Citizenship includes an awareness of the symbols of our nation. Citizenship includes an understanding of the holidays and celebrations of our nation. Citizenship includes knowledge about and a respect for the flag of the United States of America.	Citizenship and Civic Life
Rights, responsibilities, and roles of citizenship All children and adults have responsibilities at home, in school, in the classroom, and in the community. People have responsibilities as members of different groups at different times in their lives.	Citizenship and Civic Life
People making and changing rules and laws Rules affect children and adults. People make and changes rules for many reasons.	Government
People making rules that involve consideration of others and provide for the health and safety of all Families develop rules to govern and protect family members. People in school groups develop rules to govern and protect themselves.	Government

Grade 1: My Family and Other Families, Now and Long Ago

The grade 1 social studies program focuses on helping students learn about their roles as members of a family and school community. The development of identity and social interaction are stressed. The students explore self, family, and school through the five standards. Students learn about families now and long ago, as they study different kinds of families that have existed in different societies and communities. Students also begin to locate places on maps and globes and learn how maps serve as representations of physical features and objects. Building on the level K program, the grade 1 program encourages interdisciplinary learning to assist in developing the content, concepts, and skills outlined for the K-12 social studies program.

Grade 1—Content Understandings	Concepts/Themes
My family and other families Families and different kinds of families exist in all communities and societies though they may differ. Families have beliefs, customs, and traditions. Families have roles and responsibilities. Families are interdependent. Families lived in other places and at different times.	Identity Culture Interdependence

History of my family

Families have a past and they change over time; my family timeline illustrates my family's history.

Some family beliefs, customs, and traditions are based on family histories.

People of diverse racial, religious, national, and ethnic groups transmit their beliefs, customs, and traditions.

Folktales, biographies, oral histories, and legends relate family histories.

Change

Culture

My community and local region

Different events, people, problems, and ideas make up my community's history.

Folklore, myths, legends, and other cultural contributions have helped shape our community and local region.

Monuments and important places are located in my neighborhood.

Communities are connected economically and geographically.

People exchange elements of their cultures.

Change

Culture

Places and Regions

Places in my community and local region

Places can be located on maps and on a globe.

Maps and diagrams serve as representations of places, physical features, and objects.

Cardinal directions can be used to locate places and physical features.

Symbols represent places and can be used to locate geographic features and physical characteristics.

People depend on and modify their physical environments to meet basic needs.

Human Systems

Scarcity

Challenge of meeting needs and wants

Scarcity means that people's wants exceed their limited resources.

Communities provide facilities and services to help satisfy the needs and wants of people who live there.

People use tools, technologies, and other resources to meet their needs and wants.

People in communities must make choices due to unlimited needs and wants and scarce resources; these choices involve costs.

Through work, people in communities earn income to help meet their needs and wants.

Technology Needs and Wants

Economic decision making

People make decisions about how to spend the money they earn.

People work to earn money to purchase the goods and services they need and/or want.

Needs and Wants

Symbols of citizenship

Citizenship includes knowledge about and respect for the flag of the United States of America, including an understanding about its display and use.

Citizenship includes a pledge of allegiance or loyalty to the United States of America.

Citizenship and Civic Life

Rights, responsibilities, and roles of citizenship

Students, teachers, and staff are all citizens of the school community and have rights and responsibilities.

Civic Values

People making and changing rules and laws

People form governments in order to develop rules and laws to govern and protect themselves.

Key terms related to the study of government include: democracy, power, citizenship, nation-state, and justice.

People plan, organize, and make decisions for the common good.

Students can participate in problem solving, decision making, and conflict resolution.

Government

Civic Values

Decision Making

Grade 2: My Community and Other United States Communities

In the grade 2 social studies program, students explore rural, urban, and suburban communities, concentrating on communities in the United States. The student's own community can serve as an example for studying about and understanding other communities. Students study about communities from the perspectives of the five social studies learning standards. Community studies should include content examples from cultures other than the students' own, and from a variety of perspectives including geographic, socioeconomic, and ethnic. Students continue to learn how to locate places on maps and globes and how different communities are influenced by geographic and environmental factors. They also study about the rights and responsibilities of citizenship in their communities.

Grade 2—Content Understandings	Concepts/Themes
My community and region today My urban, suburban, or rural community can be located on a map. Urban, suburban, and rural communities differ from place to place. Events, people, traditions, practices, and ideas make up my urban, suburban, or rural community.	Places and Regions
Communities in the future may be different in many ways. My urban, suburban, or rural community has changed over time. Roles and responsibilities of families in rural, urban, and suburban communities change over time.	Change
People depending on and modifying the physical environment Rural, urban, and suburban communities are influenced by geographic and environmental factors. Lifestyles in rural, urban, and suburban communities are influenced by environmental and geographic factors.	Environment and Society
Challenge of meeting needs and wants Rural, urban, and suburban communities provide facilities and services to help meet the needs and wants of the people who live there. People in rural, urban, and suburban communities are producers and consumers of goods and services. People in rural, urban, and suburban communities must make choices due to unlimited needs and wants and limited resources.	Needs and Wants Factors of Production Needs and Wants
People using human, capital, and natural resources Scarcity of resources requires people to make choices in urban, rural, and suburban communities.	Factors of Production
Economic decision making Rural, urban, and suburban communities collect taxes to provide services for the public benefit. Rural, urban, and suburban communities make decisions about how to spend the taxes they collect.	Economic Systems
Symbols of citizenship Citizenship includes an understanding of the significance of the flag of the United States of America, including an understanding about its display and use. People living in urban, rural, and suburban communities celebrate various holidays.	Citizenship and Civic Life

Grade 2—Content Understandings	Concepts/Themes
Rights, responsibilities, and roles of citizenship People living in rural, urban, and suburban communities may have conflicts over rules, rights, and responsibilities. Citizens can participate in decision making, problem solving, and conflict resolution. **Making and changing rules and laws** People in rural, urban, and suburban communities develop rules and laws to govern and protect community members. Our local communities have elected and appointed leaders who make, enforce, and interpret rules and laws.	Citizenship and Civic Life Decision Making Government

Grade 3: Communities Around the World—Learning About People and Places

In the grade 3 social studies program, students study about communities throughout the world. The five social studies standards form the basis for this investigation as students learn about the social, political, geographic, economic, and historic characteristics of different world communities. Students learn about communities that reflect the diversity of the world's peoples and cultures. They study Western and non-Western examples from a variety of geographic areas. Students also begin to learn about historic chronology by placing important events on timelines. Students locate world communities and learn how different communities meet their basic needs and wants. Students begin to compare the roles of citizenship and the kinds of governments found in various world communities.

Grade 3—Content Understandings	Concepts/Themes
Cultures and civilizations What is a culture? What is a civilization? How and why do cultures change? Where do people settle and live? Why? People in world communities exchange elements of their cultures. People in world communities use legends, folktales, oral histories, biographies, autobiographies, and historical narratives to transmit values, ideas, beliefs, and traditions. People in world communities celebrate their accomplishments, achievements, and contributions. Historic events can be viewed through the eyes of those who were there, as shown in their art, writings, music, and artifacts.	Culture Empathy
Communities around the world People of similar and different cultural groups often live together in world communities. World communities have social, political, economic, and cultural similarities and differences. World communities change over time. Important events and eras of the near and distant past can be displayed on timelines. Calendar time can be measured in terms of years, decades, centuries, and millennia, using BC and AD as reference points. All people in world communities need to learn and they learn in different ways. Families in world communities differ from place to place.	Empathy Identity Change Change Culture Identity

Beliefs, customs, and traditions in world communities are learned from others and may differ from place to place.

Different events, people, problems, and ideas make up world communities.

People in world communities may have different interpretations and perspectives about important issues and historic events.

Identity
Culture

The location of world communities

World communities can be located on maps and globes (latitude and longitude).

The spatial relationships of world communities can be described by direction, location, distance, and scale.

Regions represent areas of Earth's surface with unifying geographic characteristics.

World communities can be located in relation to each other and to principal parallels and meridians.

Geographic representations such as aerial photographs and satellite-produced images can be used to locate world communities.

Earth's continents and oceans can be located in relation to each other and to principal parallels and meridians.

Places and
Regions

Physical, human, and cultural characteristics of world communities

The causes and effects of human migration vary in different world regions.

The physical, human, and cultural characteristics of different regions and people throughout the world are different.

Interactions between economic activities and geographic factors differ in world communities.

The factors that influence human settlements differ in world communities.

Human
Systems

Environment
and Society

People depending on and modifying their physical environments

People living in world communities depend on and modify their physical environments in different ways.

Lifestyles in world communities are influenced by environmental and geographic factors.

The development of world communities is influenced by environmental and geographic factors.

Physical
Systems
Environment
and Society

Challenge of meeting needs and wants in world communities

Societies organize their economies to answer three fundamental economic questions: What goods and services should be produced and in what quantities? How shall goods and services be produced? For whom shall goods and services be produced?

Human needs and wants differ from place to place.

People in world communities make choices due to unlimited needs and wants and limited resources.

People in world communities must depend on others to meet their needs and wants.

Production, distribution, exchange, and consumption of goods and services are economic decisions all societies must make.

People in world communities use human, capital, and natural resources.

People in world communities locate, develop, and make use of natural resources.

Resources are important to economic growth in world communities.

Economic
Systems

Needs and
Wants

Economic
Systems
Factors of
Production

Economic decision making in world communities

Production, distribution, exchange, and consumption of goods and services are economic decisions which all world communities must make.

Economic decisions in world communities are influenced by many factors.

Factors of
Production
Interdependence

Symbols of citizenship in world communities People in world communities celebrate various holidays and festivals. People in world communities use monuments and memorials to represent symbols of their nations.	Citizenship and Civic Life
People making and changing rules and laws People in world communities form governments to develop rules and laws to govern community members. People in world communities may have conflicts over rules, rights, and responsibilities. The processes of selecting leaders, solving problems, and making decisions differ in world communities.	Nation State Civic Values Government
Governments around the world Governments in world communities organize to provide functions people cannot provide as individuals. Governments in world communities have the authority to make, carry out, and enforce laws and manage disputes among them. Governments in world communities develop rules and laws. Governments in world communities plan, organize, and make decisions.	Nation State Decision Making Government

Grade 4: Local History and Local Government

The grade 4 social studies program builds on the students' understanding of families, schools, and communities and highlights the political institutions and historic development of their local communities with connections to New York State and the United States. The in-depth study of local government will emphasize the structure and function of the different branches and the roles of civic leaders. Students continue to learn about the rights, responsibilities, and duties of citizenship. By participating in school activities that teach democratic values, students develop a sense of political efficacy and a better understanding of the roles of supporters and leaders. Students expand their civic concepts of power, equality, justice, and citizenship as they learn about local government.

The historic study of local communities focuses on the social/cultural, political, and economic factors that helped to shape these communities. Students study about the significant people, places, events, and issues that influenced life in their local communities. Students can investigate local events and issues and connect them to national events and issues. The grade 4 program should consider the following themes and events at the local level: Native American Indians of New York State, the European encounter, the colonial and Revolutionary War period, the new nation, and the period of industrial growth and development in New York State. This chronological framework will help students to organize information about local history and connect it to United States history.

Connect local, New York State, and United States history, focusing on the following themes:

- Native American Indians of New York State
- European encounter: Three worlds (Europe, Africa, and the Americas) meet in the Americas
- Colonial and Revolutionary periods
- The new nation
- Industrial growth and expansion
- Government—local and State

Native American Indians of New York State

Native American Indians were the first inhabitants of our local region and State. Culture

The Iroquois (Haudenosaunee—People of the Longhouse) and the Algonquian were the early inhabitants of our State.

Meeting basic needs—food, clothing, and shelter Needs and Wants

Uses of the environment and how Native American Indian settlements were influenced by environmental and geographic factors

Important accomplishments and contributions of Native American Indians who lived in our community and State Culture

Three worlds (Europe, the Americas, Africa) meet in the Americas Culture

Major explorers of New York State Culture

Impacts of exploration—social/cultural, economic, political, and geographic

The slave trade and slavery in the colonies

Groups of people who migrated to our local region and into our State Environment and Society

Ways that people depended on and modified their physical environments

Colonial and Revolutionary periods

Dutch, English, and French influences in New York State Change

Lifestyles in the colonies—comparisons during different time periods Culture

Different types of daily activities including social/cultural, political, economic, scientific/technological, or religious

Ways that colonists depended on and modified their physical environments Physical Settings

Cultural similarities and differences, including folklore, ideas, and other cultural contributions that helped shape our community, local region, and State Culture

Colonial governments Government

Colonial societies were organized to answer three fundamental economic questions: What goods and services do we produce? How do we produce them? For whom do we produce them? Economic Systems

Ways of making a living in our local region and State Change

Causes for revolution: social, political, economic

Important accomplishments of individuals and groups living in our community and region

The Revolutionary War in New York State

Location of New York State Places and Regions

The significance of New York State's location and its relationship to the locations of other people and places Human Systems

Geographic features that influenced the War

Native American Indians in New York State influenced the War. Change

The war strategy: Saratoga and other local battles

Loyalists and patriots in New York State

Leaders of the Revolution

Effects of the Revolutionary War

The new nation

Foundations for a new government and the ideals of American democracy as expressed in the Mayflower Compact, the Declaration of Independence, and the Constitutions of the State of New York and the United States of America Government

The importance of the Bill of Rights Citizenship and Civic Life

Individuals and groups who helped to strengthen democracy in the United States

The roots of American culture, how it developed from many different traditions, and the ways many people from a variety of groups and backgrounds played a role in creating it

Those values, practices, and traditions that unite all Americans Culture

Industrial growth and expansion

Transportation, inventions, communication, and technology   Technology
(e.g., 1800s—Erie Canal, railroads, steamboats, turnpikes, telegraph, cable; 1900s—auto-
mobiles, subways, air travel, seaways, telephones, radios and televisions, computer)

Immigration and migration   Change
(e.g., Ellis Island; the mass starvation in Ireland, 1845-50; forced relocation of Native
American Indians in New York State)

The important contributions of immigrants to New York State

Geographic influences of industrialization and expansion   Human
(e.g., natural resources, location); the interactions between economic and geographic   Systems
factors

Urbanization: economic, political, and social impacts   Human
                                                                             Systems
Rural to urban to suburban migration
                                                                             Environment
Economic interdependence (e.g., resource use; from farm to market)   and Society

Ways of learning and public education in our community and State   Change

The labor movement and child labor

Government

Basic democratic values (Taken from: National Standards for Civics and Government)   Civic Values

The fundamental values of American democracy include an understanding of the following
concepts: individual rights to life, liberty, property, and the pursuit of happiness; the
public or common good; justice; equality of opportunity; diversity; truth; and patrio-
tism.

The fundamental values and principles of American democracy are expressed in the   Citizenship
Declaration of Independence, Preamble to the United States Constitution, Bill of Rights,   and Civic
Pledge of Allegiance, speeches, songs, and stories.   Life

Purposes of government

The basic purposes of government in the United States are to protect the rights of individuals   Government
and to promote the common good. (Taken from: National Standards for Civics and Government)

Local and State governments

An introduction to the probable consequences of the absence of government   Government

The structure and function of the branches of government of New York State and local
governments, including executive, legislative, and judicial branches

The meaning of key terms and concepts related to government, including democracy,
power, and citizenship

The United States Constitution and the Constitution of the State of New York and their   Civic Values
respective Bills of Rights were developed as written plans for organizing the functions
of government and safeguarding individual liberties.

Representatives in the legislative, executive, and judicial branches at the local, State, and   Government
national levels of government and how they are elected or appointed to office

People elect and/or appoint leaders who make, enforce, and interpret laws.

Citizenship and the rules and responsibilities of citizenship in the classroom, school, home,   Citizenship
and local community   and Civic

Citizenship includes an awareness of the holidays, celebrations, and symbols of our nation,   Life
including the flag of the United States of America, its proper display, and use.

Effective, informed citizenship involves duties such as voting, jury service, and other service
to the local community.

Citizens can participate in political decision making and problem solving at the local, State,   Nation State
and national levels.

Grade Five: The United States, Canada, and Latin America

The grade 5 social studies program stresses geographic, economic, and social/cultural understandings related to the United States, Canada, and nations in Latin America today. These perspectives build on and reinforce historic and political content about the United States included in the grade 4 social studies program. When appropriate, the grade 5 program should use contemporary examples of case studies to help students understand the content understandings that follow. The content understandings were developed to assist in selecting specific factual information and case studies. For additional guidance in selecting content, case studies, activities, evaluation questions, and resources, consult *Social Studies Program: Grade 5* (New York State Education Department, 1987).

Grade 5—Content Understandings	Concepts/Themes
History of the United States, Canada, and Latin America	
Different ethnic, national, and religious groups, including Native American Indians, have contributed to the cultural diversity of these nations and regions by sharing their customs, traditions, beliefs, ideas, and languages.	Culture
Different people living in the Western Hemisphere may view the same event or issue from different perspectives.	Empathy
The migration of groups of people in the United States, Canada, and Latin America has led to cultural diffusion because people carry their ideas and ways of life with them when they move from place to place.	Interdependence
Connections and exchanges exist between and among the peoples of Europe, sub-Saharan Africa, Canada, Latin America, the Caribbean, and the United States. These connections and exchanges include social/cultural, migration/immigration, and scientific/technological.	
Key turning points and events in the histories of Canada, Latin America, and the United States can be organized into different historical time periods. For example, key turning points might include: 18th-century exploration and encounter; 19th-century westward migration and expansion, 20th-century population movement from rural to suburban areas.	Change
Important historic figures and groups have made significant contributions to the development of Canada, Latin America, and the United States.	Identity
Industrial growth and development and urbanization have had important impacts on Canada, Latin America, and the United States.	Change
Geography of the United States, Canada, and Latin America	
Maps and other geographic representations, tools, and technologies such as aerial and other photographs, satellite-produced images, and computer models can be used to gather, process, and report information about the United States, Canada, and Latin America today.	Places and Regions
Political boundaries change over time and place.	
Different geological processes shaped the physical environments of the United States, Canada, and Latin America.	Physical Systems
The nations and regions of the Western Hemisphere can be analyzed in terms of spatial organization, places, regions, physical settings (including natural resources), human systems, and environment and society. A region is an area that is tied together for some identifiable reason, such as physical, political, economic, or cultural features.	
The physical and human characteristics of places in the United States, Canada, and Latin America today	Human Systems

Culture and experiences influence people's perceptions of places and regions in the United States, Canada, and Latin America today.	Environment and Society
The characteristics, distribution, and complexity of cultures found in the United States, Canada, and Latin America	
Human actions modify the physical environments of the United States, Canada, and Latin America.	Human Systems

The economies of the United States, Canada, and Latin American nations

Concepts such as scarcity, supply and demand, markets, opportunity costs, resources, productivity, economic growth, and systems can be used to study the economies and economic systems of the United States, Canada, and Latin America.	Economic Systems
Individuals and groups in the United States, Canada, and Latin America attempt to satisfy their basic needs and wants by utilizing scarce capital, natural, and human resources.	Needs and Wants
Types and availability of resources are important to economic development in the United States, Canada, and Latin America today.	Factors of Production
The nations of North, Central, and South America depend on one another for various resources and products they need.	Interdependence
Production, distribution, exchange, and consumption of goods and services are economic decisions which the nations of North and South America must make.	Factors of Production
Science and technology have influenced the standard of living in nations in North, Central, and South America.	
Exchanges of technologies, plants, animals, and diseases between and among nations of the Americas and Europe and sub-Saharan Africa have changed life in these regions.	Technology
Nations in North, Central, and South America form organizations and make agreements to promote economic growth and development.	Interdependence
As the economic systems of the global community have become more interdependent, decisions made in one nation or region in the Western Hemisphere have implications for all nations or regions.	Economic Systems

The governments of the United States, Canada, and Latin American nations

Across time and place, the people of the Western Hemisphere have held differing assumptions regarding power, authority, governance, and law.	Interdependence Citizenship and CivicLife
Basic civic values such as justice, due process, equality, and majority rule with respect for minority rights are expressed in the constitutions and laws of the United States, Canada, and nations of Latin America.	Civic Values Government
Constitutions, rules, and laws are developed in democratic societies in order to maintain order, provide security, and protect individual rights.	Citizenship and Civic Life
The rights of citizens in the United States are similar to and different from the rights of citizens in other nations of the Western Hemisphere.	
The roles of citizenship are defined by different constitutions in the Western Hemisphere.	
Governmental structures vary from place to place, as do the structure and functions of governments in the United States, Canada, and Latin American countries today.	Government
Concepts such as civic life, politics, and government can be used to answer questions about what governments can and should do, how people should live their lives together, and how citizens can support the proper use of authority or combat the abuse of political power. (Adapted from: *Civics Framework for the 1998 NAEP*, p. 19)	Government
Legal, political, and historic documents define the values, beliefs, and principles of constitutional democracy. In the United States these documents include the Declaration of Independence, the United States Constitution, and the Bill of Rights. In Canada these documents include the British North America Act and the Canadian Bill of Rights.	Civic Values
Citizenship in the United States, Canada, and nations of Latin America includes an awareness of the patriotic celebrations of those nations. In the United States these celebrations include:	Citizenship and Civic Life

Lincoln's Birthday, Washington's Birthday, Independence Day, Dr. Martin Luther King, Jr. Day, Labor Day, Columbus Day, Veterans Day, Thanksgiving Day, Election Day, Flag Day, Memorial Day, and Conservation Day.

International organizations were formed to promote peace, economic development, and cultural understanding. The United Nations was created to prevent war and to fight hunger, disease, and ignorance.

Government

Grade 6: The Eastern Hemisphere

The grade 6 social studies program emphasizes the interdependence of all people, keying on the Eastern Hemisphere. Many of the lessons and activities for this grade level draw on specific examples of nations and regions in the Eastern Hemisphere chosen by the district. It is highly recommended that lessons also compare and contrast this specific information with similar data from the United States, Canada, and Latin America.

The grade 6 program focuses on a social science perspective emphasizing the interaction of geography and economics. The core disciplines of geography and economics are used to develop and draw relationships and understandings about social/cultural, political, and historic aspects of life in the Eastern Hemisphere. Historical insights are used as a means of developing a total perspective rather than an organizing framework. The focus should be on major turning points that seque into the 7th-grade social history of the United States.

Each district has a responsibility for extending the student's content examples from cultures other than the student's own, and from a variety of geographic, socioeconomic, ethnic, and racial groups.

Grade 6—Content Understandings	Concepts/Themes
History of Eastern Hemisphere nations	
Time can be measured in years, decades, centuries, and millennia.	Change
Key turning points and events in the histories of Eastern Hemisphere nations can be organized into different historical time periods. The study of Eastern Hemisphere nations should include countries from each continent.	
Different peoples may view the same event or issue from different perspectives.	Identity
The Neolithic Revolution was a technological development that radically changed the nature of human society.	Change
As the river civilizations of the Eastern Hemisphere (Mesopotamia, Egypt, China, and the Indus Valley) turned to agriculture, world populations grew. (Focus on two of these.)	Needs and Wants
Across time, technological innovations have had both positive and negative effects on people, places, and regions. For example, the invention of writing made more complex civilizations and more advanced technologies possible.	Technology
Civilizations and cultures of the Eastern Hemisphere (China, India, Greece, and Rome) are explored through the arts and sciences, key documents, and other important artifacts.	Culture

Religions and other belief systems (animism, ancestor worship, Confucianism, Hinduism, Buddhism, Judaism, Christianity, Islam) have both united and divided the peoples of the Eastern Hemisphere.	Culture
The civilizations and cultures of the Eastern Hemisphere have contributed important ideas, beliefs, and traditions to the history of humankind.	Identity
From earliest times, networks of trade have connected the various civilizations of the Eastern Hemisphere.	Interdependence
Individuals and groups in the Eastern Hemisphere have played important roles and made important contributions to world history.	Culture
Slavery has existed across eras and regions in the Eastern Hemisphere.	Empathy
Internal and external factors altered civilizations in the Eastern Hemisphere and eventually contributed to their decline.	Change
During the late Middle Ages and Renaissance periods, new long distance trade routes emerged, linking the peoples of Africa, Asia, and Europe.	Interdependence
In Europe, the Renaissance was marked by major achievements in literature, music, painting, sculpture, and architecture.	Culture
The crime of genocide crosses cultures and eras. Jews and other groups experienced devastation at the hands of Nazi Germany.	Empathy/ Values

Geography of Eastern Hemisphere nations

The use of various grids, symbols, and notations makes it possible to locate specific places and indicate distance and direction in the Eastern Hemisphere.	The World in Spatial Terms
Special purpose maps can be used to show various geographic aspects of Earth's surface as seen in the Eastern Hemisphere.	
The nations and regions of the Eastern Hemisphere can be studied using maps, globes, aerial and other photographs, satellite-produced images, and models. (Taken from: *National Geography Standards*, 1994).	Human Systems
The nations and regions of the Eastern Hemisphere can be analyzed in terms of spatial organization, places and regions, physical settings (including natural resources), human systems, and environment and society.	The World in Spatial Terms
A region is an area which is tied together for some identifiable reason, such as physical, political, economic, or cultural features.	Place and Regions
Civilizations developed where geographic conditions were most favorable.	Human Systems
Geographic features and climatic conditions in the Eastern Hemisphere influence land use.	
The geographic diversity of the Eastern Hemisphere has significantly influenced physical mobility and the course of human development.	Physical Systems
The migration of groups of people has led to cultural diffusion because people carry their ideas and ways of life with them when they move from one place to another.	Human Systems
Overpopulation and widespread poverty threaten the political stability of some nations in the Eastern Hemisphere.	Nation State
Urbanization has been a characteristic of the civilizations and cultures of the Eastern Hemisphere.	Human Systems
The environment is affected by people as they interact with it.	Environment and Society
The effects of geographic conditions are moderated by technology.	Technology

Economies of Eastern Hemisphere nations

The three basic economic questions that must be addressed by every society are: What goods and services shall be produced and in what quantities? How shall goods and services be produced? For whom shall goods and services be produced?	Economic Systems
The ways resources are used impact the economic, political, and historic aspects of life throughout the world.	Scarcity
People have unlimited needs and wants which they must meet with limited resources.	Needs and Wants
A nation with limited natural resources must interact with other nations to secure its resource needs.	
In many areas of the world, improvement in life expectancy and health care have contributed to rapid population growth.	
Throughout the Eastern Hemisphere, there is great diversity in the standard of living.	
Concepts such as scarcity, supply and demand, markets, opportunity costs, resources, productivity, economic growth, and systems can be used to study the economies and economic systems of the various nations of the Eastern Hemisphere.	Economic Systems
The economic systems of the world have become an interdependent network.	Interdependence
Different economic systems have evolved to deal with economic decision making.	Economic Systems
In traditional economies, decision making and problem solving are guided by the past.	
In market economies, decisions regarding what is to be produced are based upon patterns of consumer purchases.	
In command economies, decisions regarding the control and use of the means of production and distribution are planned by the government.	
In many countries "mixed" economies have evolved to deal with economic decision making.	
Nations have joined with one another in organizations which promote economic development and growth. For example, the European Union was formed to promote free trade and a common economic policy among its members.	Interdependence
As the economic systems of the global community have become more interdependent, decisions made in one nation or region have implications for all regions.	Economic Systems
Some of the nations of the Eastern Hemisphere play leadership roles in the global economy.	Interdependence
Many of the communist nations and former communist nations in the Eastern Hemisphere are moving toward market economies.	Economic Systems

Governments of Eastern Hemisphere nations

Family, clan, and tribal groups act to maintain law and order.	Government
As settlement patterns changed, new forms of political order developed to meet the more complex needs of societies.	
Across time and place, the people of the Eastern Hemisphere have held differing assumptions regarding power, authority, governance, and law.	Values
Governments change over time and place to meet the changing needs and wants of their people.	Government
Present systems of government have their origins in the past.	
The values of Eastern Hemisphere nations affect the guarantee of human rights and how human needs are met.	Values
The values of Eastern Hemisphere nations are embodied in their constitutions, statutes, and important court cases.	
In modern political states, formalized governmental structures play a major role in maintaining social order and control.	Government

Political boundaries change over time and place.	Change
The extent to which human rights are protected becomes a key issue in totalitarian societies.	Values
International organizations were formed to promote peace, economic development, and cultural understanding. The United Nations was created to prevent war and to fight hunger, disease, and ignorance.	
Citizens of the nations of the Eastern Hemisphere have rights and responsibilities as defined by their constitutions and by other laws of their nations.	Citizenship and Civic Life

Grades 7-8 Social Studies: United States and New York State History

Social studies content in grades 7 and 8 focuses on a chronologically organized study of United States and New York State history. Course content is divided into 11 units, tracing the human experience in the United States from pre-Columbian times to the present, and tying political, geographic, economic, and social trends in United States history to parallel trends and time frames in New York State history.

Teachers are encouraged to develop and explore the 11 units of study within a two-year time frame. Knowledge of the needs of students and availability of instructional material and resources will assist in determining which units to study in which grades. The grades 7-8 course builds on and seeks to reinforce skills, concepts, and content understandings introduced in the K-6 program. It is, therefore, a vital link in the overall goals of the K-12 social studies program, and provides a solid content base in American history, allowing the grade 11 course to do greater justice to the study of the United States as a developing and fully developed industrial nation. By including hemispheric links to Canada and Mexico when appropriate, teachers will provide students a model for the global connections they will discover in the grades 9 and 10 social studies program. Mr. Henry Mueller, Niskayuna CSD; Ms. Susan Owens, East Greenbush CSD; and Ms. Elizabeth Guardenier, Bedford CSD authored the Connections column for this core curriculum.

UNIT ONE **The Global Heritage of the American People Prior to 1500**	**UNIT SEVEN** **An Industrial Society**
UNIT TWO **European Exploration and Colonization of the Americas**	**UNIT EIGHT** **The United States as an Independent Nation in an Increasingly Interdependent World**
UNIT THREE **A Nation is Created**	**UNIT NINE** **The United States Between the Wars**
UNIT FOUR **Experiments in Government**	**UNIT TEN** **The United States Assumes Worldwide Responsibilities**
UNIT FIVE **Life in the New Nation**	**UNIT ELEVEN** **The Changing Nature of the American People from World War II to the Present**
UNIT SIX **Division and Reunion**	

Source: *7 & 8 Social Studies: United States and New York State History.* The New York State Education Department, Albany, NY.

UNIT ONE: THE GLOBAL HERITAGE OF THE AMERICAN PEOPLE PRIOR TO 1500

I. HISTORY AND THE SOCIAL SCIENCES: THE STUDY OF PEOPLE

Content	Standards	Concepts/Themes	Connections

Objectives:
1. To understand the social scientific method and techniques used by social scientists to study human cultures
2. To understand how the social scientific method and techniques can be applied to a variety of situations and problems
3. To formulate social science questions and define social science issues and problems
 	
Content Outline:
A. History and the other social sciences provide a framework and methodology for a systematic study of human cultures
  1. The role of history and the historian
  2. The other social sciences including anthropology, economics, geography, political science, psychology, and sociology
B. The social scientific method as a technique for problem solving and decision making
	1,2,3,4,5	Change	ESSENTIAL QUESTIONS:
			- How do historians research the past?
			- What are primary and secondary sources?
			- How do anthropology, economics, geography, political science, psychology, and sociology assist historians as they uncover the past, research the present and forecast the future?
			
			CLASSROOM IDEAS:
			• Analyze primary and secondary source documents to understand the purpose and usefulness of both.
			• Create a web graphic organizer to demonstrate the interrelationships of the social sciences.
			
			These understandings may be introduced at the beginning of both grades 7 and 8, but should be infused and applied whenever possible in all units.

II. GEOGRAPHIC FACTORS INFLUENCE CULTURE

Content	Standards	Concepts/Themes	Connections
Objectives: 1. To describe the relationships between people and environments and the connections between people and places 2. To describe the reasons for periodizing history in different ways 3. To map information about people, places, and environments 4. To identify and compare the physical, human, and cultural characteristics of different regions and people 5. To understand the geography of settlement patterns and the development of cultural patterns			ESSENTIAL QUESTIONS: - How do maps provide information about people, places, and physical and cultural environments? - How does geography affect how and where people live? - How did geographic factors affect political, social, and economic aspects of life in the Mayan, Aztec, and Incan cultures?

II. GEOGRAPHIC FACTORS INFLUENCE CULTURE, continued

Content	Standards	Concepts/Themes	Connections

Content Outline:
A. Theories attempt to explain human settlement in the Americas
  1. Anthropologists theorize that Asians migrated across a land bridge between Asia and the Americas
  2. Native American Indians believe in indigenous development with migration patterns in both directions
B. Geographic factors affected the settlement patterns and living conditions of the earliest Americans
C. Major Native American civilizations in Central and South America
  1. The Aztecs
  2. The Mayas
  3. The Incas
	2,3
	
	2,3,4
		Movement
		World in
		  Spatial Terms
		
		Environment
		and Society
		Science and
		Technology
		Culture
		Diversity
			CLASSROOM IDEAS:
			• Use physical, topographical, political, and economic maps to compare and contrast the three early American civilizations.
			• Conduct a three-way debate to discuss the comparative contributions and accomplishments of the Mayan, Aztec, and Incan civilizations.
			• Create a timeline to track major events and dates.
			Teachers may wish to introduce the six essential elements of the national geography standards at this point (see Standard 3).
			
			Developments in Aztec, Mayan, and Incan culture (i.e., religion, government, technology) may be compared and contrasted to contemporaneous European culture (see Standard 2: Establishing time frames, exploring different periodizations. . .).

III. IROQUOIAN AND ALGONQUIAN CULTURES ON THE ATLANTIC COAST OF NORTH AMERICA

Content	Standards	Concepts/Themes	Connections
Objectives: 1. To know the social and economic characteristics such as customs, traditions, child-rearing practices, gender roles, foods, and religious and spiritual beliefs that distinguish different cultures and civilizations 2. To map information about people, places, and environments 3. To understand the worldview held by native peoples of the Americas and how that worldview developed 4. To understand the ways different people view the same event or issues from a variety of perspectives			ESSENTIAL QUESTIONS: - What are the political, social, and economic characteristics of each North American culture? - How did geography influence the development of each culture? - How did the North American world perspective differ from that of the Europeans?
Content Outline: A. Iroquois (Haudenosaunee—People of the Longhouse) and Algonquian People adapted to the environment in which they settled 1. Geographic regions of New York	3	Places and Regions	CLASSROOM IDEAS: • Use New York State maps and local resources to examine the Native American inhabitants of our region. • Examine Native American folklore, stories, and oral history as an interdisciplinary project with English.

III. IROQUOIAN AND ALGONQUIAN CULTURES ON THE ATLANTIC COAST OF NORTH AMERICA, continued

Content	Standards	Concepts/Themes	Connections
2. Diversity of flora and fauna 3. Seasons and weather patterns 4. Kinds of settlements and settlement patterns B. The Iroquois (Haudenosaunee) developed cultural patterns that reflected their needs and values 　1. Creation and religious beliefs 　2. Importance of the laws of nature and the wise use of natural resources 　3. Patterns of time and space 　4. Family and kinship 　5. Education 　6. Government: Iroquois Confederacy and political organizations at the village level (tribal organization) 　7. Conceptions of land ownership and use 　8. Language C. Algonquian Culture 　1. Spiritual beliefs 　2. Spatial patterns	1,3,4,5 1,4	Culture Human Systems Environment and Society Belief Systems Government Diversity Belief Systems	• Study the natural resources and climate of the Native American habitat as an interdisciplinary project with science. • Compare the Iroquois and the Algonquians in a Venn diagram. • Make a chart to show the political, economic, and social aspects of life in the Native American culture areas of North America. • The effects of geographic environment on culture may be examined further by comparing and contrasting Iroquois and Algonquian cultures with native people in other cultural areas, such as the Great Tribes. In later units, comparison of the effect of environment may also be made with colonists (UNIT TWO) and Preindustrial Age pioneers (UNIT FIVE).

IV. EUROPEAN CONCEPTIONS OF THE WORLD IN 1500

Content	Standards	Concepts/Themes	Connections
Objectives: 1. To understand the worldview held by Europeans prior to 1500 2. To understand the ways different people view the same event or issues from a variety of perspectives **Content Outline:** A. European knowledge was based on a variety of sources 　1. Accounts of early travelers and explorers 　2. A variety of different maps 　3. Writing of ancient scholars 　4. Guesswork 　5. Oral traditions and histories B. Different worldviews and ethnocentrism resulted in many misconceptions	2	Movement of People and Goods	ESSENTIAL QUESTIONS: - How was the European worldview demonstrated in maps, artwork, and writing from the time? - How can misconceptions lead to stereotyping? CLASSROOM IDEAS: • Rate the reliability of a variety of sources of information. • Find examples of stereotyping in historic and current events.

UNIT TWO: EUROPEAN EXPLORATION AND COLONIZATION OF THE AMERICAS

I. EUROPEAN EXPLORATION AND SETTLEMENT

Content	Standards	Concepts/Themes	Connections
Objectives: 1. To understand major turning points, such as the European exploration of and settlement in the Americas, by investigating the causes and other factors that brought about change and the results of these changes 2. To understand the impacts of European settlement on Native American Indians and Europeans 3. To investigate why people and places are located where they are located and what patterns can be perceived in these locations 4. To understand the ways different people view the same event or issues from a variety of perspectives			**ESSENTIAL QUESTIONS:** - What were the major causes and effects of European exploration? - How have the events of exploration and colonization been interpreted throughout history? Teachers may convey the changes in interpretation of history (see Standard 1: The skills of historical analysis. . .) when describing differences between "discovery" and "contact."

Content Outline:
A. Motivating factors
  1. Technological improvements in navigation
  2. Consolidation of political power within certain countries in Europe
  3. Desire to break into the Eastern trade markets
  4. Missionary zeal
B. Geographic factors influenced European exploration and settlement in North and South America
  1. Effects of weather and natural hazards on the Atlantic crossings
  2. Characteristics of different physical environments in the Americas and where different Europeans settled
  3. The development of "New England," "New France," "New Netherland," and "New Spain"
	2,4,5
	
	3
		Interdependence
		Science and Technology
		Power
		
		Environment and Society
			CLASSROOM IDEAS:
			• Draw/make models of new inventions that aided exploration.
			• Compare and contrast New England, New France, and New Spain in political, social, and economic aspects of life.
			• Study the Columbian exchange as an interdisciplinary unit with science.
			• Compare the Dutch and English settlement of the New York region, using a Venn diagram. Compare political, social, and economic characteristics of the settlements.
			<u>Suggested Document</u>: Journal of Christopher Columbus

I. EUROPEAN EXPLORATION AND SETTLEMENT, continued

Content	Standards	Concepts/Themes	Connections
C. Effects of exploration and settlement in America and Europe—human-induced changes in the physical environment in the Americas caused changes in other places 　1. Iintroduction of new diseases to the Americas was devastating 　2. The continued growth of population in the colonies resulted in the unjust acquisition of Native American lands 　3. New types of foods improved both European and Native American health and life spans 　4. Economic and political changes in the balance of power in Europe and the Americas 　5. Introduction of African slaves into the Americas	2,4	Culture Imperialism Belief Systems Economic 　Systems	The results of contact (the Columbian exchange) may be viewed in terms of positive and negative effects for all participants; however, students should be aware that some groups were unwilling participants.
D. Exploration and settlement of the New York State area by the Dutch and English 　1. Relationships between the colonists and the Native American Indians 　2. Similarities between the Europeans and Native American Indians 　　a. The role of tradition 　　b. The importance of families and kinship ties 　　c. The hierarchical nature of the community and family 　　d. The need to be self-sufficient 　3. Differences 　　a. Ideas about land ownership 　　b. Roles of men and women 　　c. Beliefs about how people from different cultures should be addressed 　4. Rivalry between the Dutch and English eventually resulted in English supremacy		Culture Imperialism Belief Systems Economic 　Systems	A look at eastern and western Long Island or settlements in the Hudson Valley can form a basis for a comparison between Dutch and English rule in New York.

II. COLONIAL SETTLEMENT: GEOGRAPHIC, POLITICAL, AND ECONOMIC FACTORS

Content	Standards	Concepts/Themes	Connections
Objectives: 1. To investigate the roles and contributions of individuals and groups in relation to key social, political, cultural, and religious practices throughout the colonial period 2. To investigate why people and places are located where they are located and what patterns can be perceived in these locations 3. To explain how societies and nations attempt to satisfy their basic needs and wants by utilizing scarce capital and natural and human resources 4. To analyze how the values of colonial powers affected the guarantee of civil rights and made provisions for human needs			ESSENTIAL QUESTIONS: - What are the political, economic, and social roots of colonial settlements in the Americas? - What role did geography play in the settlement pattern? This section includes comparisons between European nations, their colonial objectives, and the methods they used to reach their goals (see Standard 2: The study of world history requires an understanding of world cultures and civilizations. . .).

Content Outline:
A. English colonies: New England, Middle Atlantic, Southern
  1. Reviewed as a geographic region—criteria to define regions, types of regions
  2. Settlement patterns: who? when? why?
  3. Economic patterns emerge to meet diverse needs: agricultural and urban settlements
  4. Political systems: the Mayflower Compact
  5. Social order
	1,2,3,4,5	Culture
		Places and
		  Regions
		Human
		  Systems
		Economic
		  Systems
		Political
		  Systems
			CLASSROOM IDEAS:
			• Compare and contrast the English, French, and Spanish colonies, using a chart to show political, economic, and social differences.
			• Map the geography of each type of colony. Use the geography to explain differences in the types of settlements in each region.
			<u>Suggested Document</u>: The Mayflower Compact (1620): ". . .do enact, constitute, and frame, such just and equal laws. . ."

B. New Netherland; French and Spanish colonies
  1. Reviewed as a geographic region—types, connections between regions
  2. Settlement patterns: who? when? why?
  3. Economic patterns emerge to meet diverse needs
  4. Political systems and social order
	1,2,3,4,5	Culture
		Diversity
		Places and
		  Regions
		Human
		  Systems
		Economic
		  Systems
		Political
		  Systems
			• Comparison between English colonial governments and the Iroquois Confederacy

III. LIFE IN COLONIAL COMMUNITIES

Content	Standards	Concepts/Themes	Connections
Objectives: 1. To understand how European and other settlers adapted to life in the American colonies 2. To classify major developments in categories such as social, political, geographic, technological, scientific, cultural, or religious 3. To investigate the roles and contributions of individuals and groups in relation to key social, political, cultural, and religious practices throughout the American colonies 4. To present geographical information in a variety of formats, including maps, tables, graphs, charts, diagrams, and computer-generated models 5. To investigate how people in colonial communities answered the three fundamental economic questions (What goods and services shall be produced and in what quantities? How shall goods and services be produced? For whom shall goods and services be produced?) and solved their economic problems 6. To analyze how values of a people affect the guarantee of civil rights and make provision for human needs			**ESSENTIAL QUESTIONS:** - How did settlers adapt to the new environments? - How did colonial life evolve? - What kinds of political systems were created to provide order and justice? - What kinds of economic systems were created to answer the three basic economic questions: What goods and services shall be produced? How shall they be produced? For whom shall they be produced? - What kinds of social systems were created to satisfy religious and cultural needs? Teachers may emphasize the evolving nature of colonial culture that was different than that of the English mother country and resulted in a new American culture.

Content Outline:
 A. Colonial communities were the center of social, economic, and political life and tended to develop along European patterns
   1. Variations were found
     a. Religious-based
     b. Slave and free black communities
     c. Place of national origin
   2. The social structure promoted interdependence
   3. Social goals promoted community consciousness over individual rights
   4. Role of religions
     a. Puritans
     b. Quakers
	1,4	Culture
		 Diversity
		 Interdependence
		 Belief Systems
			CLASSROOM IDEAS:
			 • Recreate colonial communities on paper or in play form to show how people lived in colonial times.
			 • Case study of a colonial community.
			 • Field trip to a restored colonial village.
			 • Make maps to show geographic features that affected colonial life such as waterways, topography, climate, and natural resources.
			 • Study colonial life through historical fiction during an interdisciplinary English/social studies unit.
			 • Use primary sources such as letters, diaries, inventories, newspapers, and documents such as the Mayflower

Content	Standards	Concepts/Themes	Connections

c.   Catholics
    d.   Others
  5. Survival demanded cooperation and a strong work ethic
  6. Importance of waterways
  7. A hierarchical social order created social inequity
			Compact to bring the colonial era to life.
			• Create colonial newspapers addressing political, social, and economic issues and events in different colonies. Each paper should have a patriot or loyalist point of view.

B. Structure and roles of colonial families
  1. Nuclear families made up the basic social and economic unit
  2. Authority and obligation followed kinship lines
  3. Roles of family members
	1	Culture	Teachers may emphasize differences between New England, Middle, and Southern colonies (see Standard 3: Geography can be divided into six essential elements. . .). Differences observed in this unit may be reviewed while studying the writing of the Constitution (UNIT FOUR), sectionalism in the Preindustrial Age (UNIT FIVE), and the causes of the Civil War (UNIT SIX).

C. Life in colonial communities was a reflection of geographic and social conditions
  1. Impact of physical environments on
    a.   Travel
    b.   Communication
    c.   Settlements
    d.   Resource use
  2. Social conditions led to
    a.   Different forms of government
    b.   Varying roles of religion
    c.   Inequalities of economic conditions
    d.   Unequal treatment of blacks
  3. The impact of geographic and social conditions could be seen in the divergent landholding systems that developed in:
    a.   New England
    b.   New Netherland: patroonship system
    c.   Southern colonies: plantation system
  4. Life in French and Spanish colonies was both similar to and different from life in other colonies
	1,2,3,4
	
	1,2
		Diversity
		Places and
		  Regions
		Human
		  Systems
		Economic
		  Systems
		
		Diversity	

UNIT THREE: A NATION IS CREATED

I. BACKGROUND CAUSES OF THE AMERICAN REVOLUTION

Content	Standards	Concepts/Themes	Connections
Objectives: 1. To understand the economic, political, and social causes of the American Revolution 2. To compare and contrast different interpretations of key events and issues in New York State and United States history and explain reasons for these different accounts 3. To investigate how people in the United States and throughout the world answer the three fundamental economic questions and solve basic economic problems 4. To consider the nature and evolution of a constitutional democracy			ESSENTIAL QUESTIONS: - What are the political, economic, and social causes of the American Revolution? - How did public opinion evolve in regard to the movement for independence?

Content Outline:
A. Economic factors
  1. Growth of mercantilism: triangular trade
  2. Rise of an influential business community in the colonies
  3. Cost of colonial wars against the French
	1,3	Imperialism
		Economic
		  Systems
			CLASSROOM IDEAS:
			• Map the triangular trade route. Use a key.
			• Use primary sources such as the "Join or Die" cartoon and the text of the Albany Plan of Union to examine the French and Indian War as a cause of the Revolution.

B. Political factors
  1. The role of the British Civil War
  2. Periods of political freedom in the colonies
  3. Impact of the French and Indian War: Albany Plan of Union
  4. Political thought of the Enlightenment influenced prominent colonial leaders
	5	Decision
		  Making
			• Read writings of Enlightenment thinkers such as John Locke and Baron de Montesquieu to analyze the rationale for the movement toward independence.
			• Identify factors which led to a colonial American identity.
			
			Students should define and apply major economic concepts such as scarcity, supply and demand, markets, opportunity costs, resources, productivity, economic growth, and systems (see Standard 4).

C. New social relationships between European powers and the American colonies: development of a new colonial identity	1	Culture Identity	

II. THE SHIFT FROM PROTEST TO SEPARATION

Content	Standards	Concepts/Themes	Connections
Objectives: 1. To understand how colonists' concerns regarding political and economic issues resulted in the movement for independence 2. To compare and contrast different interpretations of key events and issues in New York State and United States history and explain reasons for these different accounts 3. To consider the nature and evolution of constitutional democracies			ESSENTIAL QUESTIONS: - How did colonial protests against Britain escalate? - What specific British policies galvanized public opinion in the colonies?

Content Outline:
A. New British attitude toward colonies following victory over France
  1. Colonies could not protect themselves
  2. Colonies were not paying a fair amount toward their support
	1,2	Imperialism	CLASSROOM IDEAS:
			• Illustrate famous quotations from the period with relevant cartoons or drawings in an interdisciplinary art/social studies unit.
			• Compare the shaping of public opinion in colonial times with modern media techniques in an interdisciplinary English/social studies unit.

B. New British policies antagonized many Americans
  1. Various acts of Parliament such as the Quebec Act
  2. New tax policies and taxes: Stamp Act and others
  3. Other acts of repression: Zenger case and others
	4,5	Economic Systems
		Scarcity
		Justice
			Role-play differing views on separation from England given differing political, economic, and social interests.
			<u>Suggested Documents</u>: Thomas Paine, *Common Sense* ; artwork, Paul Revere's engraving of the Boston Massacre (1770)

C. Public opinion was shaped in different forums
  1. Political bodies
  2. Public display and demonstration
  3. Print media
	1,5	Choice
		Decision Making
			Students should apply the concept of multiple causation while reviewing the events leading up to the American Revolution (see Standard 1: The skills of historical analysis. . .).

D. Wide variety of viewpoints evolved
  1. Complete separation
  2. More autonomy for the colonies
  3. No change in status quo: the Loyalist position
	1	Choice	

III. EARLY ATTEMPTS TO GOVERN THE NEWLY INDEPENDENT STATES

Content	Standards	Concepts/Themes	Connections
Objectives: 1. To understand how the colonists attempted to establish new forms of self-government 2. To investigate key turning points in New York State and United States history and explain why these events or developments are significant 3. To compare and contrast different interpretations of key events and issues in New York State and United States history and explain reasons for these different accounts 4. To describe how ordinary people and famous historic figures in the local community, State, and the United States have advanced the fundamental democratic values, beliefs, and traditions expressed in the Declaration of Independence, the New York State and United States constitutions, the Bill of Rights, and other important historic documents			ESSENTIAL QUESTIONS: - What political systems were established in the colonies? - How did the American Revolution parallel the move toward self-government? - What were the major documents of the independence movement and how were they produced?

Content Outline:
A. The Revolution begins
   1. Early confrontations
   2. Important leaders
   3. First Continental Congress
B. The Second Continental Congress represented the first attempt to govern the colonies
   1. "Republican" government
   2. Request for state constitutions and political systems
   3. Asserting independence
C. A movement for independence evolved from the political debate of the day
D. Declaration of Independence
   1. Origins
   2. Content
   3. Impact
   4. Ideals embodied
E. Independence creates problems for New Yorkers
   1. Organizing new State government
   2. Economic problems
   3. Political factions
   4. Slavery
   5. Recruiting soldiers for the war
	1
	
	5
	
	1,4,5
		Change
		Nationalism
		
		Political Systems
		Decision Making
		
		Change
		Nationalism
		Belief Systems
		Political Systems
			CLASSROOM IDEAS:
			• Research the lives of people who made a difference in the American Revolution.
			• After a roundtable sharing session, students can rate the individuals according to their relative contributions to the Revolution.
			• Rewrite the Declaration of Independence in modern language.
			• Write a constitution for New York State and compare it to the original 1777 version.
			• Role-play the writing of the Declaration of Independence, using words and music from *1776*.
			• Make a timeline of events in the move toward independence.
			<u>Suggested Documents</u>: Declaration of Independence (1776), New York State Constitution of 1777
			
			Student understanding of the Declaration of Independence (i.e., unalienable rights, the purpose of government) is essential in understanding such related topics as the Bill of Rights (UNIT FOUR), the Progressive movement (UNIT SEVEN), and the civil rights movement (UNIT ELEVEN).

IV. MILITARY AND POLITICAL ASPECTS OF THE REVOLUTION

Content	Standards	Concepts/Themes	Connections
Objectives: 1. To understand how the colonists were able to unite against British power to win a major military and political victory 2. To understand how events on the national level influenced and affected New Yorkers 3. To complete well-documented and historically accurate case studies about individuals and groups who represent different ethnic, national, and religious groups 4. To explain how societies and nations attempt to satisfy their basic needs and wants by utilizing capital, natural, and human resources			**ESSENTIAL QUESTIONS:** - What was the military course of the Revolutionary War? - What role did leadership, commitment, and luck play in the American victory over the British? - What political, economic, and social issues brought people together against the British?

Content Outline:
A. Strategies of the principal military engagements
  1. Washington's leadership
  2. New York as the object of strategic planning
  3. Evolution of the war from the North to the South: Lexington and Concord to Saratoga to Yorktown
	1	Change	**CLASSROOM IDEAS:**
			• Map the battle sites and create a detailed key.
			• Analyze artwork from the Revolutionary era, e.g., "Washington Crossing the Delaware" by Emanuel Leutze; analyze music from the period, e.g., "Yankee Doodle"

B. Role of the Loyalists
  1. In New York City
  2. Colonists of Nova Scotia, Quebec, and Prince Edward Island did not join the Revolution
    a. Refuge for Loyalists
    b. Staging ground for attacks on New York's patriots
	1	Identity	• Read biographies of little-known participants in the Revolution—Marquis de Lafayette, Baron von Steuben, Lydia Darragh, Peter Salem—to accent the multicultural backgrounds of the participants.
			• View a reenactment of a Revolutionary battle or engage a reenactment soldier to visit your classroom and speak about military life.

C. The outcome of the war was influenced by many factors
  1. Personalities and leadership
  2. Geography: importance of various physical features
  3. Allocation of resources
  4. Foreign aid: funds and volunteers
	3	Change
		Scarcity
			• Make supply-and-demand graphs for wartime supplies such as ammunition, shoes, wool.
			<u>Suggested Documents</u>: Thomas Paine, *The Crisis*; artwork, "Washington Crossing the Delaware,"; song, "Yankee Doodle"

5. Role of women, blacks, and Native American Indians 6. Haphazard occurrences of events: the human factor	4	Environment and Society	
7. Clash between colonial authority and Second Continental Congress	5	Power	

V. ECONOMIC, POLITICAL, AND SOCIAL CHANGES BROUGHT ABOUT BY THE AMERICAN REVOLUTION

Content	Standards	Concepts/Themes	Connections
Objectives: 1. To understand how a revolution can have a profound effect on the economic, political, and social fabric of a nation 2. To analyze how the values of a nation affect the guarantee of human rights and make provisions for human needs 3. To present information by using media and other appropriate visuals such as tables, charts, and graphs to communicate ideas and conclusions 4. To understand how different experiences, beliefs, values, traditions, and motives cause individuals and groups to interpret historic events and issues from different perspectives 5. To explain how societies and nations attempt to satisfy their basic needs and wants by utilizing capital, natural, and human resources			**ESSENTIAL QUESTIONS:** - How did the Revolution change people's lives? - How have these political, economic, and social changes been interpreted by different analysts? - Was the American Revolution a "revolution" for all of the participants? Why or why not?

Content Outline:
A. On the national level
  1. Britain gave up claims to govern
  2. Slavery began to emerge as a divisive sectional issue because slaves did not receive their independence
  3. American economy was plagued by inflation and hurt by isolation from world markets
	1,4	Change
		Scarcity
			CLASSROOM IDEAS:
			• Make a graphic organizer to show the effects of the Revolution on international, national, and state levels.
			• Classify the effects into political, social, and economic categories.

B. In New York State
  1. The effects of the American Revolution on the Iroquois Confederacy
  2. Disposition of Loyalist property and resettlement of many Loyalists after the Revolution to Canada, thus changing the French/British balance
  3. A republican ideology developed which emphasized shared power and citizenship participation
	1,5	Change
		Power	

V. ECONOMIC, POLITICAL, AND SOCIAL CHANGES BROUGHT ABOUT BY THE AMERICAN REVOLUTION, continued

Content	Standards	Concepts/Themes	Connections
C. In the Western Hemisphere 　1. Britain did not accept the notion of American dominance of the hemisphere 　2. The remaining British colonies in Canada strengthened their ties to Great Britain 　3. Many leaders in South America drew inspiration from American ideas and actions in their struggle against Spanish rule	1,2	Imperialism Nationalism	

UNIT FOUR: EXPERIMENTS IN GOVERNMENT

I. THE ARTICLES OF CONFEDERATION AND THE CRITICAL PERIOD

Content	Standards	Concepts/Themes	Connections
Objectives: 1. To understand the earliest formal structure of the United States government as expressed in the Articles of Confederation 2. To consider the nature and evolution of constitutional democracies	1,5	Political Systems	ESSENTIAL QUESTIONS: - What is a government? - How did the first United States government operate?
Content Outline: A. Need for a formal plan of union 　1. Historical precedent: the Albany Plan of Union 　2. Development of state constitutions 　3. Inadequacy of Continental Congress as a national government B. Development of a formal plan of government 　1. Draft and debate in Congress, 1776-1777 　2. Ratification by the states, 1778-1781; period of operation, 1781-1789	1,5	Choice Decision Making	CLASSROOM IDEAS: • Make a Venn diagram to show the powers of the national government and the powers of the state governments under the Articles of Confederation. • Debate the pros and cons of the Articles of Confederation. • Chart the weaknesses and achievements of the Articles of Confederation government. Suggested Documents: Albany Plan of Union (1754), Articles of Confederation
C. The structure of government under the Articles of Confederation	5	Government	

I. THE ARTICLES OF CONFEDERATION AND THE CRITICAL PERIOD, continued

Content	Standards	Concepts/Themes	Connections

1. Congress was the only branch of government
2. Each state had equal representation
3. Congress's power under the Articles included:
  a. Making war and peace
  b. Conducting foreign and Native American Indian affairs
  c. The settlement of disputes between and among states
  d. Issuance of currency and borrowing			

D. The Articles suffered from many weaknesses 1. Indirect representation 2. No coercive power; decisions more advisory than binding: e.g., Shay's Rebellion 3. Lack of national executive and judicial functions 4. Lack of taxing power 5. Difficulty in passing legislation	4,5	Scarcity Political Systems	
E. The Articles did have several achievements and contributions 1. The Land Ordinance of 1785 and the Northwest Ordinance, 1787 2. Developed the privileges and immunities of citizenship 3. Developed the concept of limited government	3,5	Human Systems Government	

II. THE NEW YORK STATE CONSTITUTION OF 1777

Content	Standards	Concepts/Themes	Connections
Objectives: 1. To understand the earliest formal structure of the New York State government, as expressed in the first New York State Constitution 2. To compare and contrast the development and evolution of the United States and New York State constitutions 3. To understand how the United States and New York State			ESSENTIAL QUESTIONS: - How did the New York State Constitution reflect the principles embodied in the Declaration of Independence? - How are the New York State Constitution and the United States Constitution alike? How are they different? - The Declaration of Independence ended the legality of colonial

Content	Standards	Theme/Concepts	Connections
constitutions support majority rule but also protect the rights of the minority			government. Students should understand that all states developed new institutions and laws and that several, such as New York, influenced the writing of the United States Constitution.

Content Outline:
A. Adopted by convention without submission to popular vote
  1. Included Declaration of Independence
  2. Influence of leaders such as John Jay
	5
	
	1,5
		Power
		
		Government
			CLASSROOM IDEAS:
			• Make a three-way Venn diagram to compare the Articles of Confederation, the New York State Constitution, and the United States Constitution.
			• Evaluate the positive and negative aspects of the State laws.
			• Diagram the three branches of the new State government.

B. Chronology of the document
  1. Draft and debate in convention, 1776-1777
  2. Period of operation, 1777-1822
	
	5
		
		Government
			Suggested Documents: United States Constitution, New York State Constitution of 1777, Articles of Confederation, Declaration of Independence

C. Form of early State government
  1. Similar to colonial government
  2. Governor with limited authority and three-year term
  3. Inclusion of rights and liberties
  4. First system of State courts
  5. Limited franchise
  6. Bicameral legislature: Senate—four-year term; Assembly—one-year term			

D. Effectiveness
  1. Smoother functioning than national government under the Articles of Confederation
  2. Cumbersome administrative procedures
  3. Excessive use of veto procedures
  4. A model for the United States Constitution of 1787
	5	Political Systems	

III. THE WRITING, STRUCTURE, AND ADOPTION OF THE UNITED STATES CONSTITUTION

Content	Standards	Concepts/Themes	Connections
Objectives:			**ESSENTIAL QUESTIONS:**
1. To understand the importance of the events that took place during the writing and adoption of the United States Constitution and to recognize their significance beyond their time and place			- Why was a new constitution necessary?
2. To explain what citizenship means in a democratic society, how citizenship is defined in the Constitution and other laws of the land, and how the definition of citizenship has changed in the United States and New York State over time			- How does the Constitution embody the principles of the Declaration of Independence?
3. To understand that the New York State Constitution, along with other documents, served as a model for the development of the United States Constitution			- How do federalism and separation of powers promote those principles in the Constitution?
4. To compare and contrast the development and evolution of the constitutions of the United States and New York State			
5. To define federalism and describe the powers granted to the national and state governments by the United States Constitution			
Content Outline:			**CLASSROOM IDEAS:**
A. Annapolis Convention, 1786	1,5	Change	• Hold a mock constitutional convention in the classroom. Assign roles.
1. Impracticality of correcting weaknesses in Articles of Confederation			• Examine compromises made by federalists and anti-federalists, slave owners and non-slave owners in the Constitution.
2. Need for an improved form of government without losing key elements of a new philosophy of government			• Write the Preamble in your own words and memorize it.
3. Decision to write a constitution			• Make a graphic organizer of Articles I, II, and III.
B. Constitutional Convention: setting and composition			• Write the Bill of Rights in your own words.
C. Major issues	5	Political Systems	• Illustrate one of the first 10 amendments.
1. Limits of power: national versus state			• Have a Bill of Rights guessing gallery.
2. Representation: slaves and apportionment			• Use primary sources such as the Federalist Papers to identify key issues in the convention debates and the ratification debates. Hold a mock ratification convention for New York State.
3. Electoral procedures: direct versus indirect election			
4. Rights of individuals			
D. The need for compromise	5	Decision	• Propose new amendments to the Constitution.
1. The issue of a "federal" or a "national" government			

III. THE WRITING, STRUCTURE, AND ADOPTION OF THE UNITED STATES CONSTITUTION, continued

Content	Standards	Concepts/Themes	Connections
2. The Great Compromise on representation 3. The three-fifths compromise on slavery 4. The commerce compromises			<u>Suggested Documents</u>: United States Constitution (1789), Bill of Rights, the Federalist Papers
E. The underlying legal and political principles of the Constitution 1. Federalism 2. Separation of powers 3. Provisions for change 4. Protection of individual rights	5	Political Systems Government	This section focuses upon the basic civic values of the American people (Standard 5: Civics, Citizenship, and Government) as implemented through laws and practices.
F. The Constitution and the functioning of the federal government 1. The Preamble states the purpose of the document 2. The structure and function of the legislative, executive, and judicial branches (Articles I, II, III) 3. The relation of states to the federal union (Article IV) 4. Assuming the responsibility for a federal system (Article VI)	5	Government	
G. The Constitution as a living document 1. The elastic clause and delegated power facilitate action 2. Amendment procedure as a mechanism for change (Article V) 3. The Bill of Rights 4. Supreme Court decision (e.g., *Tinker* v. *DesMoines School District*, 1969)	1,5	Government Justice	As a "living document," the Constitution should be revisited throughout grades 7 and 8 as questions of the federal government are examined, as well as when amendments are added.
H. The evolution of an "unwritten constitution" 1. Political parties 2. The President's cabinet 3. President's relation to Congress 4. Committee system in Congress 5. Traditional limitations on Presidential term	1,5	Change Power	

I. The ratification process
1. The debates in the states, especially New York State
2. The Federalist Papers
3. Poughkeepsie Convention
   a. Federalists—Hamilton
   b. Anti-Federalists—Clinton
4. Formal ratification of the Constitution and launching of the new government
5. The personal leadership of people like Washington, Franklin, Hamilton, Madison
	1,5	Change Decision Making	<u>Suggested Document</u>: Excerpts from the Federalist Papers

UNIT FIVE: LIFE IN THE NEW NATION

I. NEW GOVERNMENT IN OPERATION

Content	Standards	Concepts/Themes	Connections
Objectives: 1. To understand how the new nation established itself and began to operate 2. To understand how political parties emerged in response to concerns at the local, State, and national levels 3. To understand how civic values reflected in the United States and New York State constitutions have been implemented through law and practice 4. To understand the relationship between and the relative importance of United States domestic and foreign policies over time 5. To analyze the role played by the United States in international politics, past and present 6. To explain how societies and nations attempt to satisfy their basic needs and wants by utilizing scarce capital, natural, and human resources 7. To investigate how people in the United States solve the three fundamental economic questions and solve basic economic problems 8. To complete well-documented and historically correct case studies about individuals and groups who represent different ethnic, national, and religious groups, including Native American Indians in New York State and the United States			ESSENTIAL QUESTIONS: - What political, economic, and social issues did the new nation confront under the Constitution? - How did perspectives differ on the new nation's viability under the Constitution?

Content Outline:
A. Washington as President: precedents
B. Establishing stability
  1. Hamilton's economic plan
  2. The Whiskey Rebellion
  3. Preserving neutrality: the French Revolution, Citizen Genet, Jay, and Pinckney treaties
	4
	
	1,2
		Scarcity
		
		Interdependence
			CLASSROOM IDEAS:
			• Research important people and events and devise skits to show how precedents were set in the new nation, e.g., *Marbury v. Madison*, Pinckney Treaty, Louisiana Purchase, Monroe Doctrine.
			• Make a cause-and-effect diagram for the War of 1812.

I. NEW GOVERNMENT IN OPERATION

Content	Standards	Concepts/Themes	Connections

4. Political parties
5. Election of 1800
6. Judicial review: *Marbury* v. *Madison* (1803)
C. Expanding the nation's boundaries
  1. Pinckney Treaty with Spain
  2. Louisiana Purchase
  3. War of 1812: guaranteeing boundaries
  4. Monroe Doctrine: sphere of influence
  5. Purchase of Florida
  6. Native American Indian concessions and treaties
	5
	1,2,3
		Government
		Interdependence
		Places and
		  Regions
			• Map the geographic expansion westward and the ensuant expansion of slavery.
			<u>Suggested Documents</u>: Journals of Lewis and Clark; song, "The Star Spangled Banner"
			
			Teachers may describe the implementation of the new government as a period of experimentation.

D. Challenges to stability
  1. French and English trade barriers and the Embargo Act
  2. War of 1812: second war for independence
	1,2	Change	

E. The Era of Good Feelings
  1. Clay's American system
  2. Internal expansion: new roads, canals, and railroads
  3. Protective tariffs
  4. National assertions: Marshall's decision, i.e., *Gibbons* v. *Ogden* (1824)
  5. Extension of slavery by the Missouri Compromise
  6. Threats to Latin America: the Monroe Doctrine
  7. Disputed election of 1824
	1,3,5	Economic
		  Systems
		Government	

II. THE AGE OF JACKSON

Content	Standards	Concepts/Themes	Connections
Objectives: 1. To understand how an American consciousness began to develop during Jackson's administration 2. To complete well-documented and historically accurate case studies about individuals and groups who represent different ethnic, national, and religious groups, including Native American Indians, in New York State and the United States at different times and in different locations			ESSENTIAL QUESTIONS: - What was Jacksonian democracy? - How did Jackson's policies affect the political, economic, and social life of the nation? - How was Jackson viewed by different groups of people?

Content	Standards	Concepts/Themes	Connections
3. To describe how ordinary people and famous historic figures in the local community, the State, and the United States have advanced the fundamental democratic values, beliefs, and traditions expressed in the Declaration of Independence, the New York State and United States constitutions, the Bill of Rights, and other important historic documents			
4. To gather and organize information about the important achievements and contributions of individuals and groups living in New York State and the United States			
5. To develop conclusions about economic issues and problems by creating broad statements that summarize findings and solutions			
Content Outline:			CLASSROOM IDEAS:
A. The age of the "common man"	1,5	Identity	• Use primary source documents to examine differing points of view on Jackson's policies.
1. Expansion of suffrage		Citizenship	• Make cartoons to show differing viewpoints.
2. Citizenship		Power	
3. Election of 1828			• Evaluate Jackson as a President, using his actions as a basis.
4. Jackson: man, politician, President			• Write a journal as a Cherokee boy or girl traveling the Trail of Tears.
5. The "spoils system"			
6. New political parties			
B. Jackson's Native American policy reflected frontier attitudes	1,5	Diversity Human Rights	Teachers may examine the irony of Jacksonian democracy that extended suffrage while supporting Indian removal.
1. Some Native Americans resisted government attempts to negotiate their removal by treaty			
2. Government policy of forced removals (1820-1840) resulted in widespread suffering and death			Students should have the opportunity to explore interactions between Native American Indians and European Americans on the American frontier and to examine these interactions from a variety of perspectives.
3. Native American Indian territory			
C. Intensifying sectional differences	3,4,5	Places and Regions Factors of Production Government	In UNIT SIX, review growing sectionalism as an underlying cause of the Civil War.
1. Protective tariff, 1828			
2. Nullification controversy, 1828, 1832			
3. Clay's compromise tariff, 1833			

III. PREINDUSTRIAL AGE: 1790-1860s

Content	Standards	Concepts/Themes	Connections
Objectives: 1. To understand the way of life of an agrarian society 2. To understand the nature and effect of changes on society and individuals as the United States began to move from an agrarian to an industrial economy 3. To describe historic events through the eyes and experiences of those who were there 4. To explore the meaning of American culture by identifying the key ideas, beliefs, patterns of behavior, and traditions that help define it and unite all Americans 5. To define basic economic concepts such as scarcity, supply and demand, markets, resources, and economic systems 6. To understand how scarcity requires people and nations to make choices that involve costs and future considerations 7. To develop conclusions about economic issues and problems by creating broad statements that summarize findings and solutions 8. To describe the relationships between people and environments and the connections between people and places 9. To use a number of research skills (e.g., computer databases, periodicals, census reports, maps, standard reference works, interviews, surveys) to locate and gather geographical information about issues and problems			**ESSENTIAL QUESTIONS:** - How did social and economic life change as the United States began to move from an agrarian to an industrial society? - How did geographic factors contribute to this change? - How do statistics support historians as they research an era? Several of the understandings in this section (i.e., rise of technology, industrialization and urbanization, reform) are mirrored in the second half of the 19th century (UNIT SEVEN). Teachers may use examples from this section to illustrate key ideas from Standard 1 (The study of New York State and United States history requires an analysis of the development of American culture.).

Content Outline:
 A. Portrait of the United States, 1800
    1. Agriculturally based economy
    2. Urban centers on the coast
    3. Poor communication and transportation systems
    4. Self-sufficiency
    5. Regional differences
	3	Human Systems	**CLASSROOM IDEAS:**
			 • Use local resources for primary and secondary sources—statistics, documents, artwork from the time—to create a portrait of life in 1800.
			 • Produce a case study of the Erie Canal and compare it with a canal or roadway in your local area.

B. Patterns of community organization, work, and family life in agrarian America	1	Culture	• Show the interaction of social and economic changes, e.g., education, temperance, women's rights.

III. PREINDUSTRIAL AGE: 1790-1860s, continued

Content	Standards	Concepts/Themes	Connections

C. Technological changes altered the way people dealt with one another
1. Improved transportation made travel and communication easier
2. Greater ties between communities were possible
3. The Erie Canal and its impact
  a. Reasons for building the Erie Canal
  b. Technology involved in its construction
  c. Types and sources of labor: ethnic and racial labor force
  d. Results of building the Erie Canal
	3,4	Science and Technology Environment and Society	• Study the abolition movement and map the major stations on the underground railroad.
			• Examine the literature and art of the time and how it reflects American life, e.g., writings of James Fenimore Cooper, Washington Irving, Herman Melville, and Henry David Thoreau and art of the Hudson River School.
			• Map sectional differences in 1860. Show political, economic, and social differences.
			
			Teachers may wish to work with museums or local historical societies to explore this topic.

D. The impact of early industrialization and technological changes on work and workers, the family, and the community 1. An increase in the production of goods for sale rather than personal use 2. Increased purchasing of what was formerly produced at home 3. Emergence of a new work ethic	4	Factors of Production Science and Technology	
E. Family roles changed, affecting society in general 1. Changing role of women 2. Childhood became a more distinct stage of life 3. Roles of private agencies	1	Culture	Suggested Documents: Frederick Douglass, Independence Day speech at Rochester (1852): "What, to the American slave, is your Fourth of July?"; song, "The Erie Canal"

F. Slavery and abolition
1. Review the institution of slavery
2. The meaning and morality of slavery
3. Abolition movement
  a. Leadership (Harriet Tubman, Garrison, and others)
  b. Activities (e.g., freedom trail and the underground railroad)
4. Abolition in New York State
5. Canada's role
6. Effects of abolition
	5	Human Rights	

G. Social changes 1. Religious revival 2. Women's rights 3. Mental hospital and prison reform	1	Culture Change	Suggested Document: Seneca Falls Declaration of Sentiments (1848): "...that all men and women are created equal."

Content	Standards	Concepts/Themes	
4. Education			
5. Temperance			
H. An American culture begins to emerge	1	Culture	
1. Literature			
2. Art			
I. Portrait of the United States, 1860	1,3,4	Diversity Places and Regions Factors of Production	
1. Growth brought about many changes and regions—the spatial patterns of settlement in different regions in the United States			
a. The size and shape of communities			
b. Environmental impacts due to development of natural resources and industry— human modification of the physical environment			
c. The diversity of people within the larger communities and regions			
d. The ability of the political system within communities to deal with deviance			
e. The Preindustrial Age took place at different times in different places			
2. The North		Places and Regions Human Systems	
a. Industrial base			
b. Increasing population			
c. Urban centered—"causes and consequences of urbanization"			
3. The South			
a. Agricultural base (cotton)			
b. Impact of Industrial Revolution on agriculture			
c. Increasing slave population			

UNIT SIX: DIVISION AND REUNION

I. UNDERLYING CAUSES OF THE CIVIL WAR

Content	Standards	Concepts/Themes	Connections
Objectives: 1. To understand the series of events and resulting conditions that led to the American Civil War 2. To understand how different experiences, beliefs, values, traditions, and motives cause individuals and groups to interpret historic events and issues from different perspectives 3. To participate in a negotiating and compromising role-playing activity that mirrors the attempts at political compromise in the 1850s			ESSENTIAL QUESTIONS: - What political, social, and economic factors caused the Civil War? - What were the conflicting perspectives on slavery? - What kind of nation did the founding fathers create? - What is to be done with the institution of slavery? - Must sectionalism ultimately lead to disunion?

Content Outline:
A. Territorial expansion and slavery
   1. The secession of Texas, 1836
   2. The Mexican War, 1846-1848
   3. Oregon Territory
   4. The westward movement and its effects on the physical, social, and cultural environments
	1,2	Change
		
		Geography
			CLASSROOM IDEAS:
			• Categorize the causes of the Civil War.
			• Define the northern and southern perspectives on these issues.
			• Map the westward movement and its effects.
			• Use primary sources to examine art, literature, and documents relevant to the pre-Civil War period.

B. The emotional impact of slavery
   1. *Uncle Tom's Cabin*
   2. John Brown's raid on Harper's Ferry
   3. Fugitive slave laws
	1,5	Diversity
		Decision
		  Making
			• Role-play the compromises and debates.
			<u>Suggested Document</u>: Harriet Beecher Stowe, *Uncle Tom's Cabin*

C. Failure of political compromise
   1. Compromise of 1850
   2. Kansas-Nebraska Act, 1854
   3. Founding of the Republican Party, 1854-1856
   4. *Dred Scott* v. *Sanford* (1857)
   5. Lincoln-Douglas debate, 1858
   6. Election of 1860
   7. Firing on Fort Sumter, 1861
	1,5	Change
		Decision
		  Making	

II. THE CIVIL WAR BREAKS OUT

Content	Standards	Concepts/Themes	Connections
Objectives:			ESSENTIAL QUESTIONS:
1. To understand the development and progress of the Civil War			- What was the course of the Civil War?
2. To investigate key turning points in the Civil War in New York State and United States history and explain why these events or developments are significant			- What were its political, social, and economic ramifications?
3. To map information about people, places, and environments			
4. To describe the relationships between people and environments and the connections between people and places			
5. To identify and collect economic information related to the Civil War from standard reference works, newspapers, periodicals, computer databases, textbooks, and other primary and secondary sources			
Content Outline:			CLASSROOM IDEAS:
A. The Presidency of Lincoln	1,5	Power	• Biographical focus on Abraham Lincoln.
1. Personal leadership			• Analyze the strengths and weaknesses of the North and the South at the beginning of the war.
2. Opposition			
3. Emancipation Proclamation			• Categorize the advantages and disadvantages—political, economic, and social.
B. Advantages and disadvantages of each side	1,4,5	Diversity Factors of Production Government	
1. Advantages			• Use local resources to examine the role of your community in the Civil War and local attitudes toward it.
a. South			
1) Military leadership			• Use primary sources such as diaries, letters, songs, and photographs to study personalities and issues involved in the Civil War.
2) Commitment of people to preserve their way of life			
b. North			• Write the Gettysburg Address in your own words and memorize part of it.
1) Effective navy			
2) Larger army			• Map the progress of the war and make a detailed key.
3) Manufacturing			
4) Agricultural production			
5) Transportation system			Suggested Documents: Lincoln's Gettysburg Address (1863): ". . .government of the people, by the people, for the people. . .,"; Emancipation Proclamation; artwork, Matthew Brady's Civil War photographs
2. Disadvantages			
a. South			
1) Lacked manufacturing			
2) Lacked a navy			
3) Not prepared for war			
b. North			
1) Lacked quality military leadership			
2) Not prepared for war			
c. The military and political dimensions of the war			

II. THE CIVIL WAR BREAKS OUT

Content	Standards	Concepts/Themes	Connections

3. Geographic factors influenced the war's progress and out-come—role of physical and other barriers
4. Major campaigns evolved around a changing strategy on both sides
5. Wartime problems and political issues
6. Foreign policy maneuvering was crucial to the final outcome
   a. Seward's concern with Mexico
   b. Emancipation Proclamation as an element of foreign policy
7. Technology of the war
C. New York State in the Civil War
  1. Military role
  2. Political opposition in New York City
  3. Conscription laws and draft riots
   a. Undemocratic nature of the draft
   b. Conscription as a factor in racism
	3,5
	
	1,2
	
	4
	5
		Environment and Society Government
		
		Interdependence
		
		Science and Technology Government	

III. RESULTS OF THE CIVIL WAR

Content	Standards	Concepts/Themes	Connections
Objectives: 1. To understand how the Civil War affected the development of the postwar United States and influenced other countries 2. To describe how ordinary people and famous historic figures in the local community, the State, and the United States have advanced fundamental democratic values, beliefs, and traditions expressed in the Declaration of Independence, the New York State and United States constitutions, the Bill of Rights, and other important historic documents			ESSENTIAL QUESTIONS: - What were the political, social, and economic effects of the Civil War? - What happened to the South after the Civil War? - What were the long-term economic, political, and social implications of Reconstruction?

III. RESULTS OF THE CIVIL WAR, continued

Content	Standards	Concepts/Themes	Connections
3. To consider the sources of historic documents, narratives, or artifacts and evaluate their reliability 4. To value the principles, ideals, and core values of the American democratic system based upon the premises of human dignity, liberty, justice, and equality 5. To analyze the role played by the United States in international politics, past and present			

Content Outline:
A. Preservation of the Union
B. Abolition of slavery
   1. The Emancipation Proclamation
   2. Civil Rights and the 13th Amendment
C. Political power and decision making
   1. Secession
   2. States' rights
D. Reconstruction—theory, practice, and termination
   1. Lincoln's plan
   2. Johnson's plan and Congressional opposition resulted in his impeachment
   3. Congressional Reconstruction
   4. Constitutional Amendments 14 and 15 guarantee equal rights for all races except Native American Indians
   5. Problems of economic and social reconstruction led to sharecropping as a substitute for slavery
   6. The official end of Reconstruction in 1877
   7. Segregation held legal: *Plessy* v. *Ferguson* (1896)
E. The enormous human suffering and loss of life caused by the war
	1
	5
	
	5
	
	1,5
	
	1
		Change
		Nationalism
		Human Rights
		
		Power
		
		Change
		Citizenship
		Government
		Human Rights
		
		Empathy
			CLASSROOM IDEAS:
			• Analyze primary source documents such as the Emancipation Proclamation and the Civil War Amendments.
			• Debate Lincoln's plan, Johnson's plan, and the Radical Republicans' plan for Reconstruction.
			• Compare the impeachment of Andrew Johnson with that of William Jefferson Clinton.
			Suggested Documents: Civil War Amendments 13, 14, 15

UNIT SEVEN: AN INDUSTRIAL SOCIETY

I. THE MATURING OF AN INDUSTRIAL SOCIETY IN THE SECOND HALF OF THE 19TH CENTURY

Content	Standards	Concepts/Themes	Connections

Objectives:
1. To understand how industrialization led to significant changes in the economic patterns for producing, distributing, and consuming goods and services
2. To explain how societies and nations attempt to satisfy their basic needs and wants by utilizing scarce capital, natural, and human resources
3. To define basic economic concepts such as scarcity, supply and demand, markets, resources, and economic growth
4. To understand how scarcity requires people and nations to make choices that involve costs and future considerations
5. To understand how people in the United States and throughout the world are both producers and consumers of goods and services
			ESSENTIAL QUESTIONS:
			- What are the causes and effects of scarcity?
			- How did the United States respond to the three basic economic questions in the late 1800s?
			  - What goods and services shall be produced and in what quantities?
			  - How shall goods and services be produced?
			  - For whom shall goods and services be produced?

Content Outline:
A. Problems and progress in American politics: Framework for a changing United States
  1. New problems created a changing role for government and the political system
  2. Scandals, depressions, and limitations of traditional politics resulted in reluctant change, e.g., civil service
  3. National politics were dominated by the Democratic and Republican parties, but third parties occasionally arose to meet special interests
  4. New York State and New York City in an era of machine politics, e.g., the Tweed Ring and Tammany Hall
  5. Prevailing attitude of noninterference ("laissez-faire") as the appropriate role for
	1,5	Change
		Government
		
		Economic Systems
			CLASSROOM IDEAS:
			• Compare the industrialization, urbanization, and reforms of the last half of the 19th century to similar developments during the first half of that century.
			• Identify ideas associated with the American economy and list the costs and benefits of each.
			- individual entrepreneurship
			- laissez-faire economy
			- cheap labor
			- free enterprise
			- monopolies
			- government regulation
			• Analyze political cartoons of the era. What was the role of journalists in exposing corruption?

Content	Standards	Concepts/Themes	Connections
government, with some regulations to meet excesses			
B. The United States developed as an industrial power	4	Factors of Production Science and Technology	• In 1876 the nation celebrated its 100th birthday. Describe an event or invention of this period that changed methods of transportation, communication, business, or manufacturing.
1. Changes in the methods of production and distribution of manufactured goods			• Analyze photographs of city slums, such as those taken by Jacob Riis. Describe conditions, speculate about causes, and suggest solutions.
a. Transportation developments and their effects on economic developments, 1865-1900			
b. Communication developments, 1865-1900			
c. Industrial technology, 1865-1900			
d. Rise of banking and financial institutions			
2. Increase in the number and size of firms engaged in manufacture and distribution of goods			
3. Increase in the number and skill level of workers; new labor markets			
4. Expansion of markets for manufactured goods			
5. The growth and emerging problems of the cities		Urbanization	
C. Growth of the corporation as a form of business organization: Case studies—oil, railroads, steel	4,5	Factors of Production Power	
1. One of several forms of business organization			
2. Many firms maintained traditional ways of doing business			
3. Advantages and disadvantages of a corporation			
D. Government response to industrial development and abuses	4,5	Factors of Production Government	• Organize a debate of the topic: How much government regulation of the economy is enough?
1. Laissez-faire versus regulation			
2. Interstate commerce: state and national control			
3. Sherman Antitrust Act: bigness as a threat			
E. Changing patterns of agricultural organization and activity in the United States and New York State	3,4	Environment and Society Factors of Production	• Make maps showing those parts of the country being farmed in 1850 as compared to 1900. Graph the agricultural population and compare it to the total population. Identify a trend.
1. Unprecedented growth in agriculture			• Create advertisements for new farm tools and methods.
2. Changes in the methods of production and distribution of farm products—spatial distribution of economic activities			

I. THE MATURING OF AN INDUSTRIAL SOCIETY IN THE SECOND HALF OF THE 19TH CENTURY, continued

Content	Standards	Concepts/Themes	Connections
3. Efficient use of resources combined with competition and the profit motive to improve methods of production			
F. Occurrence of many significant and influential changes 1. Communities grew in size and number 2. Interdependence increased 3. Decision-making procedures changed 4. Technology advanced 5. Adaptation of, rather than to, the environment—human modifications of the physical environment 6. Perceptions of time became more formal, e.g., railroad schedules 7. Political machines influenced daily life	1,3,4,5	Change Interdependence Environment and Society Power	• Using census data from 1850 to 1900, graph the growth of population in the United States. Use maps to show the shift in the center of population. • Select one of the changes listed in the content outline and find before-and-after pictures.
G. The response of labor to industrialization 1. Industrialization created a larger workforce and more complex work 2. Working conditions underwent extensive change, which often placed hardships on the workers; roles of women, children, minorities, disabled changed 3. Early attempts to unionize the workforce met with resistance and failure, e.g., the Knights of Labor and the Haymarket Riot, American Railway Union, the Industrial Workers of the World 4. Roots of modern labor unionism, e.g., the American Federation of Labor 5. Labor as a reform movement in other aspects of society	1,4,5	Identity Factors of Production Decision Making	• Compare child labor in the 1800s to that which occurs today. Present findings as a photo collage, skit, news report, or video. • Examine pictures of people doing different jobs in the late 1800s. Which show self-sufficiency and which show interdependence? • Compare labor unions in the past with unions that exist today. What are differences and similarities?
H. The response of the farmer to industrialization 1. Expanding agricultural production and railroads 2. Cheap money and high railroad rates 3. The Grange and state reforms 4. The Populist movement 5. The closing of the frontier—limitations of physical environment	1,3,4,5	Identity Factors of Production Decision Making Environment and Society	• Read accounts of the lives of an upstate farmer, a Midwest farmer, and a Southern sharecropper. Role-play a meeting in which they discuss their lives. Suggested Documents: Emma Lazarus, "The New Colossus"; artwork, photographs from Jacob Riis, *How the Other Half Lives*

II. CHANGES IN THE SOCIAL STRUCTURE ALTERED THE AMERICAN SCENE

Content	Standards	Concepts/Themes	Connections
Objectives: 1. To understand how industrialization altered the traditional social pattern of American society and created a need for reform 2. To investigate key turning points in New York State and United States history and explain why these events or developments are significant 3. To complete well-documented and historically accurate case studies about individuals and groups who represent different ethnic, national, and religious groups, including Native American Indians, in New York State and the United States at different times and in different locations 4. To consider the sources of historic documents, narratives, or artifacts and evaluate their reliability 5. To describe historic events through the eyes and experiences of those who were there 6. To understand how scarcity requires people and nations to make choices that involve costs and future considerations			ESSENTIAL QUESTIONS: - Is there an American culture? - How is cultural diversity both a benefit and a problem? - How did massive immigration lead to new social patterns and conflicts? - Why do some people view the same event differently? - Why was the United States a magnet to so many people?

Content Outline:
A. The immigration experience
  1. Two distinct waves occurred, from the 1840s to the 1890s, and from the 1890s to the early 1920s; migration streams over time
  2. Differences were based on national origins, cultural patterns, and religion
  3. Similarities included motivations for coming and patterns of community settlement
  4. Initial clashes ended in varying degrees of acculturation
  5. Occupational and political experiences varied
	1,2,3	Movement of People and Goods
		Culture
		Places and Regions
			CLASSROOM IDEAS:
			• Write a letter as a new immigrant back to your homeland. How has America met your expectations?
			• Explain the "push-pull" theory of immigration.

B. Case studies of the immigrant experience in the United States and New York State—population characteristics 1. A comparison of European immigrants and the black slave experience—human migration's	1,2,3,4	Culture Diversity Places and Regions Scarcity	• Do a case study of a particular immigrant group. Use demographic information, maps, and interviews. Determine the effect this group had on American society and culture.

Content	Standards	Concepts/Themes	Connections
effects on the character of different places and regions 2. Immigrants as rural settlers in the Midwest 3. The Chinese experience in the Far West 4. Mexicans in the Southwest 5. New York City's ethnic neighborhoods 6. French-Canadian settlement in northern New York State 7. Immigration patterns and experiences throughout New York State 8. Irish immigration: Mass starvation in Ireland, 1845-1850 9. Immigrants in the local community			• Essay topic: Compare immigration past and present. Compare countries of origin, reasons for emigration, and degree of acceptance by Americans. • Interview a recent immigrant to the United States. <u>Suggested Document</u>: Chinese Exclusion Act, 1882
C. Legal basis for citizenship in the United States 1. Citizenship by the "law of the soil" 2. Citizenship by birth to an American parent 3. Citizenship through naturalization	5 5	Citizenship Citizenship	• Investigate the steps to becoming a United States citizen. • Explain and rewrite the naturalization oath.

D. Responsibilities of citizenship
1. Civic: A citizen should be:
  a. Knowledgeable about the process of government
  b. Informed about major issues
  c. A participant in the political process
2. Legal: A citizen should:
  a. Be knowledgeable about the law
  b. Obey the laws
  c. Respect the rights of others
  d. Understand the importance of law in a democratic society
3. The changing role of the citizen			

E. America becomes an increasingly mobile society 1. Motivated by new economic opportunities 2. Changing patterns of movement, e.g., blacks begin to move North 3. Westward settlement 4. The disappearance of the frontier—physical limits of geography	1,3	Change Movement of People and Goods Human Systems	• Explain the conflict between Native Americans, farmers, and cowboys over scarce resources in the West. What was the role of the cavalry and Buffalo Soldiers? • Show how the movement of people from one geographic area to another creates both opportunity and conflict.

II. CHANGES IN THE SOCIAL STRUCTURE ALTERED THE AMERICAN SCENE, continued

Content	Standards	Concepts/Themes	Connections

F. America developed as a consumer society
  1. Improved standard of living increased consumption
  2. Greater variety of goods available
  3. Continually rising expectations
	4	Needs and Wants	

G. Leisure activities reflected the prevailing attitudes and views of the time
  1. Greater variety of leisure activities became available as less time was spent on work
  2. Leisure activities reflected general characteristics of modern society, i.e., organized use of technology, emphasis on the individual role, and reliance on experts
	1,4	Culture
		Needs and Wants
			• Research a particular activity of the time period or provide a demonstration. Some suggestions might be vaudeville, amusement parks, Buffalo Bill shows, a particular fad of the time, or dime novels.

III. THE PROGRESSIVE MOVEMENT, 1900-1920: EFFORTS TO REFORM THE NEW SOCIETY

Content	Standards	Concepts/Themes	Connections
Objectives: 1. To understand how industrialization led to a need for reevaluating and changing the traditional role of government in relation to the economy and social conditions 2. To investigate key turning points in New York State and United States history and explain why these events or developments are significant 3. To gather and organize information about the important achievements and contributions of individuals and groups living in New York State and the United States 4. To classify major developments into categories such as social, political, economic, geographic, technological, scientific, cultural, or religious 5. To describe historic events through the eyes and experiences of those who were there			ESSENTIAL QUESTIONS: - What specific social, economic, and political problems needed reform in the late-19th century? - How can an individual help to bring about change in society? - What is the amendment process? - How did the federal government help the reform movement through amendments and legislation? Do these problems exist today? To what extent?
Content Outline: A. Social ills 1. The Muckrakers—exposing corruption and abuses in industry,	1,4,5	Change Belief Systems	

III. THE PROGRESSIVE MOVEMENT, 1900-1920: EFFORTS TO REFORM THE NEW SOCIETY, continued

Content	Standards	Concepts/Themes	Connections

government, and urban living conditions
  2. Fighting racial discrimination, e.g., the formation of the NAACP
  3. Temperance and prohibition
  4. Settlement houses
		Decision Making	

B. Efforts to reform government and politics
  1. Need for responsive government, e.g., primary elections, the initiative, the referendum, the recall election
  2. Progressive leaders, e.g., LaFollette, Theodore Roosevelt, Taft, Debs
  3. The Socialist Party challenges the political establishment
  4. Direct election of Senators—the 17th Amendment
  5. Women's suffrage—the 19th Amendment
	1,5	Change
		Decision Making
		Civic Values
			CLASSROOM IDEAS:
			• Select one reform movement, identify leaders, and create a broadside inviting people to one of their meetings.
			• Create mock interviews of reformers of the time period.

C. Economic reform efforts
  1. Labor-related legislation, e.g., minimum wage laws, workmen's compensation insurance, safety regulations, child labor laws
  2. Prosecuting trusts
  3. Government regulation of the railroads
  4. The Federal Reserve Act
  5. Graduated income tax—the 16th Amendment
	1,4,5	Change
		Factors of Production
		Government
			• Research organizations and individuals who are seeking to reform conditions in the United States today and compare them to reformers in the past.
			Suggested Documents: Upton Sinclair, *The Jungle*,; Ida Tarbell, *The History of the Standard Oil Company*; artwork, photographs from Jacob Riis, *How the Other Half Lives*

UNIT EIGHT: THE UNITED STATES AS AN INDEPENDENT NATION IN AN INCREASINGLY INTERDEPENDENT WORLD

I. THE UNITED STATES EXPANDS ITS TERRITORIES AND BUILDS AN OVERSEAS EMPIRE

Content	Standards	Concepts/Themes	Connections
Objectives: 1. To understand how and why the United States grew during the 19th century 2. To recognize that American territorial and economic growth had widespread economic, political, and social impacts both at home and abroad			ESSENTIAL QUESTIONS: - What were the causes and effects of United States involvement in foreign affairs at the turn of the 20th century? - What were the domestic and foreign issues of this time period?

3. To describe the reasons for periodizing history in different ways
4. To understand the relative importance of United States domestic and foreign policies over time
5. To analyze the role played by the United States in international politics, past and present
6. To compare and contrast different interpretations of key events and issues in New York State and United States history and offer reasons for these different accounts

Content	Standards	Concepts/Themes	Connections

Content Outline:
A. Growth of imperialist sentiment was caused by several factors
   1. A belief that the nation had a right to the land, i.e., Manifest Destiny—"people's differing perceptions of places, people, and resources"
   2. Perceived moral obligations to extend America's way of life to others, i.e., ethnocentrism and racism
   3. American citizens were already migrating into new lands in North America—the effects of human migration on the characteristics of different places
   4. Increased foreign trade led to a growing interest in gaining control over some foreign markets
   5. Fear that other foreign nations would gain control of strategic locations at the expense of the United States
   6. Developing technology in transportation and communication contributed to American expansion potential—the importance of location and certain physical features
	1,2,4,5	Nationalism
		Imperialism
		Scarcity
		Power
			CLASSROOM IDEAS:
			• Make comparisons between the economic, political, and social motives for 19th-century imperialism and the European colonization of the Americas.
			• Given our own history, debate the pros and cons of American imperialism.
			• Make a cultural comparison collage of the United States and lands acquired in Latin America and the Pacific.

B. The Spanish-American War signaled the emergence of the United States as a world power
   1. The war's origins lay in Cuban attempts to gain freedom from Spain
   2. Concerns of the United States,
	1,2,5	Nationalism
		Imperialism
		Power
			• Demonstrate the causes and effects of the ideas of Manifest Destiny.
			• Map the battles of the Spanish-American War.
			• Create headlines regarding foreign or domestic problems today in the style of yellow journalism.

I. THE UNITED STATES EXPANDS ITS TERRITORIES AND BUILDS AN OVERSEAS EMPIRE, continued

Content	Standards	Concepts/Themes	Connections

i.e., pro-expansionist sentiment, Cuba's location, Spanish tactics
  3. Newspapers shaped public opinion over the Maine incident—"yellow journalism"
  4. Conduct of the war created domestic and international problems
  5. Opposition to American imperialist movement
C. Victory in the Spanish-American War created a need for a new foreign policy
  1. Acquisition of land far from America's shores—importance of resources and markets
  2. Emphasis on doing what the government felt was necessary and possible to protect American interests, i.e., maintaining a strong navy, gaining control of other strategic locations, advocating equal trading rights in Asia, e.g., the Open Door Policy
  3. Actions created conflict with Filipinos and Japanese
	3,4,5
	
	1,2,3,4,5
		Human Systems Factors of Production	• Write an account of the Spanish-American War in the Philippines from the perspective of an American, a Spaniard, and a Filipino.
			• Review the constitutional foreign policy roles of the President and Congress.

D. United States policies in Latin America
  1. The United States attempted to control a number of locations in Latin America for economic and political reasons
  2. The quest for Latin American stability through the Roosevelt Corollary to the Monroe Doctrine: Panama Canal
  3. Armed intervention in Latin America
		Imperialism
		Science and Technology
		Power
			• Make maps showing the growth of the United States from 1783 to 1867 and from 1868 to 1914.
			• Create the front page of a newspaper reporting on the building of the Panama Canal.
			<u>Suggested Document</u>: Frederick Jackson Turner, *The Turner Thesis*

II. THE UNITED STATES BEGINS TO TAKE A ROLE IN GLOBAL POLITICS

Content	Standards	Concepts/Themes	Connections
Objectives: 1. To understand how American relations with other nations developed between the end of the Civil War and the end of World War I 2. To describe the reasons for periodizing history in different ways 3. To understand the relative importance of United States domestic and foreign policies over time 4. To analyze the role played by the United States in international politics, past and present 5. To describe the relationships between people and environments and the connections between people and places			**ESSENTIAL QUESTIONS:** - What are the costs and benefits of neutrality and foreign intervention? - How did the role of the United States in foreign affairs change at the turn of the century?

Content Outline:
A. United States policy on noninvolvement in European political affairs was based on a number of factors
  1. Tradition dating back to the earliest days of the country
  2. Focus on the international problems of the new nation
  3. Recognition of United States military unpreparedness
  4. Impacts of geography (e.g., location, resources) on United States foreign policy
	1,2,3	Choice
		Environment and Society
			CLASSROOM IDEAS:
			• Create a timeline that indicates periods of United States isolationism and foreign involvement from 1900 to the present.
			• Show areas of the world in which the United States was involved at the turn of the 20th century.

B. Pre-World War I involvements
  1. Application of the Monroe Doctrine to the Western Hemisphere
  2. Threats to American foreign trade
  3. Roosevelt's Treaty of Portsmouth
	1,2	Interdependence	

C. World War I occurred as a result of international problems
  1. Intense nationalism
  2. Power struggles among European nations
  3. A failure of leadership
  4. European alliances
	1,2,5	Nationalism
		Power
			• Debate: Was the United States neutral in practice as well as policy (1913-1917)?

D. Events led to United States involvement in World War I 1. The American people were divided in ways that made involvement difficult	1,2,4,5	Interdependence Scarcity Decision Making	• List the causes of United States involvement in World War I. • Analyze World War I posters and identify the propaganda techniques used.

II. THE UNITED STATES BEGINS TO TAKE A ROLE IN GLOBAL POLITICS, continued

Content	Standards	Concepts/Themes	Connections
2. Fear that United States involvement would increase intolerance at home			• Write a letter home from the perspective of a soldier in Europe, a German immigrant, or an African-American who moved North.
3. Initial attempts to follow traditional policy of neutrality failed			
4. Unwillingness of warring nations to accept President Wilson as a mediator			
5. England was a major United States trade partner			
6. Despite varied ethnic backgrounds in the United States, leaders felt closer to the English than to the Germans			
7. While both sides attempted to restrict United States trade with their opponent, Germany did so by sinking American ships			
8. Recognition that the United States would have no say at any peace conference if it remained neutral			
E. The United States entered the war	1,2,4	Nationalism Factors of Production Science and Technology	• Examine themes such as major events and battles, roles played by great leaders; the effect of the war on diverse people, new weapons technology, the role of women, and contributions of African-Americans to the war effort.
1. Combining new technology with old strategies e.g., chemical warfare led to the death of millions			
2. The war was supported by the majority of Americans			
3. The war effort created changes on the home front, e.g., economic controls, the role of women in the workforce, black migrations to the North, and attempts to organize labor to improve conditions			
4. War promoted intolerance, e.g., the Espionage Act of 1917 and the Sedition Act of 1918; "hyphenated Americans" have their loyalty questioned			
F. The United States and the peace negotiations	1,2,5	Choice Nation state	• Convene a mock Versailles Peace Conference with students representing each country. <u>Suggested Documents</u>: The Versailles Treaty; songs, "Over There," "Oh, How I Hate to Get Up in the Morning," "The Marine Hymn"
1. Wilson's failed attempts to establish leadership with his Fourteen Points			
2. Senate opposition to the League of Nations			
3. The Versailles Treaty			
G. The Bolshevik Revolution	1,2	Change	
1. Effect of World War I			
2. Civil war in Russia			
3. Western intervention			
4. Threat of international communism			

I. THE ROARING TWENTIES REFLECTED THE SPIRIT OF THE POSTWAR PERIOD

Content	Standards	Concepts/Themes	Connections
Objectives: 1. To understand the economic, social, and political development of America in the period between World War I and World War II 2. To understand the relative importance of United States domestic and foreign policies over time 3. To analyze the role played by the United States in international politics, past and present 4. To classify major developments into categories such as social, political, economic, geographic, technological, scientific, cultural, or religious 5. To understand how people in the United States and throughout the world are both producers and consumers of goods and services			ESSENTIAL QUESTIONS: - What were the economic, political, and social changes of the 1920s? - How was Prohibition an outgrowth of the earlier temperance movement? - How did the role of government change from the 1920s to the 1930s?

Content Outline:
A. Prohibition and the 18th Amendment
  1. End of reform era
  2. The rise of organized crime
  3. Economic, social, political effects
	1,4,5	Culture
		Needs and Wants
		Decision Making
			CLASSROOM IDEAS:
			• Debate the pros and cons of Prohibition.

B. The Republican decade
  1. Political developments
    a. Back to "normalcy"; the election of 1920
    b. Scandals
    c. Coolidge: austerity and integrity
    d. Government and business: laissez-faire and protection
    e. Election of 1928
	1,5	Choice
		Government
			• Research, list, and illustrate the "firsts" that occurred in the 1920s; e.g., the first trans-Atlantic flight.

C. Relative isolation of the United States in world political affairs
  1. General policy of noninvolvement in European affairs; the League of Nations controversy
  2. Limited participation in international activities
    a. World Court
    b. Naval disarmament 1924
    c. Efforts for peace; Kellogg-Briand Pact, 1928
    d. Postwar reparation talks
	1,2,3,4	Interdependence
		Movement of People and Goods
		Human Systems
		Scarcity
			• Predict the effects of United States noninvolvement in foreign affairs as the world became more interdependent.

Content	Standards	Concepts/Themes	Connections

e. Relief efforts in Europe
  3. Expansion of international trade and tariffs
  4. Restrictions on immigration, e.g., Quota Act, 1924			

D. A rising standard of living resulted in the growth of a consumer economy and the rise of the middle class
  1. Increase in single-family homes; move to nuclear families
  2. Emergence of suburbs
  3. Spread of middle-class values
  4. Increased use of credit
	1,4	Urbanization
		Belief Systems
			• Compare and contrast trends described in this section (i.e., rising standard of living, changes in the workplace, immigration, use of leisure time) with similar trends in the late-19th century.

E. Changes in the workplace
  1. Shift from agrarian to industrial workforce
  2. Lessened demand for skilled workers
  3. Working conditions and wages improved
  4. Increase in white-collar employees
  5. Women continued to increase their presence in the workforce
	4	Factors of Production	• Using advertisements, determine what consumer goods a family of the 1920s would have owned.
			• Make a chart of the percentage of people in farming and nonfarming occupations from 1840 to 1930. Determine the trend.

F. Problems developed in the midst of unprecedented prosperity
  1. Not all groups benefited equally
    a. Low farm prices
    b. High black unemployment
    c. Millions of poor
  2. New trends conflicted with tradition
  3. Environmental balance was jeopardized
	3,4	Factors of Production
		Enviroment
			• How did the plight of farmers foreshadow the Great Depression?

G. Foreign immigration and black migration resulted in a very diverse population and an increase in social tensions—the effects of human migrations on the nature and character of places and regions
  1. Restrictions on immigration
  2. Black migration to Northern cities
  3. Growth of organizations to fight discrimination; e.g., NAACP
  4. Growth of black art, music, and cultural identity; e.g., the Harlem Renaissance
  5. Generational conflicts
  6. Widespread emergence of retired workers
  7. Right-wing hate groups
	1,5	Diversity
		Movement of People and Goods
		Justice
			• Essay topic: How were the 1920s an age of intolerance toward immigrants and African-Americans?
			• Defend the statement: Not all Americans enjoyed the fruits of economic prosperity during the 1920s.
			• Research the writings of such African-American writers as Claude McKay, Countee Cullen, James Weldon Johnson, and Langston Hughes.

I. THE ROARING TWENTIES REFLECTED THE SPIRIT OF THE POSTWAR PERIOD, continued

Content	Standards	Concepts/Themes	Connections
H. New ideas about the use of leisure time emerged 　1. Impact of the automobile: Henry Ford 　2. Organized sports: Babe Ruth 　3. Search for heroes and heroines: Lindbergh, Amelia Earhart 　4. Motion pictures 　5. Popular literature 　6. Fads and fashion 　7. Changes in social behavior	1	Culture	• Compare and contrast the growth of celebrity culture and mass media in the 1920s to current trends in these areas. • Create a "Meeting of the Minds" of personalities from the 1920s. Have students research their lives and answer questions in character.
I. The stock market crash marked the beginning of the worst economic time the country has ever known 　1. National prosperity had been structured on the investments of the wealthy 　2. There were problems with the economic structure 　3. People lost faith in the system 　4. The government was unwilling or unable to correct the downturn 　5. The economic depression that followed was the worst in our history	1,4,5	Change Factors of 　Production Scarcity Government	• Assign students a stock and have them find out its price before October 1929 and after the market crashed.

II. THE GREAT DEPRESSION

Content	Standards	Concepts/Themes	Connections
Objectives: 1. To understand the economic, political, and social impacts of the Great Depression on the United States 2. To understand the economic, political, and social changes that took place in the world during the 1930s 3. To explain how societies and nations attempt to satisfy their basic needs and wants by utilizing scarce capital, natural, and human resources 4. To understand how scarcity requires people and nations to make choices that involve costs and future considerations 5. To evaluate economic data by differentiating fact from opinion and identifying frames of reference			ESSENTIAL QUESTIONS: - Why did the crash of the market affect those who did not own stock? - How did the concept of checks and balances relate to the New Deal? - How was New York a model for federal programs? - What parts of the New Deal legislation are still in effect today?

II. THE GREAT DEPRESSION, continued

Content	Standards	Concepts/Themes	Connections
6. To develop conclusions about economic issues and problems by creating broad statements that summarize findings and solutions			
Content Outline:			
A. Contributing factors	4	Needs and Wants	
1. Economic growth declined during the late 1920s		Factors of Production	
2. Stock purchases were made on margin/credit		Scarcity	
3. Corporations and individuals became overextended			
4. The stock market crash led to a cycle of low demand and high unemployment			CLASSROOM IDEAS:
B. Responses to deepening economic woes	5	Government	• Compare Hoover's attempt to solve economic problems with Roosevelt's.
1. Hoover administration response: too little, too late			
2. Local and State actions			
a. Soup kitchens and outstretched hands			
b. A modified "new deal" in New York			
3. Election of 1932; question of confidence			
C. The New Deal	1,4,5	Change	• Use the Constitution to examine why the New Deal was considered unconstitutional.
1. Psychological boost; FDR at the fireside		Economic Systems	
2. Relieving human suffering; providing for dignity and jobs		Government	• Chart New Deal legislation in terms of relief, recovery, and reform efforts.
3. Helping business and industry recover			
4. Adjusting the economic system to prevent recurrence			
a. Government regulation of business and banking			
b. Instituting Social Security			
c. Providing a guaranteed labor voice: the Wagner Act			
5. Other voices			• Write a persuasive article from the point of view of a political activist of the 1930s.
a. Court-packing scheme			
b. Alternative solutions: Father Coughlin, the Townsend Plan, Huey Long, socialism, communism			Suggested Document: Roosevelt's first inaugural address (1933): "This nation asks for action, and action now. . ."
1) The economics of war versus depression conditions; climbing out of depression and into war			

Content	Standards	Concepts/Themes	Connections
D. Effects on work, family, and communities	1,4	Change Scarcity Needs and Wants	• Have students interview someone who lived during the Great Depression.
1. Even though unemployment reached new heights, most people continued to hold jobs but at reduced hours and lower wages			• Use newspaper archives to examine the economic, social, and political impact of the Great Depression on your local community.
2. The loss of jobs fell unequally on women, blacks, and the unskilled			
3. The threat of possible job loss was a psychological strain on those who were employed			
4. Unemployment affected the traditional male role of provider, especially for those who equated success at work with success as a husband and father			
5. Charities' resources were inadequate			
6. Local communities attempted to meet the needs of their people			
7. The Dust Bowl and the Okies—human modification of the physical environment	3	Environment and Society Culture	
E. The cultural environment during the Great Depression	1,5	Government	• Make a cultural scrapbook incorporating literature, music, and art from the 1930s.
1. The times were reflected in the arts and literature			• Read selections from *The Grapes of Wrath*. Write a journal describing your journey as a migrant teen in the 1930s.
2. Escapism was popular in fiction and the cinema			
3. Many works of social commentary and criticism appeared			
4. Federal government supported the arts through the Works Project Administration (WPA)			
F. Effects of the Great Depression on industrialized Europe	1,2,4	Interdependence Scarcity	• Have groups of students research different countries and the conditions they faced during the Great Depression. Compare Hitler with Roosevelt. Use a Venn diagram.
1. Trade and loans tied Western economies together			Suggested Documents: Speeches of Franklin Roosevelt; Studs Turkel, *Hard Times*; song, "Brother, Can You Spare a Dime?"
2. The Great Depression followed similar patterns in affected nations			
a. Tighter credit			
b. Business failures			
c. Decreased money supply			
d. Lowered demand			
e. Lower production			
f. Widespread unemployment			
3. Developing totalitarian responses: Germany, Italy,	2,5	Nationalism Change Political Systems	

II. THE GREAT DEPRESSION, continued

Content	Standards	Concepts/Themes	Connections
Spain, Japan; intensified communism characterized by: a. One-party governments headed by a strong individual b. Armies and police forces fostered national goals and eliminated opposition c. Use of propaganda in the media and schools to support national goals d. Art and literature were used to endorse official policies in totalitarian countries G. European conflicts resulted in several basic problems for United States policy makers 1. The question of whether to shift focus from domestic problems to foreign policy 2. Issue of neutrality versus the growing power of totalitarian states 3. Continued efforts to improve Latin American relations through the "Good Neighbor Policy" without losing influence in that area's affairs	1,2	Interdependence	

UNIT TEN: THE UNITED STATES ASSUMES WORLDWIDE RESPONSIBILITIES

I. WORLD WAR II

Content	Standards	Concepts/Themes	Connections
Objectives: 1. To understand why World War II began and how it changed the lives of millions of people 2. To be aware of the much different world left as a legacy of World War II 3. To investigate key turning points in New York State and United States history and explain why these events or developments are significant			ESSENTIAL QUESTIONS: - How did the Versailles Treaty lead to World War II? - How could the use of the first atomic bomb be considered a turning point in United States history? - Why is World War II considered a "total war" affecting all aspects of American life?

I. WORLD WAR II, continued

Content	Standards	Concepts/Themes	Connections
4. To understand the relative importance of United States domestic and foreign policies over time 5. To analyze the role played by the United States in international politics, past and present 6. To describe historic events through the eyes and experiences of those who were there			

Content Outline:
A. Origins of the war
  1. The Versailles Treaty
  2. The Great Depression
  3. Rise of totalitarianism; expansionism and persecution
  4. The rearming of Germany
  5. Isolationism
  6. Failure of the League of Nations
	1,2	Change
		Choice
			CLASSROOM IDEAS:
			• Compare and contrast the origins of World War I and World War II.
			• Debate the topic: United States membership in the League of Nations would have prevented World War II.
			• Make a timeline of major events that occurred during the war.

B. Prewar alliances
  1. Axis powers
  2. Allied powers
  3. Role of the United States
	1,2	Interdependence	• On a world map, indicate the Allied and Axis powers.

C. Failure of peace
  1. Aggression by Germany in Europe, Italy in Europe and Africa, and Japan in Asia
  2. Appeasement; Chamberlain in Munich
  3. German attack on Poland; World War II begins
  4. United States role to 1941—guarded isolation, aid to allies
	1,2	Change
		Choice	

D. The United States in World War II
  1. Japanese attack on Pearl Harbor
  2. A two-front war
    a. Europe—Eisenhower
    b. Pacific—MacArthur
	1,2	Change	• Write a news report about the bombing of Pearl Harbor from the American and Japanese points of view.

E. New aspects of the war
  1. German blitzkrieg
  2. Aerial bombing
  3. New technology and its impact on people and the physical environment
  4. Atomic bomb—the Manhattan Project
  5. The Nazi Holocaust
  6. Concept of unconditional surrender
	1,2,4	Science and Technology
		Empathy
			• Take the role of one of the following—a soldier in the Pacific, a Jewish person in Europe, a Japanese-American, or a student in high school. How might the war have affected their lives?
			• Interview those who lived during World War II and those who did not. Compare their attitudes toward the dropping of the atomic bomb.

I. WORLD WAR II, continued

Content	Standards	Concepts/Themes	Connections
F. The home front 　1. Total mobilization of resources 　2. Rationing 　3. Role of women 　4. War bonds 　5. Internment to incarceration of Japanese-Americans 　6. Limited progress toward economic, political, and social equality for black Americans, i.e., Roosevelt's Executive Order 8802	1,4,5	Nationalism Diversity Scarcity Human Rights	• Explain the causes and effects of rationing during World War II. • Have groups research how the war affected minorities.
G. End of the war 　1. Allied agreement—Yalta Conference 　2. Defeat of Germany 　3. Defeat of Japan	1,2	Change	
H. Impact of the war 　1. Entire countries were physically and demographically devastated—effects of physical and human geographic factors 　2. Millions of families suffered the loss of loved ones 　3. The Nazi Holocaust—Hitler's "Final Solution"; worldwide horror; human rights violations 　4. United States response to the Holocaust: Fort Ontario; Oswego, New York 　5. The Nuremberg Trials 　6. Global impact; rise of nationalism in Africa and Asia 　7. Advent of the United Nations 　8. Advent of the nuclear age	1,2,3,5	Environment and Society Empathy Decision Making Nationalism	• Chart the casualties of the war. What were the human and economic costs? • Compare the League of Nations and the United Nations in a Venn diagram. Suggested Documents: United Nations Charter; United States military recruitment posters, and Rosie the Riveter posters; songs, "God Bless America," "This is the Army, Mr. Jones," "This Land is Your Land," and "Praise the Lord and Pass the Ammunition"

II. THE UNITED STATES AS LEADER OF THE FREE WORLD

Content	Standards	Concepts/Themes	Connections
Objectives: 1. To understand why the United States assumed a leadership role in the post-World War II world 2. To appreciate the historical background for the formation of United States foreign policy of this era 3. To understand the relative importance of United States domestic and foreign policies over time			ESSENTIAL QUESTIONS: - How and why did the leadership role of the United States differ after World War II and World War I? - How and why did the United States help the nations of Europe after World War II? - What was the Cold War? How was it different from previous wars?

II. THE UNITED STATES AS LEADER OF THE FREE WORLD, continued

Content	Standards	Concepts/Themes	Connections
4. To analyze the role played by the United States in international politics, past and present **Content Outline:** A. Role of the United Nations 1. Human rights issues; United Nations Universal Declaration of Human Rights (1948)—role played by Eleanor Roosevelt on the United Nations Commission on Human Rights 2. Actions of the United Nations to promote peace	1,2,5	Human Rights Interdependence	CLASSROOM IDEAS: • Research human rights violations since World War II and the United Nations' response to them.
B. United States and the Soviet Union emerge as world leaders 1. The Cold War 2. Truman Doctrine and Marshall Plan 3. Alliance systems: e.g., NATO, Warsaw Pact	1,2,4,5	Interdependence Economic Systems Political Systems	• Make a chart comparing the United States and the Soviet Union in size, population, government, allies, economy, and religion.
C. Communist expansion leads to United States policy of containment 1. In Europe: Berlin airlift, Berlin Wall 2. In Asia: Communist China, Korean War 3. In Latin America: Cuban missile crisis 4. In Southeast Asia: Vietnam War	1,2,3,5	Interdependence Places and Regions Decision Making	• Create an illustrated timeline of Cold War events. • List the causes and results of the Korean War. • Invite a Korean War veteran to class. • Examine foreign policy issues of the Cold War and actions taken by presidents of the United States. Suggested Document: United Nations Universal Declaration of Human Rights, December 10, 1948
D. Superpower rivalry 1. The spread of nuclear weapons 2. The arms race 3. From Sputnik to astronauts on the Moon	1,2,5	Nationalism Decision Making	

III. THE UNITED STATES IN THE POST-COLD WAR WORLD

Content	Standards	Concepts/Themes	Connections
Objectives: 1. To understand the historic, political, and social context in which United States foreign policy has evolved during the post-Cold War era 2. To understand the relative importance of United States domestic and foreign policy over time 3. To analyze the role played by the United States in international politics, past and present			ESSENTIAL QUESTIONS: - How were World War II and the Vietnam War different? - How were the Vietnam War and the Gulf War different? - How has our relationship with Latin America changed?

III. THE UNITED STATES IN THE POST-COLD WAR WORLD, continued

Content	Standards	Concepts/Themes	Connections

Content Outline:
A. Shifting foreign policies help lead to the end of the Cold War
  1. Detente and arms control beginning with President Nixon
  2. Military buildup and treaties to bring about reductions
  3. Fall of the Berlin Wall (1989) and the collapse of the Soviet Union
	1,2,5	Change
		Interdependence
		Political Systems	

B. The United States seeks a new role in the world
  1. Arab-Israeli conflicts; Camp David Accord
  2. Persian Gulf War
  3. Peacekeeping missions; Somalia, Bosnia
	1,2,3,5	Change
		Places and Regions
		Power
			CLASSROOM IDEAS:
			• Make a poster comparing the weapons of World War I, the Vietnam War, and the Gulf War. Draw conclusions.
			• Use the study of current events to convey the ongoing nature of United States foreign policy.
			• Research a timeline to show involvement in the Middle East.
			• Research products made in Mexico and Latin America. Analyze the economic effects on business and labor in the United States.

C. Western Hemisphere relations
  1. Economic competition and cooperation: NAFTA
  2. Immigration patterns between the United States and Mexico, Latin America
  3. Spread of democratic principles in Latin America
	1,2,4,5	Interdependence
		Movement of People and Goods
		Scarcity
		Factors of Production
		Political Systems
			Suggested Documents: Gulf of Tonkin Resolution; song Pete Seeger, "Where Have All the Flowers Gone?"

UNIT ELEVEN: THE CHANGING NATURE OF THE AMERICAN PEOPLE FROM WORLD WAR II TO THE PRESENT

I. POSTWAR SOCIETY CHARACTERIZED BY PROSPERITY AND OPTIMISM

Content	Standards	Concepts/Themes	Connections
Objectives: 1. To understand that the period immediately following World War II was a prolonged period of prosperity with a high level of public confidence in the United States 2. To investigate key turning points in New York State and United States history and explain why these events or developments are significant 3. To compare and contrast different interpretations of key events and issues in New York State and United States history and explain reasons for these different accounts			ESSENTIAL QUESTIONS: - How did the Cold War affect the lives of people in the United States? - How did the United States deal with the assassination of one president and the resignation of another?

Content	Standards	Concepts/Themes	Connections
Content Outline: A. Changing patterns of production and consumption resulted in economic expansion 　1. Increased productivity, a result of improving technology and rising consumer demand, led to higher wages and declining unemployment 　2. Number of service jobs, women in the workforce increased 　3. Poverty continued to exist in the midst of plenty	1,4,5	Change Factors of 　Production Justice Citizenship	CLASSROOM IDEAS: • Graph the economic cycles of prosperity and recession after World War II.
B. Families and communities underwent significant changes 　1. Postwar baby boom had major effects on social and economic decisions made by families 　2. Growth of suburbs paralleled by movement from major cities 　3. Effect of automobiles reflected in interstate highway system, shopping centers, increased commuting to work	1,3,4	Change Places and 　Regions Science and 　Technology	• Show how the baby boom generation has affected the social, economic, and political life of the United States.
C. Civil rights movement placed focus on equality and democracy 　1. Important executive and judicial decisions supported equal rights 　2. *Brown* v. *Board of Education of Topeka* (1954) overturned legal basis of segregation 　3. Activists and leaders such as Dr. Martin Luther King, Jr. developed strategies to secure civil rights for African-Americans 　4. Women, Native American Indians, and others also sought greater equality 　5. Supreme Court moved to protect individual rights: *Miranda* v. *Arizona* (1966), *Tinker* v. *Des Moines Independent School District* (1969)	1,5	Diversity Justice Civic Values Human Rights	• Analyze the conflict between federal and State law concerning the issue of school desegregation, using primary source documents. • What method did minority groups use in their attempts to gain equal rights? • Create a poster indicating the significant people and events in the struggle for equal rights of a particular minority group. <u>Suggested Documents</u>: Dr. Martin Luther King, Jr.'s address at the Lincoln Memorial (1963): "I have a dream. . . ,"; Kennedy's inaugural speech; song, "We Shall Overcome"
D. Self-confidence of early postwar years eroded by series of events 　1. Assassinations of major leaders: Kennedy, King 　2. Nation split over involvement in Vietnam War 　3. Groups in society turn to violence to reach their goals 　4. Resignation of President Nixon 　5. Oil crisis and skyrocketing inflation	1,2,5	Change Power	

II. THE UNITED STATES BEGINS A NEW CENTURY

Content	Standards	Concepts/Themes	Connections
Objectives: 1. To understand the economic, social, and political trends that shaped the end of the 20th century and point to the 21st century 2. To investigate problems and opportunities the United States faces in its immediate future			ESSENTIAL QUESTIONS: - How has the fall of communism changed the balance of power in the world? - What will be the role of the United States in the 21st century?

Content Outline:
A. The United States competes in a world economy
  1. Competition from Europe, Asia, rest of Western Hemisphere
  2. Effects on economy of the United States
	1,2,4	Interdependence
		Factors of
		  Production
			CLASSROOM IDEAS:
			• Read the labels on your clothing. Where were the clothes made? How does this affect supply and demand in the American economy?

B. Federal and state governments reevaluate their roles
  1. Fiscal and monetary policies: taxation, regulation, deregulation
  2. Social programs: health, welfare, education
	1,5	Change
		Government
		Decision Making	

C. Technology changes: the home and the workplace	1	Science and Technology	

D. Old and new problems must be addressed
  1. Violent crime and substance abuse
  2. Protection of the environment
  3. Growing number of elderly Americans
  4. The continuing struggle for economic and social justice for all citizens
  5. Balancing the ideals of national unity with growing cultural diversity
  6. Civic and legal responsibilities of citizenship
	1,2,3,4	Culture
		Environment
		  and Society
		Needs and
		  Wants
		Justice
		Citizenship
			• Research an enduring problem or issue from different points of view.
			• Compare the beginning of the 20th century with that of the 21st century.

Global History and Geography

The global history and geography core curriculum is designed to focus on the five social studies standards, common themes that recur across time and place, and eight historical units. Each unit lists the content, concepts and themes, and connections teachers should use to organize classroom instruction and plan for assessment. This curriculum provides students with the opportunity to explore what is happening in various regions and civilizations at a given time. In addition, it enables students to investigate issues and themes from multiple perspectives and make global connections and linkages that lead to in-depth understanding. As students explore the five social studies standards, they should have multiple opportunities to explore the content and intellectual skills of history and the social science disciplines.

Introductory Notes

TEACHER'S NOTE: For each historical era, students will investigate global connections and linkages. These global connections and linkages include:

 Cultural Diffusion (Ideas/Technology/Food/Disease)

 Belief Systems

 Migrations

 Trade

 Multi-Regional Empires

 Conflict

The Regents examination for global history and geography will be based on the content column in this core curriculum. The following concepts and themes in global history and geography are emphasized in this curriculum.

Belief Systems	Factors of Production	Nationalism
Change	Human and Physical	Nation State
Citizenship	Geography	Needs and Wants
Conflict	Human Rights	Political Systems
Culture and Intellectual Life	Imperialism	Power
Decision Making	Interdependence	Scarcity
Diversity	Justice	Science and Technology
Economic Systems	Movement of People and	Urbanization
Environment and Society	Goods	

Suggested Documents: Throughout the global history and geography core curriculum, teachers will find lists of suggested documents. In this context, the term "document" includes:

- books and monographs
- newspapers, periodicals, magazines, and scholarly journals
- government documents
- manuscripts, archival materials, journals, diaries, and autobiographies
- maps; visual materials (paintings, drawings, sculptures, architectural drawings, films, posters, prints, engravings, photographs, etc.)
- music
- artifacts.

The suggested documents are indicative of the kinds of primary and secondary sources that can be used in a global history and geography program. They do not comprise a mandatory listing but rather represent the kinds of documents that can be used in document-based questions. In a few cases, specific websites for listed documents are included. A fuller listing of websites can be found in the Appendix of this document.

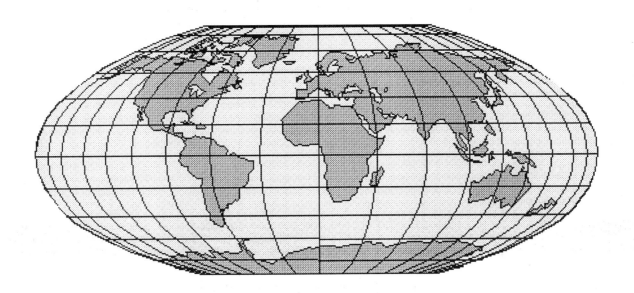

Content reviews were provided by Dr. Jo Margaret Mano, Department of Geography, State University of New York, New Paltz, Dr. Ronald G. Knapp, Professor and Chair, Department of Geography, State University of New York, New Paltz, D. Joseph Corr, Shaker High School, Latham, New York, and Steven Goldberg, New Rochelle Central School District, New Rochelle, New York.

METHODOLOGY OF GLOBAL HISTORY AND GEOGRAPHY

Content	Standards	Concepts/Themes	Connections

A. History
  1. Skills of historical analysis
    a. Investigate differing and competing interpretations of historical theories—multiple perspectives
    b. Hypothesize about why interpretations change over time
    c. Explain the importance of historical evidence
  2. Understand the concepts of change and continuity over time
  3. The connections and interactions of people across time and space
  4. Time frames and periodization
  5. Roles and contributions of individuals and groups
  6. Oral histories
	1,2	Belief Systems
		Change
		Conflict
		Cultural/
		  Intellectual
		  Life
		Diversity
		Human Rights
		Interdependence
		Imperialism
		Nationalism
		Urbanization
			TEACHER'S NOTE: This introductory unit is designed to introduce students to the five social studies standards and the essential questions associated with each standard. Many teachers may choose to infuse this introduction into the body of the course.
			
			TEACHER'S NOTE: While this core curriculum presents a chronological approach to global history and geography, it may be necessary at times to suspend chronology. In some instances, events overlap historical eras. An example would be European feudalism that has been placed in UNIT TWO: Expanding Zones of Exchange and Encounter (500-1200); Japanese feudalism is placed in UNIT THREE: Global Interactions (1200-1650). The teacher may wish to place Japanese feudalism in UNIT TWO with European feudalism so that students can better compare and contrast the two. This is a local curriculum decision.
			
			TEACHER'S NOTE: Over this two-year course of study, students should develop a sense of time, exploring different periodization systems and examining themes across time and place. This ability is critical in understanding the course and being able to make the fundamental connections and linkages.

METHODOLOGY OF GLOBAL HISTORY AND GEOGRAPHY, continued

Content	Standards	Concepts/Themes	Connections

B. Geography
  1. Elements of geography
    a. Human geography
    b. Physical geography
    c. Political geography
    d. Migration
    e. Trade
    f. Environment and society
    g. The uses of geography
  2. Critical thinking skills
    a. Asking and answering geographic questions
    b. Analyzing theories of geography
    c. Acquiring, organizing, and analyzing geographic information
  3. Identifying and defining world regions
	3	Human/Physical Geography
		Movement of People and Goods
		Environment and Society
		Change
		Needs and Wants
		Interdependence
		Culture
			TEACHER'S NOTE: Prior to the completion of the two-year global history and geography program, students should have a clear understanding of the human and physical geography. They should have multiple opportunities to explore the impact of geography on the past and present. Students should be able to make, use, and apply geographic generalizations. They should be able to use data to construct maps, graphs, charts, etc.
			- What impact does geography have on history?
			- How do physical and human geography affect people and places?
			- To what extent are terms such as "Far East" and "Middle East" a reflection of a European perspective on regions?

C. Economics
  1. Major economic concepts (scarcity, supply/demand, opportunity costs, production, resources)
  2. Economic decision making
  3. The interdependence of economics and economic systems throughout the world
  4. Applying critical thinking skills in making informed and well-reasoned economic decisions
	4	Economic Systems
		Decision Making
		Factors of Production
		Interdependence
		Needs and Wants
		Scarcity
		Science and Technology
			TEACHER'S NOTE: Students should be able to apply the three basic questions of economics to situations across time and place.
			- What goods and services shall be produced and in what quantities?
			- How shall goods and services be produced?
			- For whom shall goods and services be produced?

D. Political science
  1. The purposes of government
  2. Political systems around the world
  3. Political concepts of power, authority, governance, and law
  4. Rights and responsibilities of citizenship across time and space
  5. Critical thinking skills
    a. Probing ideas and assumptions
    b. Posing and answering analytical questions
    c. Assuming a skeptical attitude toward questionable political statements
    d. Evaluating evidence and forming rational conclusions
    e. Developing participatory skills
	5	Decision Making
		Justice
		Nation State
		Citizenship
		Political Systems
		Power
		Nationalism
			- What are the basic purposes of government?
			- What assumptions have different groups made regarding power, authority, governance, and law across time and place?
			- How is citizenship defined and how do different societies view the rights and responsibilities of citizenship?
			- How do concepts of justice and human values differ across time and place?
			- How are decisions made under different political systems?

UNIT ONE: ANCIENT WORLD—CIVILIZATIONS AND RELIGIONS (4000 BC - 500 AD)

Content	Standards	Concepts/Themes	Connections
A. Early peoples 1. Human and physical geography 2. Hunters and gatherers—nomadic groups 3. Relationship to the environment 4. Migration of early human populations a. Out of Africa b. Other theories 5. Early government a. Purposes b. Decision making c. Move toward more complex government systems	2,3,4 5	Human/ Physical Geography Movement of People and Goods Scarcity Needs and Wants Environment Political Systems	- What was the relationship between early peoples and their environment? - What reasons can you pose to explain why early peoples migrated from place to place? - What does the use of tools tell us about a society?
B. Neolithic Revolution and early river civilizations 1. Compare and contrast (Mesopotamia, Egypt, the Indus Valley, and Yellow River civilizations) a. Human and physical geography of early river civilizations	2,3,4	Human/ Physical Geography Urbanization Technology	TEACHER'S NOTE: Throughout global history, students should know and be able to analyze critical turning points in history. They should be able to explain how technological change affects people, places, and regions. TEACHER'S NOTE: When studying early river civilizations, students investigate at least two civilizations in depth. It is not necessary that all civilizations be addressed to the same extent. The model presented here for the study of early river civilizations can be used in the study of any civilization. Students should be able to analyze important ideas, social and cultural values, beliefs, and traditions. - Why was the introduction of agriculture referred to as the Neolithic Revolution? Why was this a turning point? - What political systems developed in early river civilizations? - How was the rise of cities related to the Neolithic Revolution and the development of early civilizations?

Content	Standards	Concepts/Themes	Connections

b. Traditional economies
c. Political systems
d. Social structures and urbanization
e. Contributions
  1) Writing systems
  2) Belief systems
	2,3,4,5	Economic System
		Political System
		Cultural and Intellectual Life
		Decision Making
			- What is meant by the term "traditional economy"?
			- In what ways have science and technology helped humankind meet its basic needs and wants?
			<u>Suggested Documents</u>: Timelines, photographs and/or models of temples, pictures of artifacts, palaces, and neolithic villages; record-keeping systems; creation stories such as *The Epic of Gilgamesh*

3) Early technology—irrigation, tools, weapons
  4) Architecture
  5) Legal systems—Code of Hammurabi
2. Identify demographic patterns of early civilizations and movement of people—Bantu migration (500 BC - 1500 AD)
  a. Human and physical geography
  b. Causes of migration
  c. Impact on other areas of Africa
	2,3,4	Science and Technology
		Justice
		Culture and Intellectual Life
		Change
			- What caused the Bantu to migrate south and east from their west African origins?
			- How did this migration change sub-Saharan Africa?

C. Classical civilizations
1. Chinese civilization
  a. Human and physical geography
  b. Chinese contributions (engineering, tools, writing, silk, bronzes, government system)
  c. Dynastic cycles
  d. Mandate of Heaven
2. Greek civilization
  a. Human and physical geography
  b. The rise of city-states—Athens/Sparta
  c. Contributions: art, architecture, philosophy, science—Plato, Socrates, Aristotle
  d. Growth of democracy in Athens versus the Spartan political system
  e. Alexander the Great and Hellenistic culture—cultural diffusion
	2,3,4,5	Human/Physical Geography
		Cultural/Intellectual Life
		Political Systems
			TEACHER'S NOTE: Have students develop timelines and maps to illustrate the parallel development of classical civilizations.
			- What have been the contributions of classical civilizations to the history of humankind?
			- What forces caused the rise and fall of classical civilizations?
			- What were the status and role of women in these civilizations?
			- What was the Mandate of Heaven? Why did the Chinese define their history in terms of dynastic cycles?
			- How are contemporary democratic governments rooted in classical traditions?
			- What impacts did Greece and Rome have on the development of later political systems?
			- How did geography affect the rise of city-states in Greece and the rise of the Roman Empire?
			- How did the institution of slavery fit within the Athenian concept of democracy?

Content	Standards	Concepts/Themes	Connections

3. Roman Republic
  a. Human and physical geography
  b. Contributions—law (Twelve Tables), architecture, literature, roads, bridges
4. Indian (Maurya) Empire
  a. Human and physical geography (monsoons)
  b. Contributions—government system
		Decision Making Citizenship	Suggested Documents: Hammurabi's Code, Hebrew law, the Twelve Tables of Rome (http://members.aol.com/pilgrimjon/private/LEX/12tables.html), the Golden Rule, *The Odyssey*, Ptolemaic maps, for Ashoka of the Maurya Empire see http://www.fordham.edu/halsall/india/ashoka-edicts.html
			- What impact did monsoons have on the historic and economic development of the sub-continent?

5. Rise of agrarian civilizations in Mesoamerica—Mayan (200 BC - 900 AD)
  a. Human and physical geography
  b. Contributions (mathematics, astronomy, science, arts, architecture, and technology)
  c. Role of maize
  d. Religion
6. The status and role of women in classical civilizations
	2,3,4,5	Human/ Physical Geography Factors of Production Needs and Wants Belief Systems Culture and Intellectual Life	TEACHER'S NOTE: The Mayan civilizations span the time period and are placed here to introduce students to developments in the Western Hemi-sphere from an early date.
			- How did agriculture arise in the Americas?
			- What were the earliest crops in the Americas?
			- How did the Mayan civilizations compare to river valley and classical civilizations of Eurasia?
			- How did the decline of the Mayans compare to the fall of the Han and Roman empires?
			- What brought about the decline of the Mayans?

7. The growth of global trade routes in classical civilizations
  a. Phoenician trade routes
  b. Silk Road
  c. Maritime and overland trade routes
    1) Linking Africa and Eurasia
    2) Linking China, Korea, and Japan
	2,3,4	Movement of People and Goods
		
		Interdependence
			TEACHER'S NOTE: The study of economics includes the investigation of interdependent economies throughout the world over time and place. Students should be able to trace the maritime and overland trading routes that linked civilizations and led to interdependence and cultural diffusion.
			- Why did the Silk Road extend from Korea across Central Asia?
			- What goods were being traded? Why?
			Suggested Documents: Maps of classical civilizations and early trade routes

D. The rise and fall of great empires
1. Han Dynasty
  a. Human and physical geography
  b. Factors leading to growth
  c. Contributions
  d. Causes of decline
  e. Role of migrating nomadic groups from Central Asia
2. Roman Empire
		Human/ Physical Geography Cultural and Intellectual Life Movement of People and Goods Technology Power	- What caused the fall of the Han and Roman empires?
			- What role did migrating nomadic groups play in the fall of the Han and Roman empires?

Content	Standards	Concepts/Themes	Connections
a. Human and physical geography b. Factors leading to growth (engineering, empire building, trade) c. Contributions d. Causes of decline e. Role of migrating nomadic groups from Central Asia f. Pax Romana			

E. The emergence and spread of belief systems
1. Place of origin and major beliefs
  a. Animism—African
  b. Hinduism
  c. Buddhism
  d. Chinese philosophies (Confucianism, Daoism)
  e. Judaism
  f. Christianity
  g. Islam
  h. Legalism
  i. Shintoism
  j. Jainism
2. Expansion of Christianity, Islam, Confucianism, and Buddhism
		Belief Systems
		Human/
		  Physical
		  Geography
		Conflict
		Diversity
		Cultural and
		  Intellectual
		  Life
			TEACHER'S NOTE: When analyzing the world's major religions and philosophies, it may be best to suspend a strict adherence to chronology in favor of comprehensively exploring belief systems as a theme. On the other hand, you may teach this subject in its historical context. This study involves learning about the important roles and contributions made by individuals and groups. It is important to make linkages to the present.
			- In what ways are these varying belief systems similar and different?
			- How do these belief systems affect our lives today?
			- In what ways does a culture's arts reflect its belief system?
			- What individuals and groups are associated with the major religions of the world?
			- What holy books or texts are associated with the major religions of the world?
			- What role did missionaries, traders, and conquerors play in the spread of religions?
			- How did the expansion of Islam, Confucianism, Christianity, and Buddhism encourage the encounter and exchanges of peoples, goods, and ideas?
			Suggested Documents: Maps showing spread of religions, Old Testament, Torah, New Testament, the Lawbook of Manu: the Caste System, the Bhagavad-Gita, Life of Buddha, the Analects, Daoist poems, the Koran (Qur'an), Confucius, *Analects* http://www.wsu.edu:8080/~wldciv/world_civ_reader/world_civ_reader_1/confucius.html

UNIT TWO: EXPANDING ZONES OF EXCHANGE AND ENCOUNTER (500 - 1200)

Content	Standards	Concepts/Themes	Connections
A. Gupta Empire (320-550 AD) 1. Human and physical geography 2. Artistic, scientific, and mathematical contributions 3. Ties to Hinduism 4. Organizational structure	2,3	Human/ Physical Geography Cultural and Intellectual Life	TEACHER'S NOTE: Students should be able to interpret and analyze documents and artifacts related to global history. Using graphic organizers, they can compare and contrast civilizations. - What contributions to human history have been made by the Gupta Empire, the Tang and Song Dynasty, Byzantine Empire, and medieval Europe? - What role did women play in the Gupta Empire? the Tang and Song Dynasty?
B. Tang and Song Dynasty (618-1126 AD) 1. Human and physical geography 2. Contributions 3. Chinese influence on Korea and Japan 4. Cultural flowering 5. Growth of commerce and trade	2,3	Human/ Physical Geography Cultural and Intellectual Life	Suggested Documents: Photographs of Gupta, Tang, and Song arts; remains of material culture; timelines; and maps
C. Byzantine Empire (330-1453 AD) 1. Human and physical geography 2. Achievements (law—Justinian Code, engineering, art, and commerce) 3. The Orthodox Christian Church 4. Political structure and Justinian Code 5. Role in preserving and transmitting Greek and Roman cultures 6. Impact on Russia and Eastern Europe D. Early Russia 1. Human and physical geography 2. Trade 3. Kiev 4. Russian Orthodox Church	2,3,4,5	Human/ Physical Geography Interdependence Diversity Justice Belief Systems	TEACHER'S NOTE: Students should understand the development and connectedness of civilizations and cultures. The study of the Byzantine Empire is particularly suited to this approach because it encompasses lands from more than one region. - What role did the Byzantine Empire play in the preservation and transmission of Greek and Roman knowledge and culture? of Roman concept of law? - What impact did the Byzantine Empire have in the development of historical Russia? of Russia today? - What impact did the fall of Constantinople (1453) have on Western Europe? To what extent was this event a turning point in global history? - How did the location of Constantinople make it a crossroads of Europe and Asia? - How did geography affect early Russia? Suggested Documents: Justinian Code, pictures of Hagia Sophia, mosaics, reservoirs, etc.
E. The spread of Islam to Europe, Asia, and Africa 1. Human and physical geography 2. Organizational structure		Human/ Physical Geography	TEACHER'S NOTE: Through their inquiry, students should gain an appreciation for the vastness of the various Muslim empires, the ability of Islam to

Content	Standards	Concepts/Themes	Connections
3. The development of Islamic law and its impact 4. Social class: women and slavery in Muslim society 5. Position of "people of the book"	2,3	Conflict Interdependence Diversity Justice and Human Rights Political Systems Economic Systems Belief Systems	successfully rule very diverse populations, and the role of Islam in cultural innovation and trade. - What contributions did Islamic culture make to global history? - What was the status of women under Islamic law? - How did Islam link Eastern and Western cultures?

6. The golden age of Islam
  a. Contributions to mathematics, science, medicine, art, architecture, and literature
  b. Role in preserving Greek and Roman culture
  c. Islamic Spain
7. Trade
	2	Cultural and Intellectual Life
		Science and Technology
			- What was the role of Islamic missionaries in Africa? in other regions?
			- How did Islam art and architecture reflect a blend of many different cultures?
			<u>Suggested Documents</u>: Maps showing trade in and around the Indian Ocean and Central Asia, Islamic art and architecture, and calligraphy

F. Medieval Europe (500-1400)
1. Human and physical geography
2. Frankish Empire—Charlemagne
3. Manorialism
4. Feudalism
  a. Social hierarchy and stratification
  b. Role of men and women
5. Spiritual and secular role of the Church
6. Monastic centers of learning
7. Anti-Semitism
8. Art and architecture
	2,3,4,5	Economic Systems
		Factors of Production
		Political Systems
		Belief Systems
			- What assumptions did medieval Europe make regarding power, authority, governance, and law?
			- How did the roles of men and women differ in medieval society?
			- What role did individual citizens play in feudal society?
			- How were decisions made about the use of scarce resources in medieval Europe?
			- What principles were the basis of these decisions?
			<u>Suggested Documents</u>: Photographs and architectural drawings, details of paintings showing everyday life, diagrams and charts of monasteries and manors, and diagrams of social pyramids

G. Crusades 1. Causes 2. Impacts on Southwest Asia, Byzantium, and Europe 3. Perspectives 4. Key individuals—Urban II, Saladin, and Richard the Lion-Hearted	2,3,4	Human/ Physical Geography Change Nation-states Interdependence Movement of People and Goods Needs and Wants Science and Technology Conflict	TEACHER'S NOTE: Students should be able to analyze the causes of the Crusades and their impact. They should understand the diverse ways Muslims, Byzantines, and Christians viewed this period. They should appreciate that one dimension of a society's growth is its connection to neighboring and competing societies. Students should explore how places have taken on symbolic meaning throughout history, e.g., Jerusalem as a holy city. <u>Suggested Documents</u>: Portolan charts, various kinds of other maps, and first-hand accounts

UNIT THREE: GLOBAL INTERACTIONS (1200 - 1650)

Content	Standards	Concepts/Themes	Connections
A. Early Japanese history and feudalism 1. Human and physical geography 2. Early traditions (Shintoism) 3. Ties with China and Korea: cultural diffusion, Buddhism, and Confucianism 4. Tokugawa Shogunate 5. Social hierarchy and stratification 6. Comparison to European feudalism 7. Zen Buddhism	1,2,3,4,5	Human/ Physical Geography Political Systems Cultural and Intellectual Life Belief Systems	TEACHER'S NOTE: Students should be able to compare and contrast the social, political, and economic dimensions of the Japanese and European feudal systems. They should understand the impact of cultural diffusion on Japanese culture. Additional case studies might include Chinese and Korean feudalism. - How are Japanese and European feudalism similar? dissimilar? - How did location impact Japanese history? Suggested Documents: *The Way of Samurai*, and other literary works; materials on Kabuki theatre; Japanese wood-block prints; diagrams of the social system
B. The rise and fall of the Mongols and their impact on Eurasia 1. Human and physical geography 2. Origins—Central Asian nomadic tribes 3. The Yuan Dynasty: a foreign non-Chinese dynasty 4. Extent of empire under Ghengis Khan and Kublai Khan 5. Impact on Central Asia, China, Korea, Europe, India, Southwest Asia 6. Impact on the rise of Moscow 7. Interaction with the West and global trade, Pax Mongolia (e.g., Marco Polo) 8. Causes of decline	2,3,4,5	Human/ Physical Geography Interdependence Diversity Urbanization Movement of People and Goods Conflict	TEACHER'S NOTE: Students should understand the development and connectedness of civilizations and cultures. They should understand the global significance and great diversity encompassed by the Mongol Empire. This era saw the growing importance of cities as centers of trade and culture. - How did geography contribute to the success of the Mongols? - What forces led to the rise and fall of the Mongols? - How were a nomadic people able to conquer more advanced civilizations? - Why was the Mongol defeat in Japan significant? - How did the Mongols in China change? Suggested Documents: Descriptions of Mongols by such travelers as Marco Polo (see http://www.fordham.edu/halsall/source/mpolo44-46.html) and others; visuals, maps

C. Global trade and interactions
1. Resurgence of Europe
  a. Hanseatic League and Italian city-states
  b. Trade fairs and towns
  c. Medieval guilds
  d. Commercial revolution
2. Major trading centers—Nanjing/ Calicut/Mogadishu/Venice
3. Ibn Battuta
4. Expansion of the Portuguese spice trade to Southeast Asia and its impact on Asia and Europe
	2,3,4	Economic Systems
		Change
		Urbanization
		Factors of Production
		Movement of People and Goods
			TEACHER'S NOTE: Students should be able to trace the rise and evolution of capitalism as an economic system. They should understand that capitalism was made possible by changes within the European economic system and by overseas expansion.
			- What was the relationship between the rise of capitalism and the decline of feudalism?
			- What role did a class of merchants and bankers play in the rise of capitalism?

Content	Standards	Concepts/Themes	Connections
			- In a market economy, how does the system determine what goods and services are to be produced and in what quantities? and for whom? - How did a capitalist economy change the way men and women worked? - Why did cities like Venice and Mogadishu become trading centers? - What were the major land and sea trade routes of the early 1400s? - What goods were being traded? Suggested Documents: Maps, descriptions of medieval guilds, town charters, journals

D. Rise and fall of African civilizations: Ghana, Mali, Axum, and Songhai empires
  1. Human and physical geography
  2. Organizational structure
  3. Contributions
  4. Roles in global trade routes
  5. Spread and impact of Islam—Mansa Musa
  6. Timbuktu and African trade routes
	2,3,4	Human/ Physical Geography Economic Systems Change Urbanization Belief Systems Movement of People and Goods	TEACHER'S NOTE: Students should study development and interactions of social/cultural/political/economic/ religious systems in different regions of the world.
			- What role did African kingdoms play in overland and maritime trade routes of the era?
			- What impact did Islam have on these kingdoms?
			- What forces contributed to the rise and fall of African kingdoms? How did they compare with the rise and fall of other empires?
			- How did traditional art reflect the beliefs of African kingdoms?
			Suggested Document: Leo Africanus; Description of Timbuktu from *The Description of Africa* see http://www.ws u.edu:8080/~wldciv/world_civ_reader/ world_civ_reader_2/leo_africanus.html

E. Social, economic, and political impacts of the plague on Eurasia and Africa	2,3,4,5	Human/ Physical Geography Change	- What role did the plague play in major demographic and social shifts in Eurasia and Africa? Suggested Documents: Maps showing the global spread and extent of the plague, written accounts by Europeans and others (Jean deVenette; Ibn al-wardi; Giovanni Boccaccio, *The Decameron*)

F. Renaissance and humanism
  1. Human and physical geography
  2. Shift in worldview—other-worldly to secular
  3. Greco-Roman revival (interest in humanism)
  4. Art and architecture (e.g., da Vinci and Michelangelo)
	2,3,5	Human/ Physical Geography Cultural and Intellectual Life Science and Technology	TEACHER'S NOTE: Students should understand that the Renaissance represented a shift from the emphasis on spiritual concerns in the medieval period to more secular ones. Humanism emphasized the importance of individual worth in a secular society.
			- What impact did capitalism have on the Renaissance?

Content	Standards	Concepts/Themes	Connections
5. Literature (e.g., Dante, Cervantes, Shakespeare) 6. Political science (e.g., Machiavelli) 7. New scientific and technological innovations (Gutenberg's moveable type printing press, cartography, naval engineering, and navigational and nautical devices)		Decision Making Power	- How did the Renaissance differ from the medieval period? How was it similar? Suggested Documents: Diagrams of the printing press; nautical devices; maps and historical atlases—the historic maps of Ptolemy, Abraham Ortelius, Gerardus Mercator, Johann Blaeu, Georg Braun, and Franz Hogenberg; Renaissance art; excerpts from Renaissance literature; Machiavelli, *The Prince;* works by Dante, Cervantes, and Shakespeare
G. Reformation and Counter Reformation 1. Human and physical geography 2. Martin Luther's *Ninety-Five Theses*: the challenge to the power and authority of the Roman Catholic Church 3. Anti-Semitic laws and policies 4. Henry VIII and the English Reformation 5. Calvin and other reformers 6. Counter Reformation (Ignatius Loyola, Council of Trent) 7. Roles of men and women within the Christian churches 8. Religious wars in Europe: causes and impacts	2	Human/ Physical Geography Belief Systems Conflict Change Nationalism	TEACHER'S NOTE: Students should be provided with opportunities to look at issues from multiple perspectives (e.g., the conflict between the Roman Catholic Church and secular rulers, nationalism, and the unifying role of the Roman Catholic Church). The Reformation challenged the traditional power and authority of the Roman Catholic Church. Students should analyze different kinds of maps of Europe during this time period. - How did religious reform lead to conflict? To what extent were these conflicts resolved? - What role did Elizabeth I play in the English Reformation? Suggested Documents: Exerpts from Shakespeare, *The Merchant of Venice;* Martin Luther, *The Ninety-five Theses,* Loyola, *Spiritual Exercise*
H. The rise and impact of European nation-states/decline of feudalism Case studies: England—Elizabeth I: France—Joan of Arc a. Forces moving toward centralization b. Role of nationalism	5	Nationalism Nation State Conflict Political Systems Power Decision Making	- What forces led to the rise of nation-states? - In what ways did nationalism support centralized governments headed by powerful rulers? - What forces opposed absolute monarchies? - How did nationalism lead to conflict between secular and ecclesiastical powers? Suggested Documents: Different kinds of maps including Ptolemaic, Mercator, Blaeu, Braun, and Hogenberg, and Ortelius; pictures of cities

UNIT FOUR: THE FIRST GLOBAL AGE (1450 - 1770)

Content	Standards	Concepts/Themes	Connections

A. The Ming Dynasty (1368-1644)
  1. Human and physical geography
  2. Restoration of Chinese rule, Chinese world vision
  3. The impact of China on East Asia and Southeast Asia
  4. China's relationship with the West
  5. Contributions
  6. Expansion of trade (Zheng He, 1405-1433)
	2,3,4	Human/ Physical Geography
		Cultural and Intellectual Life
		Movement of People and Goods
			- What were the Ming achievements in science and engineering?
			- What impact did China's self-concept of the "middle kingdom" have on its political, economic, and cultural relationships with other societies in Eastern and Southeastern Asia?
			- To what extent was Europe more interested in trade with China, than China was interested in trade with the West? Why?
			- What factors made the Ming turn away from expeditions of trade and exploration?
			Suggested Documents: Photographs of blue and white porcelain, map showing voyages of Zheng He; excerpts from the novel *Journey to the West*; Matteo Ricci, *The Art of Printing* http://academic.brooklyn. cuny.edu/core9/phalsall/texts/ric-prt.html

B. The impact of the Ottoman Empire on the Middle East and Europe
  1. Human and physical geography
  2. Contributions
  3. Suleiman I (the Magnificent, the Lawgiver)
  4. Disruption of established trade routes and European search for new ones
  5. Limits of Ottoman Europe
	2,3,4
	
	5
	
	2
		Human/ Physical Geography
		Belief Systems
		Change
		Political Systems
		Movement of People and Goods
			TEACHER'S NOTE: Students should have a clear understanding of the extent of the Ottoman Empire at its height. They should investigate the factors that brought about change within the Ottoman Empire and its long-term impacts on global history.
			- What factors contributed to the rise and fall of the Ottoman Empire?
			- What impact did Ottoman domination have on Eastern Europe? What impact continues today?
			- To what extent were the fall of Constantinople to the Ottomans and Columbus's voyages major turning points in global history?
			- Why was Suleiman I called the Magnificent by Westerners and Lawgiver by Ottomans?
			- How did Suleiman I compare to other absolute rulers (Akbar, Louis XIV, Peter the Great)?
			- How did Ottoman law compare with other legal systems?

C. Spain and Portugal on the eve of the encounter
  1. Human and physical geography
  2. Reconquista under Ferdinand and Isabella
	5	Human/ Physical Geography	- What were Spain and Portugal like on the eve of the encounter?
			- In what ways was 1492 a turning point in global history?

Content	Standards	Concepts/Themes	Connections
3. Expulsion of Moors and Jews 4. Exploration and overseas expansion a. Columbus b. Magellan circumnavigates the globe		Movement of People and Goods Human Rights Conflict	- What impact did the encounter have on demographic trends in the Americas, Africa, and Europe? - How did life change as a result of this encounter? - How did the standard of living in Europe change as a result of the encounter? - What technologies made European overseas expansion possible? What were the original sources of those technologies? - How did Jews and Muslims view the Reconquista? the Inquisition?
D. The rise of Mesoamerican empires: Aztec and Incan empires before 1500 1. Human and physical geography 2. Organizational structure 3. Contributions 4. Trade	2,3,4,5	Human/Physical Geography Cultural and Intellectual Life Diversity Urbanization	TEACHER'S NOTE: Here is another instance in which strict adherence to chronology is suspended in order for students to acquire a broader knowledge of the rise and fall of diverse civilizations. Students should be able to compare and contrast the empires of Mesoamerica with the empires of Afro-Eurasia. They should understand that on the eve of the encounter, the peoples of the Americas already had complex societies. - To what extent can the Aztec and Incan empires be compared to earlier Afro-Eurasian classical civilizations in terms of their organization and achievements? - How widespread were Aztec and Incan trade?
E. The encounter between Europeans and the peoples of Africa, the Americas, and Asia Case study: The Columbian exchange 1. Human and physical geography 2. European competition for colonies in the Americas, Africa, East Asia, and Southeast Asia—The "old imperialism" 3. Global demographic shifts Case study: The triangular trade and slavery 4. The extent of European expansionism 5. European mercantilism 6. Spanish colonialism and the introduction of the Encomienda system to Latin America 7. Dutch colonization in East Asia (Japan and Indonesia) 8. Exchange of food and disease	2 5 3 4	Human/Physical Geography Conflict Economic Systems Human/Physical Geography Movement of People and Goods	TEACHER'S NOTE: Students should understand that the encounters between peoples in the 15th and early-16th centuries had a tremendous impact upon the worldwide exchange of flora, fauna, and diseases. - What forces came together in the mid-1400s that made the Age of European Exploration possible? - What impact did European technology, food, and disease have on the Americas? - What impact did food and diseases introduced from the Americas have on Europe, Africa, and Asia? - What impact did the introduction of American foodstuffs (corn, sweet potatoes, peanuts) have on the increase in Chinese population? - What impact did mercantilism have on European colonies? on Europe? <u>Suggested Documents</u>: Maps of transatlantic trade showing the exchange of goods; various diaries; Bartolomé de las

Content	Standards	Concepts/Themes	Connections
F. Political ideologies: global absolutism 1. Human and physical geography 2. Thomas Hobbes, *The Leviathan* 3. Jacques-Benigne Bossuet: Absolutism and Divine right theory 4. Case studies: Akbar the Great, Suleiman the Magnificent, Philip II, Louis XIV, Ivan the Terrible, and Peter the Great	2,5	Human/ Physical Geography Political Systems Power	Casas, *The General History of the Indies* TEACHER'S NOTE: Students should understand that in the 16th and 17th centuries, the monarchies of Western Europe sought to centralize political power. Political absolutism supported that trend. Students should be able to compare and contrast absolutism in Europe with absolutism in Asia and Africa. Suggested Documents: Maps of Russian expansion, other political maps; Extracts from Bossuet's Work on Kingship, http://history.hanover.edu/early/bossuet.htm
G. The response to absolutism: The rise of parliamentary democracy in England 1. Background—Magna Carta 2. Divine Right of Monarchy—Stuart rule 3. Puritan Revolution—Oliver Cromwell 4. Glorious Revolution—John Locke and the English Bill of Rights	5	Conflict Culture and Intellectual Life Decision Making Power Citizenship	TEACHER'S NOTE: The tradition of sharing political power and natural law had its roots in Greek and Roman practice and was expressed in documents that limited royal power such as the Magna Carta and the English Bill of Rights. - What impact did the Puritan Revolution have on the Enlightenment and subsequent political events in Europe and the Americas? Suggested Documents: Thomas Hobbes, *The Leviathan*; Niccolo Machiavelli, *The Prince*; James I, *Justification of Absolute Monarchy*; John Locke, *Two Treatises of Government*; and the English Bill of Rights

UNIT FIVE: AN AGE OF REVOLUTION (1750 - 1914)

Content	Standards	Concepts/Themes	Connections
A. The Scientific Revolution 1. The development of scientific methods 2. The work of Copernicus, Galileo, Newton, and Descartes	2	Science and Technology Change	TEACHER'S NOTE: Students should understand that the Scientific Revolution in Europe, with its emphasis on observation, experimentation, investigation, and speculation, represented a new approach to problem solving. This philosophy became synonymous with modern thought throughout the world. - What role did science and technology play in the changes that took place in Europe from 1450 to 1770? - To what extent was the Scientific Revolution a rejection of traditional authority?

Content	Standards	Concepts/Themes	Connections
			- To what extent does this tension still exist? - To what extent did Europeans apply this approach to traditional values and institutions? Suggested Documents: Nicolaus Copernicus, *On the Revolutions of the Heavenly Spheres*; Galileo Galilei, *Letter to the Grand Dutchess Christina* and *Dialogue Concerning the Two Chief World Systems*; René Descartes, *Discourse on Method*
B. The Enlightenment in Europe 　1. The writings of Locke, Voltaire, Rousseau, and Montesquieu 　2. The impact of the Enlightenment on nationalism and democracy 　3. The enlightened despots—Maria Theresa and Catherine the Great	5	Cultural and Intellectual Life Citizenship Decision Making Political Systems	TEACHER'S NOTE: Students should understand that during the Enlightenment, Europeans moved toward new assumptions regarding power, authority, governance, and law. These assumptions led to the new social and political systems during the Age of Revolution. Suggested Documents: John Locke, *Two Treatises of Government*; Jean-Jacques Rousseau, *The Social Contract*; Voltaire, Treatise on Toleration; René Descartes, *Discourse on Method*; for writings of Catherine the Great see http://www.fordham.edu/halsall/mod/18catherine.html
C. Political revolutions 　1. Human and physical geography of revolutions 　2. American Revolution 　　a. Impact of the Enlightenment on the American Revolution 　　b. Impact of the American Revolution on other revolutions 　3. French Revolution 　　a. Causes 　　b. Key individuals (Robespierre and Louis XVI) 　　c. Impact on France and other nations 　　d. Rise to power of Napoleon and his impact (Napoleonic Code) 　4. Independence movements in Latin America 　Case studies: Simon Bolivar, Toussaint L'Ouverture, José de San Martín 　　a. Causes 　　b. Impacts	1,2,3,4,5 1,2,3,4,5	Human/ Physical Geography Conflict Change Political Systems Economic Systems Nationalism Nation State	TEACHER'S NOTE: Students should focus on the impact of the Enlightenment on American political thought and, in turn, the impact of the American Revolution on subsequent revolutions. Students should not engage in an in-depth analysis of the battles and phases of the American Revolution. The American, French, and Latin American revolutions were turning points in global history. Students should be able to identify the forces that brought about these changes and their long-term effects. TEACHER'S NOTE: Each of these revolutions, both political and economic, provides students with multiple opportunities for examination of issues from multiple perspectives. - To what extent was the Scientific Revolution related to the Enlightenment? - In what ways did the French Revolution overturn the balance of power that had existed in Europe? - To what extent are the stages of the American, French, and Latin American revolutions similar? dissimilar?

Content	Standards	Concepts/Themes	Connections

D. The reaction against revolutionary ideas
1. Human and physical geography
2. Balance of power politics and the Congress of Vienna (Klemens von Metternich)
3. Revolutions of 1848
4. Russian absolutism: reforms and expansion
  a. Impact of the French Revolution and Napoleon
  b. 19th-century Russian serfdom
  c. Expansion of Russia into Siberia
	1,2,3,4,5	Human/ Physical Geography
		Change
		Nation State
			Suggested Documents: Thomas Paine, *Common Sense*; the Declaration of Independence; the Bill of Rights; the Declaration of the Rights of Man and of Citizens; Edmund Burke, *Reflections on the Revolution in France*; Simon Bolivar, *Message to the Congress of Angostura* http://www.fordham.edu/halsall/mod /1819bolivar.html
			- What impact did the Congress of Vienna and conservative reaction across Europe have on the establishment of democratic states in Europe?
			- What reactions against revolutionary ideas occurred in Europe, Russia, and Latin America?
			- What forces led to the 19th-century failure of democracy in Latin America and Russia?
			- What role did the individual citizen play in these revolutions?
			Suggested Documents: Political maps of these revolutions reflecting adjustments and boundary changes, before and after the Congress of Vienna

E. Latin America: The failure of democracy and the search for stability
1. Human and physical geography
2. Roles of social classes: land-holding elite, creoles, mestizos, native peoples, and slaves
3. Roles of the Church and military
4. Role of cash crop economies in a global market
5. The Mexican Revolution (1910-1930)
  a. Cause and effect
  b. Roles of Porfirio Diaz, Francisco "Pancho" Villa, and Emiliano Zapata
  c. Economic and social nationalism
	2,3,4,5	Nationalism
		
		Economic Systems
		
		Factors of Production
		
		Change
		Conflict
		Human Rights
			- What were the perspectives of various social classes on the revolutions in Latin America?
			
			- What role did peasants play in the Mexican Revolution?
			- How successful was this revolution?
			- What role did nationalism play in this revolution?

F. Global nationalism
1. Human and physical geography
2. Role in political revolutions
3. Force for unity and self-determination
  a. Unification of Italy and Germany (Camillo Cavour, Otto von Bismarck)
  b. Asian and Middle Eastern nationalism
   1) India (Indian National
	2,3,4,5	Human/ Physical Geography
		Change
		Conflict
		Nationalism
			TEACHER'S NOTE: Students should be able to define nationalism and analyze the impact of nationalism as a unifying and divisive force in Europe and other areas of the world. They should also be able to examine nationalism across time and place.
			- What role did nationalism play in Europe, Eastern Europe, Asia, Africa, and Latin America?
			- What role does nationalism play today in these regions?

UNIT FIVE: AN AGE OF REVOLUTION (1750 - 1914), continued

Content	Standards	Concepts/Themes	Connections

Congress, Moslem League)
 2) Turkey—Young Turks
 4. Zionism
 5. Force leading to conflicts
   a. Balkans before World War I
   b. Ottoman Empire as the pawn of European powers
			<u>Suggested Documents</u>: Giuseppe Mazzini, *Young Italy*; Carl Schurz, *Revolution Spreads to the German States*

G. Economic and social revolutions
 1. Human and physical geography
 2. Agrarian revolution
 3. The British Industrial Revolution
   a. Capitalism and a market economy
   b. Factory system
   c. Shift from mercantilism to laissez-faire economics—Adam Smith, *The Wealth of Nations*
   d. Changes in social classes
   e. Changing roles of men, women, and children
   f. Urbanization
   g. Responses to industrialization
    1) Utopian reform—Robert Owen
    2) Legislative reform
    3) Role of unions
	2,3,4,5	Human/ Physical Geography Change Economic Systems Urbanization Factors of Production
		
		 Environment Human Rights Conflict
		
		 Environment
			TEACHER'S NOTE: Students should understand that the Agrarian and Industrial revolutions, like the Neolithic Revolution, led to radical change. Students should realize that the process of industrialization is still occurring in developing nations.
			 -What role did the Industrial Revolution play in the changing roles of men and women?
			 - What impact did the Industrial Revolution have on the expansion of suffrage throughout the late-19th and early-20th centuries?
			 - To what extent did the Industrial Revolution lead to greater urbanization throughout the world?
			 - What geographic factors explain why industrialization began in Great Britain?
			 - How did the European arts respond to the Industrial Revolution?
			 - In what ways did social class impact on the ways various groups looked at the Industrial Revolution?
			 - What impact did industrialization have on the environment?
			 - In what ways did the abuses of the Industrial Revolution lead to such competing ideologies as liberalism, conservatism, socialism, and communism?
			 TEACHER'S NOTE: Students should be able to compare social and economic revolutions with political revolutions. In looking at the Industrial Revolution, students should be provided with the opportunity to investigate this phenomenon in at least two nations.
			 - To what extent is the Industrial Revolution still occurring in the non-Western world?

Content	Standards	Concepts/Themes	Connections
4) Karl Marx and Friedrich Engels and command economies		Urbanization	- What is meant by postindustrial economy?
5) Sadler Report and reform legislation			TEACHER'S NOTE: Students should understand that Marx and Engels proposed an economic system that would replace capitalism.
6) Parliamentary reforms— expansion of suffrage			Suggested Documents: Resource maps, Sadler Commission, *Report on Child Labor*; Friedrich Engels, *The Conditions of the Working Class in England*; Karl Marx and Friedrich Engels, *Communist Manifesto*; Thomas Malthus, *Essay on the Principles of Population*; Adam Smith, *The Wealth of Nations*; Charles Dickens, *Hard Times* and *Oliver Twist*; Emile Zola, *Germinal*
7) Writers (Dickens and Zola)			
8) Global migrations (19th century)		Movement of People and Goods	
9) Writings of Thomas Malthus (*Essay on the Principles of Population*)		Human Rights Nationalism	
3. Mass starvation in Ireland (1845-1850)		Change Conflict	TEACHER'S NOTE: A response by individuals to industrialization was the mass migration of Europeans to other parts of the world. Look at other examples of migration.
a. Growth of Irish nationalism			
b. Global migration			TEACHER'S NOTE: Students may want to look at industrialization in other nations.
H. Imperialism	2,3,4,5	Imperialism	TEACHER'S NOTE: Using primary and secondary sources, students should be able to analyze and evaluate conflicting viewpoints regarding imperialism.
1. Reasons for imperialism—nationalistic, political, economic, "The White Man's Burden", Social Darwinism		Economic Systems	- To what extent is there a relationship between industrialization and imperialism?
2. Spatial characteristics—"new imperialism"		Factors of Production	- Why did Japan turn to imperialism and militarism in the late-19th and early-20th centuries? Here again, students should have a clear appreciation of the world in spatial terms.
3. British in India			
a. British, East India Company			
b. Sepoy Mutiny		Political Systems	
4. British, French, Belgians, and Germans in Africa			
a. Scramble for Africa			- What was the relationship between nationalism, industrialization, and imperialism?
b. The Congress of Berlin			
c. African resistance—Zulu Empire			Suggested Documents: Maps of migration, charts, graphs, rural and urban demographics, maps of colonial possessions, journals, writings of people and groups showing contending perspectives on imperialism, Sun Yixian, *History of the Chinese Revolution*; Rudyard Kipling's, "The White Man's Burden"
d. Boer War			
e. Cecil Rhodes			
f. 19th-century anti-slave trade legislation			
5. European spheres of influence in China			
a. Opium Wars (1839 - 1842 and 1858 - 1860) and the Treaty of Nanjing			
1) Unequal treaties			
2) Extraterritoriality			

Content	Standards	Concepts/Themes	Connections

b. Boxer Rebellion
c. Sun Yat-sen (Sun Yixian) and the Chinese Revolution (1910-1911)
6. Multiple perspectives toward imperialism
  a. Immediate/long-term changes made under European rule
  b. Long-term effects in Europe and the rest of the world			

I. Japan and the Meiji restoration
  1. Human and physical geography
  2. The opening of Japan
    a. Commodore Matthew Perry
    b. Impact upon Japan of Treaty of Kanagawa
  3. Modernization, industrialization
	2,3,4,5	Change
		Human/
		  Physical
		  Geography
		Imperialism
		Conflict
		Economic
		  Systems
			TEACHER'S NOTE: Students should analyze the Meiji Restoration in terms of the political, economic, and social changes that were introduced. Students should be able to compare and contrast English and Japanese industrialization. Have students compare industrialization and westernization in Japan and the Ottoman Empire and other non-Western nations and Europe.
			- Why did the Industrial Revolution occur in Japan before other Asian and African nations?
			- What caused the conflicts between China, Russia, and Japan?

4. Japan as an imperialist power
    a. First Sino-Japanese War (1894 - 1895)
    b. Russo-Japanese War
    c. Annexation of Korea
    d. Dependence on world market
			- What impact did the Russo-Japanese War have on the relative power of Russia? Japan?
			- Why did Japan annex Korea? What policies did Japan follow in Korea (1910-1945)?
			- How does Japanese imperialism of the past influence Japan's relations with her Asian neighbors today?
			<u>Suggested Documents</u>: Political maps of Japan and East Asia; Millard Fillmore, *Letter to the Emperor of Japan*; Ito Hirobumi, *Reminiscence on Drafting of the New Constitution*; 19th-century Japanese prints showing contact with the West

UNIT SIX: A HALF CENTURY OF CRISIS AND ACHIEVEMENT (1900 - 1945)

Content	Standards	Concepts/Themes	Connections

A. World War I
  1. Europe: the physical setting
  2. Causes
  3. Impacts
  4. Effects of scientific/technological advances on warfare
  5. Armenian Massacre
  6. Collapse of the Ottoman Empire
  7. The war as reflected in literature, art, and propaganda
	2,3,4,5	Human/
		Physical
		Geography
		Conflict
		Nationalism
		Imperialism
		Diversity
		Political
		Systems
		Cultural and
		Intellectual
		Life
		Science and
		Technology
			Students analyze documents and artifacts related to the study of World War I. They should be asked to consider which events of the first half of the 20th century were turning points.
			- What role did nationalism and imperialism play in World War I?
			- What role did technology play?
			- To what extent were the issues that caused World War I resolved?
			- In what ways did World War I raise fundamental questions regarding justice and human rights?
			- To what extent were World War I and the Russian Revolution turning points?
			- What role did women play in the war?
			- To what extent was the collapse of the Ottoman Empire like the fall of the Han and Roman empires and the collapse of the Soviet Union?
			Why might the Germans, French, and British view the causes of World War I differently?
			<u>Suggested Documents</u>: Erich Maria Remarque, *All Quiet on the Western Front*; Mustafa Kemal, *Proclamation of the Young Turks*; videotapes

B. Revolution and change in Russia—causes and impacts
  1. Czar Nicholas II
  2. The Revolution of 1905
  3. March Revolution and provisional government
  4. Bolshevik Revolution
  5. V.I. Lenin's rule in Russia
  6. Stalin and the rise of a modern totalitarian state: industrialization, command economy, collectivization
  7. Russification of ethnic republics
  8. Forced famine in Ukraine
  9. Reign of Terror
	2,3,4,5	Change
		Justice and
		Human
		Rights
		Political and
		Economic
		Systems
		Conflict
			TEACHER'S NOTE: Students should understand that Lenin and Stalin used the work of Marx to create a command economy.
			- What were the causes of the Russian Revolution?
			- Why did a communist revolution occur in Russia rather than a more industrialized nation?
			- What steps did the Communists take to industrialize the Soviet Union?
			- To what extent were the human rights of Russians and other ethnic and national groups respected by the Stalinist regime?
			- How did various groups view the Russian Revolution?
			- How does Russian industrialization compare with that of Western Europe?

Content	Standards	Concepts/Themes	Connections

C. Between the wars
  1. Human and physical geography
  2. Treaty of Versailles and the League of Nations
  3. Modernization and westernization of a secular Turkey—Kemal Atatürk
  4. Women's suffrage movement
  5. Great Depression—causes and impacts
  6. Weimar Republic and the rise of fascism as an aftermath of World War I
  7. Japanese militarism and imperialism
    a. Manchuria, 1931
    b. Second Sino-Japanese War (1937-1945)
  8. Policy of appeasement—Munich Pact
  9. Colonial response to European imperialism
    Case studies: Mohandas Gandhi, Reza Khan, Jiang Jieshi (Chiang Kai-shek), Mao Zedong.; Zionism, Arab nationalism, the Amritsar massacre—Indian nationalism, Salt March, civil disobedience
  10. Arabic and Zionist nationalism
	2,3,4,5	Human/
		Physical
		Geography
		Justice and
		Human
		Rights
		Change
		Economic
		Systems
		
		Imperialism
		Nationalism
		Conflict
			Suggested Documents: Communist political posters and art; V.I. Lenin, *The Call to Power*; Joseph Stalin, *The Hard Line*; Nikita S. Khrushchev, Address to the Twentieth Party Congress; for the Abdication of Nikolai II see http://www.dur.ac.uk/~dml0www/abdicatn.html
			- To what extent did communism and fascism challenge liberal democratic traditions?
			
			- What impact did Japanese occupation have on China?
			
			Suggested Documents: Political maps of the Post World War I time period; Woodrow Wilson's speeches; Mao Zedong, *Strategic Problems of China's Revolutionary War*; Mohandas Gandhi, *Indian Opinion* and *The Essential Gandhi: An Anthology*; Arthur James Balfour, *The Balfour Declaration*

D. World War II—causes and impact
  1. Human and physical geography
  2. The Nazi and Japanese states
  3. Key individuals—Hitler, Mussolini, Stalin, Churchill, and Roosevelt
  4. Key events—Dunkirk, the Blitz, D-Day, Hitler's second front, the war in the Pacific
  5. The Nazi Holocaust: the extermination of Jews, Poles, other Slavs, Gypsies, disabled, and others
  6. Resistance
  7. Japan's role—Nanjing, Bataan, Pearl Harbor
  8. War in China—Long March
  9. Impacts of technology on total war
  10. Hiroshima and Nagasaki
  11. War crime trials
  12. Global spatial arrangements—post-World War II world
	1,2,3,4,5
	
	1,2,3,4,5
		Human/
		Physical
		Geography
		Change
		Economic and
		Political
		Systems
		Science and
		Technology
		Conflict
		Human Rights
		Justice
			- What roles did Churchill, Roosevelt, Stalin, Hitler, and Mussolini play in the outcome of World War II?
			- As nations moved toward war, what roles did individual citizens play in the Third Reich and in Western democracies?
			- To what extent did science and technology redefine the latter half of the 20th century?
			- How did geography affect the conduct of World War II?
			- In what ways did the Germans, Soviets, British, French, and Americans view the causes of World War II differently?
			Suggested Documents: Maps, World War II photographs, *Teaching About the Holocaust and Genocide* : The Human Rights Series Volumes I-III (New York State Education Department); Benito Mussolini, *Fascist Doctrines*; Adolf Hitler, *Mein Kampf*, Thomas Mann, *An Appeal to Reason*, Rudolf Hoess, *Commandant of Auschwitz*; Elie Wiesel, *Reflections of a Survivor*; Winston Churchill, "Blood, Toil, Tears, and Sweat" speech; John Hersey, *Hiroshima*

Content	Standards	Concepts/Themes	Connections
A. Cold War balance of power 　1. Human and physical geography 　2. The world in 1945: physical setting 　3. United States occupation of Germany and Japan 　　a. The adoption of democratic systems of government 　　b. Economic rebuilding of Germany and Japan 　4. Emergence of the superpowers 　5. Political climate of the Cold War 　　a. Marshall Plan 　　b. Truman Doctrine 　　c. Berlin airlift and a divided Germany 　　d. North Atlantic Treaty Organization (NATO)/Warsaw Pact—expanding membership and role of NATO 　　e. Hungarian Revolt 　　f. Soviet invasion of Czechoslovakia 　　g. Nuclear weapons and space 　　h. Surrogate superpower rivalries Case studies: (Egypt, Congo, Angola, Chile, Iran, Iraq, Vietnam, Guatemala) 　　i. Role of nonaligned nations	1,2,3,4,5	Human/ Physical Geography Political Systems Conflict Decision Making Science and Technology	TEACHER'S NOTE: Students should understand that the defeat of Germany and Japan in World War II had fundamental impacts on the future political development of both these powers. Germany's and Japan's new constitutions reflect these wartime and post-wartime experiences. - What impact did the failure of democracy in Germany in the 1930s and 1940s play in post-World War II Germany? - What did Germany learn from its Holocaust experience? - What reasons can you pose for Germany's adoption of one of Europe's most liberal asylum laws? - What is the nature of Germany's diplomatic relations with Israel? - How was Japan's new constitution developed? TEACHER'S NOTE: Choose examples that best fit your local curriculum and the needs of your students. Students should investigate superpower rivalries in at least two different settings. - What impact did the conflict between the superpowers have on the rest of the world? - What was the global impact of the Cold War? - Why did nations like Greece and Turkey become important in this struggle? TEACHER'S NOTE: Students should examine the Cold War from the perspectives of Great Britain, France, Germany, the Soviet Union, the satellite nations of Eastern Europe, and the developing nations of Africa, Asia, and Latin America. <u>Suggested Documents</u>: Winston Churchill's "Iron Curtain" speech, memoirs; newspapers; books of the leading figures of the Cold War era; geopolitical maps; videotapes

UNIT SEVEN; THE 20TH CENTURY SINCE 1945, continued

Content	Standards	Concepts/Themes	Connections
6. Korean War a. United States role in the division of Korea b. Comparison of Korea and Germany c. Conduct of the war B. Role of the United Nations 1. Peace keeping 2. Social and economic programs 3. Contemporary social conditions	1,2,3,4,5	Human/ Physical Geography Justice Human Rights Conflict	- What role did the United Nations play in Korea? - How did Korean expectations of what would happen to their country after the war differ from that of the Super Powers? - What possibility is there for the reunification of Korea? - What threat does North Korea pose today? The United Nations was created to prevent war and to fight against hunger, disease, and ignorance. - How successful has the United Nations been in achieving its goals? <u>Suggested Documents</u>: The United Nations Declaration of Human Rights; for Cold War documents see http://metalab.unc.edu/expo/soviet.exhibit/coldwar.html
C. Economic issues in the Cold War and Post-Cold War era 1. Human and physical geography 2. A comparison of market versus command economies (Western Europe versus Soviet Union) 3. Economic recovery in Europe and Japan a. Western Germany becomes a major economic power b. European economic community/ Common Market/ European Union—steps toward European integration c. Japan becomes an economic superpower 4. Organization of Petroleum Exporting Countries (OPEC): oil crisis in the 1970s 5. Pacific Rim economies/economic crisis 6. North America Free Trade Agreement (NAFTA), 1997		Science and Technology Economic Systems Environment Change Needs and Wants Factors of Production Conflict	TEACHER'S NOTE: Students should understand that the Cold War was more than a military rivalry; it was a struggle for survival and supremacy by two basically different ideologies and economic systems. TEACHER'S NOTE: You might wish to have students compare and contrast industrialization in Europe and Japan with that in Egypt, India, or Korea. - What role did science and technology play in this conflict? - Why did the United States play such a vital role in the economic recovery of Europe and Japan? <u>Suggested Documents</u>: Resource maps, graphs, charts, cartograms, GDP maps, World Bank Allocations
D. Chinese Communist Revolution 1. Human and physical geography 2. Communist rise to power (1936-1949); Jiang Jieshi (Chiang Kai-shek), Mao Zedong 3. Communism under Mao Zedong	2,3,4,5	Conflict Change Needs and Wants Economic and Political Systems	TEACHER'S NOTE: Students should be given the opportunity to hypothesize about why democratic reforms failed in China and why Marxism was adopted. Like Russia, China was not an industrialized nation. - How did China alter Marxist theory? - To what extent are the stages of the

Content	Standards	Concepts/Themes	Connections

a. Great Leap Forward
b. The Cultural Revolution and the Red Guard
4. Communism under Deng Xiaoping
  a. Economic reforms—Four Modernizations
    1) Limited privatization
    2) Dismantling of Communes
    3) Introduction of "responsibility system"
    4) Foreign investment
  b. Fifth modernization—democracy
    1) April/May 1989
    2) Tiananmen Square
5. Return of Hong Kong—July 1,1997
6. The social system in communist China versus dynastic China
		Factors of Production
		Human Rights
		Decision Making
			Communist Revolution in China similar to those of other revolutions?
			- What roles did such individuals as Jiang Jieshi (Chiang Kai-shek) and Mao Zedong play in the Communist Revolution in China?
			- How successful was Mao in meeting the needs of the Chinese?
			- What were the successes of the Chinese Revolution under Mao?
			- How might a Chinese perspective of "liberation" differ from that of a Westerner?
			- Why were the Communists under Deng Xiaoping willing to adopt elements of the West's market economies but not their concept of human rights?
			- What role does the citizen play in the Chinese communist system?
			- What hope does democracy have in a post-Deng China?
			- What role will cities such as Hong Kong, Shanghai, and Guangzhou play in the 21st-century global economy?
			- How did the role of women change?
			- What has happened to such practices as foot binding?
			<u>Suggested Documents</u>: Maps showing expansion of communism (1936-1940); writings, speeches, memoirs of Mao Zedong, Deng Xiaoping, and others
			Imperialism had played a major role in the global history of the 19th and 20th centuries.

E. Collapse of European imperialism
1. Human and physical geography
2. India—independence and partition
  a. Political system
  b. Muslim/Hindu conflicts
  c. Status of the caste system
  d. Roles of Mohandas Gandhi and Jawaharlal Nehru
  e. Nonalignment
  f. Kashmir and Punjab
3. African independence movements and Pan Africanism
  a. Changing political boundaries in Africa (Nigeria, Ghana, and Kenya)
	2,5	Human/ Physical Geography
		Imperialism
		Urbanization
		Conflict
		
		Human/ Physical Geography
		Imperialism
		Nationalism
			- Why did the colonial empires collapse after World War II?
			-What role does the caste system play in India today?
			<u>Suggested Documents</u>: Maps, memoirs, speeches of Gandhi, Nehru, and others; videotapes
			- What forces brought about the collapse of European imperialism in the post-World War II world?
			- What role did non-Western nationalism play in the collapse?
			- To what extent have all ties between imperialistic nations and former colonies been completely broken?

Content	Standards	Concepts/Themes	Connections

b. Roles of Jomo Kenyatta and Kwame Nkrumah
c. Continuance of economic linkages with former colonial powers
d. Ethnic tensions versus nationalism: Nigeria and civil war
e. Apartheid—policy of racial separation and segregation
  1) Historical circumstances
  2) African National Congress
  3) Leadership—Nelson Mandela, Desmond Tutu, F. W. de Klerk
f. Political and economic instability—Congo (Zaire) or any other examples
		Change
		Political Systems
		Economic Systems
		Human Rights
		Justice
			<u>Suggested Documents</u>: Nelson Mandela, *The Rivonia Trial Speech to the Court*; Kwame Nkrumah, *I Speak of Freedom: A Statement of African Ideology*

g. Ethnic tensions: Rwanda—Hutu-Tutsi 4. Southeast Asia a. Vietnam/Ho Chi Minh b. Cambodia/Pol Pot/Khmer Rouge c. Aung San Suu Kyi—Myanmar		Human Rights	TEACHER'S NOTE: Students should have the opportunity to examine the multiple perspectives at play in Southeast Asia. - To what extent can the war in Vietnam be seen as an anti-imperialist revolt? <u>Suggested Documents</u>: Maps, speeches, and memoirs of Ho Chi Minh, Pol Pot, Aung San Suu Kyi, and others

F. Conflicts and change in the Middle East
1. Human and physical geography
2. The creation of the State of Israel, Arab Palestinians, and Israel's Arab neighbors
3. Roles of individuals—Golda Meir, Yasir Arafat, Anwar Sadat, King Hussein, Yitzhak Rabin, Palestine Liberation Organization (PLO)
a. Arab-Israeli wars
b. Peace treaties
4. Role of terrorism
5. Turkey and Iraq—Kurds
6. Migration of Jews from Europe, the United States, the Soviet Union, and Africa
7. The Iranian Revolution
a. Causes and impact
b. Ayatollah Ruhollah Khomeini versus Reza Pahlavi
8. Persian Gulf War—Saddam Hussein
	1,2,3,4,5
	
	2
		Human/
		  Physical
		  Geography
		Political Systems
		Economic
		  Systems
		Interdependence
		Conflict
		
		Nationalism
		Justice and
		  Human Rights
		Diversity
		Conflict
			TEACHER'S NOTE: Students should examine Islamic fundamentalism from multiple perspectives in at least two nations. Students should also study fundamentalist groups in other religions and regions.
			- To what extent has the migration of Jews to Israel been similar to earlier migrations? similar to other migrations going on today?
			- Why has it proven so difficult to resolve conflict in the Middle East?
			- Why is this region so important to the world's global economy?
			- What role have the United States, United Nations, and Egypt played in trying to resolve Arab-Israeli conflicts?
			<u>Suggested Documents</u>: Maps, speeches, cartoons, treaties, eyewitness accounts, and videotapes

Content	Standards	Concepts/Themes	Connections
9. Islamic fundamentalism (Iran, Libya, Afghanistan, Algeria, Turkey)			- What role does Islamic fundamentalism play in modern Turkey?
G. Collapse of communism and the breakup of the Soviet Union 1. Human and physical geography 2. Background events, 1970 to 1987 3. Poland's Solidarity and Lech Walesa 4. Mikhail Gorbachev (perestroika and glasnost) 5. Fall of the Berlin Wall and the reunification of Germany—causes and impacts 6. Ethnic conflict in former satellite states, e.g., Kosovo, Bosnia 7. Changing political boundaries 8. Challenges faced by post-communist Russia—the world of Boris Yeltsin	1,2,3,4,5 4	Human/ Physical Geography Economic and Political Systems Decision Making Conflict Citizenship	- To what extent was the collapse of communism in the Soviet Union a major turning point in global history? - In what ways can it be compared to the fall of the Roman Empire and the Han Dynasty? - What caused the collapse of communism in the Soviet Union? - What was the impact of the collapse on the West? on Cuba? - What role did nationalism play in the collapse of communism and the breakup of the Soviet Union? - What historic ties did Eastern Europe have with Western Europe? - Why did communism as an economic system collapse in the Soviet Union? - What problems does Russia face as it moves toward capitalism? <u>Suggested Documents</u>: Writings and speeches of Vaclav Havel, Mikhail S. Gorbachev, Boris Yeltsin, and Lech Walesa

H. Political and economic change in Latin America
1. Latin America: physical setting
2. Argentina
  a. Peron
  b. The Mothers of the Plaza De Maya
3. Fidel Castro's Cuban Revolution—causes and impact
4. Nicaragua and the Sandinistas
5. Guatemala and the indigenous peoples
6. Changing role of the Roman Catholic Church in Latin America
7. Latin American immigration to the United States
8. Return of the Panama Canal
	5	Human/ Physical Geography Conflict Change Political Systems Decision Making	- What is the future of a post-Cold War Cuba?
			<u>Suggested Documents</u>: Political and economic maps of Latin America, speeches and memoirs of Fidel Castro, Carlos Salinas de Gortari, Jose Napoleon Duarta, Violeta Barrios de Chamorro; Camilo Torres, *Communism and Revolution in Latin America*

UNIT EIGHT: GLOBAL CONNECTIONS AND INTERACTIONS

Content	Standards	Concepts/Themes	Connections
A. Social and political patterns and change 1. Human and physical geography	1,2,3	Human/ Physical Geography Movement of People and Goods Conflict Human Rights	Students should be able to investigate the characteristics, distributions, and migrations of human populations on the Earth's surface. - What patterns of migration are emerging in the late-20th/early-21st century? - To what extent are these patterns global?

2. Population pressures and poverty (China, India, Africa, and Latin America)
  a. One-child policy—China
  b. Family planning—India
  c. Mother Theresa
  d. Cycles of poverty and disease
	3,4		- What is the relationship between the migration of people and ethnic tensions?
			- What is the relationship between ethnic tensions and nationalism?
			- What opposition has arisen to migration? Why?
			- To what extent are current migrations similar to early migrations? How are they different?

3. Migration
  a. Urbanization
  b. Global migration
    Suggested case studies: Turkish, Italian, and Russian immigration to Germany, North African immigration to France, Latin American and Asian immigration to the United States, and Hutu and Tutsis immigration
			TEACHER'S NOTE: In most societies there is a tension between tradition and modernization. Traditional societies that are modernizing frequently develop conflicts regarding the secularization of the political system and the assumption of nontraditional roles by men and women. Non-Western nations often look to technology to resolve their social, political, and economic problems and at the same time they want to maintain their traditional culture and values. You may want to examine industrialization in one or two developing nations in depth.

4. Modernization/tradition—finding a balance
  a. Japan
  b. Middle East (Saudi Arabia, Egypt, Afghanistan, and Algeria)
  c. African
  d. Latin America
	1,2,3,4,5	Change	- What impact did the scientific and technological advances of the period have on life expectancy, war, and peace?
			- What would Thomas Malthus have said about these changes?

5. Scientific and technological advances
  a. Treatment of infectious diseases
  b. Improved standard of living
	2		- To what extent is the process of industrialism similar from one nation to the next?

6. Urbanization—use and distribution of scarce resources (Africa, India, Latin America)	3,4	Science and Technology	- What role does democracy play in Latin America? - What problems are posed by increased modernization and urbanization in developing nations?

7. Status of women and children
  a. Economic issues, e.g., child labor
  b. Social issues, e.g., abuse and access to education
	5	Urbanization
		Needs and
		Wants
			Urbanization and population pressures are issues facing all nations. Students

Content	Standards	Concepts/Themes	Connections
c. Political issues, e.g., participation in the political process		Factors of Production Environment Human Rights	need to understand how nations use and distribute scarce resources. Urbanization, modernization, and industrialization are powerful agents of social change in developing nations. - What factors determine whether or not a nation is overpopulated? - What strategies are nations taking to overcome the adverse aspects of urbanization and overpopulation? - To what extent has the status of women advanced throughout the 20th century? <u>Suggested Documents</u>: Official United Nations documents from the Beijing Conference on Women (1995); Amnesty International, *Political Murder;* Paul Kennedy, *Demographic Explosion*
8. Ethnic and religious tensions: an analysis of multiple perspectives a. Northern Ireland b. Balkans: Serbs, Croats, and Muslims c. Sikhs and Tamils d. Indonesian Christians e. China—Tibet f. Indonesia—East Timor	2,4,5	Conflict Change	
B. Economic issues 1. North/South dichotomy: issues of development (post-colonialism) a. Africa b. Latin America 2. Korea's economic miracle 3. Economic interdependence 4. World hunger	1,2,4	Change Economic Systems Needs and Wants Factors of Production Scarcity Interdependence	TEACHER'S NOTE: Students should understand that as global economic systems become more interdependent, economic decisions made in one nation or region have implications for all regions. Economic development for all nations depends upon a wise use of globally scarce resources. - What is meant by the term "post-colonialism"? - What is the relationship between former colonies and the nations that once controlled them? -How has the global economy changed since 1945? - What weaknesses do many developing economies face? - What made Korea's economic miracle possible? -To what extent is Latin America moving from a cash crop economy to a diversified industrial economy? - On what basis are economic decisions being made in developing nations? in industrialized nations? (Compare/contrast.) - How has economic decision making become more global as the world economy becomes increasingly interdependent? - To what extent have economic disparities between developed and developing nations persisted or increased?

Content	Standards	Concepts/Themes	Connections

C. The environment and sustainability
  1. Pollution—air, water, toxic waste (Europe)
  2. Deforestation (Amazon Basin)
  3. Desertification (Sahel)
  4. Nuclear safety (Chernobyl)
  5. Endangered species (Africa)
	1,2,3,4,5	Interdependence
		Environment and Society
		Technology
		Economic Systems
			- How do societies balance their desire for economic development with the pressures such development places on the environment?
			- To what extent does conflict exist between developed and developing nations over environmental issues?
			- What is the responsibility of developing nations on the depletion of resources?

D. Science and technology
  1. Information age/Computer Revolution /Internet
  2. Impact of satellites
  3. Green Revolution
  4. Space exploration
  5. Literacy and education
  6. Medical breakthroughs—disease control/life expectancy/genetics
  7. Epidemics—AIDS
	1,2,3,4,5	Human/ Physical Geography
		Environment
		Science and Technology
		Change
			- What is the relationship between scientific/technological development and ethics?
			- What is the impact of the Green Revolution on population and poverty?
			- What would Thomas Malthus have thought about the impacts of science and technology on life spans and health?
			Suggested Documents: USGS, NASA, and National Geographic Web sites (www.nationalgeographic.com); World Bank, World Development Report,1992

8. Nuclear proliferation	2,4	Conflict	TEACHER'S NOTE: Students should have the opportunity to compare and contrast the nuclear threat at the end of World War II with that threat at the end of the 20th century. - What nations can be described as nuclear powers? - What nations have an undeclared nuclear capacity? - What nations are suspected of having secret nuclear weapons? -What role does nationalism play in nuclear proliferation? - What threat does nuclear proliferation pose for world peace? - What impact has the collapse of communism had on nuclear proliferation?

UNITED STATES HISTORY AND GOVERNMENT

U nited States history is the history of a great experiment in representative democracy. The basic principles and core values expressed in the Declaration of Independence became the guiding ideas for our nation's civic culture. United States history since the Declaration of Independence has witnessed continued efforts to apply these principles and values to all people. Adoption of the United States Constitution codified these principles, but, as the history of our nation shows, that document and its amendments represented only the first step in achieving "liberty and justice for all."

One major goal of the State social studies curriculum, K-11, calls for students to learn about the structure and function of governments and to learn how to take on their roles as citizens. Students should understand those basic principles and the cultural heritage that support our democracy so that they can become informed, committed participants in our democracy. This core curriculum lists examples that describe how individuals and groups throughout history have challenged and influenced public policy and constitutional change. These examples and this course of study should help students understand how ordinary citizens and groups of people interacted with lawmakers and policy makers and made a difference.

This core curriculum is organized into seven historical units. Each unit lists the content, concepts and themes, and connections teachers should use to organize classroom instruction and plan for assessment. The State Regents examination for United States History and Government will be based on the content column in this core curriculum. The following concepts and themes in United States history are also emphasized in this curriculum:

Change
Citizenship
Civic Values
Constitutional Principles
Culture and Intellectual Life
Diversity
Economic Systems
Environment
Factors of Production
Foreign Policy
Government
Human Systems
Immigration and Migration
Individuals, Groups, Institutions
Interdependence
Physical Systems
Places and Regions
Reform Movements
Presidential Decisions and Actions
Science and Technology

Since this curriculum emphasizes government and basic constitutional principles, students should understand the importance of key United States Supreme Court decisions. The following required Supreme Court decisions have had significant impact on our nation's history:

Marbury v. *Madison* (1803)

McCulloch v. *Maryland* (1819)

Gibbons v. *Ogden* (1824)

Worcester v. *Georgia* (1832)

Dred Scot v. *Sanford* (1857)

Civil Rights Cases (1883)

Wabash, St. Louis & Pacific R.R. v. *Illinois* (1886)

United States v. *E.C. Knight Co.* (1895)

In Re Debs (1895)

Plessy v. *Ferguson* (1896)

Northern Securities Co. v. *United States* (1904)

Lochner v. *New York* (1905)

Muller v. *Oregon* (1908)

Schenck v. *United States* (1919)

Schechter Poultry Corporation v. *United States* (1935)

Korematsu v. *United States* (1944)

Brown v. *Board of Education of Topeka* (1954)

Watkins v. *United States* (1957)

Mapp v. *Ohio* (1961)

Baker v. *Carr* (1962)

Engle v. *Vitale* (1962)

Gideon v. *Wainwright* (1963)

Heart of Atlanta Motel v. *United States* (1964)

Miranda v. *Arizona* (1966)

Tinker v. *Des Moines* (1969)

New York Times v. *United States* (1971)

Roe v. *Wade* (1973)

United States v. *Nixon* (1974)

New Jersey v. *TLO* (1985)

Cruzan v. *Director, Missouri Department of Health* (1990)

Planned Parenthood of Southeastern Pennsylvania, et. al. v. *Casey* (1992)

Vernonia School District v. *Acton* (1995)

Briefs of these cases are available in *U. S. Supreme Court Decisions: A Case Study Review for U.S. History and Government*, developed by Project P.A.T.C.H. of the Northport-East Northport U.F.S.D. and the Law, Youth, and Citizenship Program. The book can be accessed on the internet at http://www.tourolaw.edu/patch/CaseSummary.html where the briefs are linked to the full text of each case.

The connections column for this core curriculum was developed by Ms. Alice Grant, Pelham U.F.S.D. and Mr. Walter J. Gable, Seneca Falls C.S.D. Content reviews were provided by Dr. Gregory S. Wilsey, Director, Law, Youth, and Citizenship Program of the New York State Bar Association and the New York State Education Department and Dr. James G. Basker, President, Gilder Lehrman Institute of American History.

UNIT ONE: Introduction

I. GEOGRAPHY

Content	Concepts/Themes	Connections

A. The physical/cultural setting in the Americas
  1. Size and location
  2. Major zones/areas
    a. Climate zones
    b. Vegetation zones
    c. Agricultural areas
    d. Natural resources
  3. Factors that shaped the identity of the United States
    a. Major mountain ranges
    b. Major river systems
    c. Great Plains
    d. Atlantic/Pacific oceans
    e. Coastlines
    f. Climate
    g. Abundance of natural resources
  4. Barriers to expansion/development
    a. Climate
    b. Mountain ranges
    c. Arid lands
    d. Great Plains
	Places and Regions
	
	Physical Systems
	
	Physical Systems
	
	Physical Systems
		Note: Sections A-1 to A-3 are suggested as a combination review and overview of United States geography that should introduce this course of study. Sections A-4 to D-5 are incorporated into the content outline of this core curriculum at the appropriate historical points. The Connections column suggests where these geographic concepts and themes can be integrated into the study of United States history and government.
		
		Use climate and physical feature maps to illustrate physical setting, regions, and features of different places in the United States.

B. Role/influence of geography on historical/-cultural development
  1. Influences on early Native American Indians
  2. Influence on colonization patterns and colonial development
  3. Territorial expansion
  4. Impact during wartime
  5. Effect of location on United States foreign policy
	Environment
	Human Systems
		Use maps showing the stages of the expansion of the United States to demonstrate the importance of strategic location and to explain economic need to secure the port of New Orleans in the Louisiana Purchase (1803) or the need to obtain a natural boundary to the West such as the Mississippi River in the Treaty of Paris (1783). (Study in greater detail in UNIT TWO.)
		Discuss the influence of geography on settlement/demographic patterns in the United States, e.g.,
		- the fact that the Great Plains area was settled in the period after the Civil War (UNIT THREE);
		- lack of settlement in the arid lands of the Mexican Cession (UNIT TWO and UNIT THREE);
		- influence of mountain ranges such as Appalachians and Rocky Mountains on westward travel and settlement (UNIT TWO and UNIT THREE);

I. GEOGRAPHY, continued

Content	Concepts/Themes	Connections
		- midwestern: effect of the Dust Bowl on agriculture (UNIT FIVE); - impact of the energy crisis of the 1970s on the development and demographic growth of the Southeast and Southwest (UNIT SEVEN). - lure of the so-called sun belt states for the increasing numbers of retired people (UNIT SEVEN) Illustrate the importance of strategic location in foreign policy discussions, e.g., - interest in protecting the Western Hemisphere with Monroe Doctrine (UNIT TWO) and Roosevelt Corollary (UNIT FOUR); - interest in building the Panama Canal to link the Atlantic and Pacific trade (UNIT FOUR); - annexation of Hawaii as a potential naval base (UNIT FOUR); - acquisition of the Philippines in relation to China trade (UNIT FOUR); - Gulf War in terms of protecting oil resources of the Persian Gulf region (UNIT SEVEN).

C. Geographic issues today
   1. Waste disposal
   2. Water/air pollution
   3. Shifting populations
   4. Energy usage
   5. Urban problems/challenges
 	
 D. Demographics
   1. Characteristics
     a. Gender
     b. Age
     c. Ethnicity
     d. Religion
     e. Economic variables
     f. Nature of household
     g. Marital status
   2. Immigration
   3. Migration
   4. Population relationships/trends since 1865
     a. Population growth
     b. Distribution
     c. Density
   5. Current issues
     a. Graying of America
     b. Effects of the baby boom generation
     c. Changing composition of populations
	Science and Technology
	
	 Human Systems
	
	 Change
	
	 Immigration and Migration
	
	 Diversity
		Discuss these geographic issues as they relate to the United States' adjustment to industrial and demographic change (UNITS THREE - SEVEN). Consider demographic change in discussing stages of settlement and impacts of new waves of immigrants (UNITS THREE - SEVEN). Consider the impact of demographic change and political, economic, and social life, for example:
		 - implications of baby boom generation at the early stages of their life cycle (increased demands for housing after WWII);
		 - pressure on educational resources of the 1950s, 1960s, and 1970s;
		 - graying of the population and its effects on Social Security and Medicare (UNIT SIX and UNIT SEVEN).

UNIT TWO: CONSTITUTIONAL FOUNDATIONS FOR THE UNITED STATES DEMOCRATIC REPUBLIC

I. THE CONSTITUTION: THE FOUNDATION OF AMERICAN SOCIETY

Content	Concepts/Themes	Connections

A. Historical foundations
  1. 17th- and 18th-century Enlightenment thought
    a. European intellectuals (Locke, Montesquieu, Voltaire, Rousseau)
    b. Key events (Magna Carta, habeas corpus, English Bill of Rights, Glorious Revolution)
	Citizenship
	Civic Values
		Students should understand that American political rights and institutions are derived from (1) British political traditions, (2) 18th-century Enlightenment thought, and (3) developments during the colonial period.

2. The peoples and peopling of the American colonies (voluntary and involuntary)
    a. Native American Indians (relations between colonists and Native American Indians, trade, alliances, forced labor, warfare)
    b. Slave trade
    c. Varieties of immigrant motivation, ethnicities, and experiences
	Civic Values	<u>Suggested Documents</u>: Mayflower Compact, Albany Plan of Union, Declaration of Independence, New York State Constitution

3. Colonial experience: political rights and mercantile relationships
    a. Colonial charters and self-government: Mayflower Compact, town meetings, House of Burgesses, local government, property rights, enforceable contracts, Albany Plan of Union
    b. Native American governmental systems
    c. Colonial slavery (evolution and variation of slavery in Chesapeake, South Carolina and Georgia, lower Mississippi Valley, middle colonies, and the North; slave resistance; influence of Africa and African-American culture upon colonial cultures; contradiction between slavery and emerging ideals of freedom and liberty)
    d. Freedom of the press: the Zenger case
    e. Salutary neglect, rights of English citizens in America
	Government	

4. The Revolutionary War and the Declaration of Independence
    a. Causes of the Revolution
    b. Revolutionary ideology (republican principles, natural rights)
    c. Revolutionary leaders: Benjamin Franklin, George Washington, John Adams, Samuel Adams, Patrick Henry
	Civic Values
	Change
		Students should understand the American Revolution as the result of colonial resistance to changes in British imperial policy after 1763. To what extent did the Declaration of Independence reflect Enlightenment thought and colonial experiences?
		<u>Suggested Document</u>:Thomas Paine, *Common Sense*

I. THE CONSTITUTION: THE FOUNDATION OF AMERICAN SOCIETY, continued

Content	Concepts/Themes	Connections
d. Slavery, African-Americans, and the outcome of the American Revolution (African-American role in the Revolution, growth of the "free black" population)		

5. New York State Constitution based on republican principles
  a. New York State Constitution
  b. State constitutions (ratification by the people, unicameral versus bicameral legislatures, branches of government)
  c. Guaranteeing religious liberty (disestablishment of churches, the growth of religious pluralism)
  d. The abolition of slavery in the North
	Civic Values	- What features from state constitutions, including New York's, were incorporated into the United States Constitution?

6. Articles of Confederation		- Why was this time called the "critical period"? - Why were the powers of the national government purposely limited? What were the major strengths and weaknesses of the government under the Articles? How did the authors of the Constitution remedy these weaknesses?
7. Northwest Ordinance		

B. Constitutional Convention
  1. Representation and process
    a. Framers of the Constitution (James Madison)
    b. Plans of government (Virginia plan, New Jersey plan, Connecticut plan)
  2. Conflict and compromise: seeking effective institutions
    a. Protecting liberty against abuses or power
    b. Power separated and balanced
    c. The Constitution, slavery, and fear of tyrannical powers of government
  3. The document: structure of government
	Government	Students should understand that the Philadelphia convention addressed weaknesses of the Articles while at the same time trying to avoid a tyrannical national government.
		- What kinds of men were delegates? Why?
		- Why were no women or African-Americans included? How does this help to explain some of the resulting provisions?
		- Upon what principles of government did the authors agree? disagree?
		- What were the important compromises reached?
		- How did the compromises deal with slavery issues?
		- How was the national government under the Constitution different from that under the Articles?

4. Ratification
  a. The Federalist Papers—a New York activity with widespread influence
  b. The debate: Federalist and Anti-Federalist arguments
C. The Bill of Rights
	Civic Values	Students should understand the major arguments expressed in the Federalist Papers to gain support for the proposed Constitution. Students could examine Federalist Papers 51 and 78 and write a paper in support of ratification.
		Students should understand why the Bill of Rights was added to the

I. THE CONSTITUTION: THE FOUNDATION OF AMERICAN SOCIETY, continued

Content	Concepts/Themes	Connections
		Constitution, what the contents of the various amendments are, and how the Supreme Court has interpreted and applied the wording in specific cases. (Note: Teachers might consider discussing Bill of Rights cases listed later in the core curriculum while studying the Bill of Rights provisions.) - How did the Bill of Rights satisfy the Anti-Federalist argument? - What specific provisions have been interpreted by the Supreme Court?
D. Basic structure and function: three branches and their operation	Government	Students should understand the powers of each of the three branches of government as well as the system of checks and balances. Students could list the powers of each branch and explain current examples of checks and balances.

E. Basic constitutional principles
   (1) national power—limits and potentials
   (2) federalism—balance between nation and state
   (3) the judiciary—interpreter of the Constitution or shaper of public policy
   (4) civil liberties—protecting individual liberties from governmental abuses; the balance between government and the individual
   (5) criminal procedures—the balance between the rights of the accused and protection of the community and victims
   (6) equality—its historic and present meaning as a constitutional value
		Students should understand basic constitutional principles and monitor their application throughout the course. After completing work on sections A-E, students could prepare a chart of several specific ideas expressed in the original Constitution and Bill of Rights. For each of these ideas, the students should (1) explain the meaning of the idea, (2) identify its historical origin(s), and (3) cite specifically where that idea is found in the Constitution and/or Bill of Rights.
		 <u>Suggested Documents</u>: Federalist Papers, United States Constitution, Bill of Rights

(7) the rights of women under the Constitution
   (8) the rights of ethnic and racial groups under the Constitution
   (9) Presidential power in wartime and in foreign affairs
   (10) the separation of powers and the capacity to govern
   (11) avenues of representation
   (12) property rights and economic policy
   (13) constitutional change and flexibility
	Diversity	

F. Implementing the new constitutional principles
   1. Creating domestic stability through sound financial policies: Hamilton's financial plans
   2. Development of unwritten constitutional
	Government	Students should understand that the Constitution provided only the basic framework for our government. In the early years under the Constitution, several important practical details of government were added.

I. THE CONSTITUTION: THE FOUNDATION OF AMERICAN SOCIETY, continued

Content	Concepts/Themes	Connections

government under Washington, Adams, and Jefferson: cabinet, political parties, judicial review, executive and Congressional interpretation, lobbying; the Marshall Court (*Marbury v. Madison*, 1803, *McCulloch v. Maryland*, 1819, and *Gibbons v. Ogden*, 1824)
 	
3. Establishing a stable political system
  a. The Federalist and Republican parties (philosophies of Hamilton and Jefferson)
  b. Suppressing dissent (the Whiskey Rebellion, the Alien and Sedition Acts)
4. Neutrality and national security, Washington through Monroe: foreign affairs, establishing boundaries
  a. Neutrality: A key element of American foreign policy—influence of geography
  b. A new nation in a world at war
  c. Economic pressures as a tool of diplomacy
  d. The failure of Republican diplomacy: War of 1812 (significance of the War for Native American Indians, Spain, the growth of industry)
  e. Monroe Doctrine
	Foreign Policy	- How did Hamilton's financial plans contribute to economic growth?
		- How did Jefferson's and Madison's opposition to Hamilton's plans contribute to the rise of political parties?
		- How did the different geographic regions react to the economic debate?
		- How was the "necessary and proper" clause involved in the debate? How has this clause been used throughout our nation's history?
		- What roles did Washington, Adams, and Jefferson play in shaping the office of President which had been vaguely defined in the Constitution?
		- How did the rulings of the Marshall Court in *Marbury v. Madison, McCulloch v. Maryland,* and other cases strengthen the power of the Supreme Court compared to the other two branches? How did the Marshall Court influence the elements of federalism?
		- What motives influenced the conduct of United States foreign policy in the following periods?
		  Federalist Era: 1789-1800; 1801-1812; Post War of 1812; Monroe Doctrine, Manifest Destiny
		- How did geography contribute to each of these foreign policy decisions?
		- How did the debate over foreign policy influence the development of political parties?
		- How did Jefferson, a strict constructionist and a devotee of limited government and frugality in terms of government spending, justify the purchase of Louisiana?
		- Was the War of 1812 a "second war for independence," a war of expansion, or a war for maritime rights?
		- To what extent did the Monroe Doctrine reflect isolationist/neutrality sentiment? United States national concerns? the concerns of the new Latin American republics?
		- To what extent was Manifest Destiny a philosophical justification for other, more complex social, political, and economic motives?

I. THE CONSTITUTION: THE FOUNDATION OF AMERICAN SOCIETY, continued

Content	Concepts/Themes	Connections
		- What regional tensions are evident in the debate over such issues as the Louisiana Purchase, Embargo Act of 1807, War of 1812, and Manifest Destiny? - In the attempt to obtain more secure national boundaries, what areas were acquired by war? by treaty and purchase? - What geographic factors were involved in acquisition and settlement of new territories?

II. THE CONSTITUTION TESTED: NATIONALISM AND SECTIONALISM

Content	Concepts/Themes	Connections

A. Factors unifying the United States, 1789-1861
  1. The first and second two-party systems
  2. The market economy and interstate commerce
  3. The Marshall Court
	Diversity	Students should understand that there were forces contributing to national unity as well as sectionalism.
		- What factors contributed to the growing economic interdependence of the United States at this time?
		- How did the further development of political parties reflect the growing economic and regional differences?
		- How did the rulings of the Marshall Court help to strengthen the national government and thereby help to unite the country?

B. Constitutional stress and crisis
  1. Developing sectional differences and philosophies of government
    a. The growth of urban and industrial patterns of life in the North
      (1.) the transportation revolution (Erie Canal, rise of the port of New York, New York City's rise as a trade and manufacturing center)
      (2.) the introduction of the factory system
      (3.) working conditions
      (4.) women and work
      (5.) urban problems
    b. Middle-class and working-class life in the pre-Civil War North (families, gender roles, schooling, childhood, living conditions, status of free blacks)
	Government
	
	Factors of Production
		- What geographic and economic factors contributed to sectional differences?
		- How did the question of the admission of new territories such as Missouri and later the Mexican Cession threaten national unity?
		- How was the character of America altered by conquest and annexation of the (1) Louisiana Purchase and (2) Mexican Cession?
		- What compromises were reached in 1820, 1833, and 1850 to resolve these sectional differences and avert constitutional crisis?
		- What characterized the early immigrant experience?

II. THE CONSTITUTION TESTED: NATIONALISM AND SECTIONALISM, continued

Content	Concepts/Themes	Connections

c. Foreign immigration and nativist reactions (Jews; Irish mass starvation, 1845-1850; Germans; 1848 refugees; Know Nothings)
d. Patterns of Southern development (growth of cotton cultivation, movement into the Old Southwest, women on plantations)
e. Life under slavery (slave laws; material conditions of life; women and children; religious and cultural expression; resistance)
2. Equal rights and justice: expansion of franchise; search for minority rights; expansion of slavery; abolitionist movement; the underground railroad; denial of Native American Indian rights and land ownership
  a. Political democratization: national political nominating convention, secret ballot
  b. The rise of mass politics (John Quincy Adams, Andrew Jackson, the spoils system, the bank war, Martin Van Buren)
  c. Native Americans
    (1.) History of Indian relations from 1607
    (2.) Native American cultural survival strategies (cultural adaptation, cultural revitalization movements, Pan-Indian movements, resistance)
    (3.) The removal policy: *Worcester* v. *Georgia*, 1832
  d. The birth of the American reform tradition (religious and secular roots; public schools; care for the physically disabled and the mentally ill; the problems of poverty and crime; antislavery; women's rights movement)
3. The great constitutional debates: states' rights versus federal supremacy (nullification); efforts to address slavery issue (Missouri Compromise, Compromise of 1850, fugitive slave law, *Dred Scott* v. *Sanford*, 1857); preservation of the Union
	Immigration and Migration
	
	Diversity
	
	Civic Values
	
	Reform Movement
		- What roles did these immigrant groups play in pre-Civil War American society—Irish, German, Scandinavian, and Chinese?
		- Where did these immigrant groups settle and why?
		- How did new arrivals change the composition of a region?
		Students should understand the causes (push and pull factors) of Irish immigration to the United States during this period and the impacts of that migration on both Ireland and the United States. Students should understand that the Age of Jackson led to a series of democratic/humanitarian reform movements.
		- To what extent were reforms realized in the areas of voting rights, the abolition of slavery, women's rights, and property rights for Native American Indians?
		Suggested Documents: Seneca Falls Declaration and Resolutions on Woman's Rights, 1848
		
		- Did the Supreme Court ruling in *Dred Scott* v. *Sanford* make a civil war inevitable? Was "compromise" possible?
		- Why did Southerners see the election of Lincoln in 1860 as such a threat?
		- On what basis did Southerners justify their secession? How did this viewpoint compare with that of the Founding Fathers?
		- How did Lincoln and Buchanan differ regarding their constitutional powers as President?
		- In addition to slavery, what factors contributed to the Civil War?
		Suggested Document: *Dred Scott* v. *Sanford*, 1857

C. Territorial expansion through diplomacy, migration, annexation, and war; Manifest Destiny 1. The Louisiana Purchase	Immigration and Migration	

Content	Concepts/Themes	Connections

2. Exploring and settling the West (explorers, Lewis and Clark expedition, naturalists, trappers and traders, trailblazers, missionaries, pioneers, the Mormon Church)
 3. The Spanish, Mexican, and Native American West
 4. Motives for and implications of expansion and western settlement
 5. Politics of western expansion (Manifest Destiny, the Texas and Oregon questions, the Mexican War)
 6. Impact of western expansion upon Mexicans and Native Americans
 D. The Constitution in jeopardy: The American Civil War
   1. United States society divided
     a. Party disintegration and realignment and sectional polarization (Kansas-Nebraska Act, disintegration of the Whig Party and the rise of the Republican Party, *Dred Scott* decision, John Brown's raid)
     b. Abraham Lincoln, the secession crisis, and efforts at compromise (Lincoln-Douglas debates, election of 1860, secession, compromise plans, Fort Sumter)
   2. Wartime actions
     a. Military strategy, major battles (Antietam, Gettysburg), and human toll
     b. Impact of war on home front (civil liberties during the Civil War, women's roles)
     c. Government policy during the war (wartime finances, creating a national currency, transcontinental railroad, Homestead Act)
     d. Lincoln and Emancipation (the Emancipation Proclamation, the Gettysburg Address, African-American participation in the Civil War, the 13th Amendment)
	Civic Values
	 Constitutional Principles
	
	 Change
		- Was the Civil War necessary to resolve the conflict over federalism?
		 - To what extent were the powers of the President expanded as Lincoln attempted to deal with the crisis of civil war?
		 <u>Suggested Documents</u>: The Emancipation Proclamation, the Gettysburg Address

UNIT THREE: INDUSTRIALIZATION OF THE UNITED STATES

I. THE RECONSTRUCTED NATION

Content	Concepts/Themes	Connections

A. Reconstruction plans
  1. Lincoln's plan
  2. Congressional Reconstruction
  3. Post-Civil War amendments (13th, 14th, and 15th)
  4. Impeachment of Andrew Johnson
  5. The reconstructed nation and shifting relationships between the federal government, state governments, and individual citizens
	Change
	Constitutional
	  Principles
	Citizenship
		- In what ways were the Congressional Republican plans for Reconstruction more "radical" than those of Abraham Lincoln and Andrew Johnson? What were their views on secession, amnesty and pardon, and procedures for readmission of the Confederate states?
		- How might the debate over Reconstruction have been seen as an attempt to restore the balance of power between Congress and President that had been eroded by Lincoln's wartime measures?
		- Why did the Radical Republicans want to impeach Andrew Johnson? What are the constitutional grounds for impeachment? Had Johnson been removed from office through the impeachment process, how might our government system have changed?
		- What are the specific provisions of the 13th, 14th, and 15th amendments? In spite of the passage of these amendments, how did the Southern states deprive African-Americans of these rights for over 100 years?
		- What impact did the withdrawal of federal support for enforcement of these amendments have upon the status of freedmen?

B. The North
  1. Economic and technological impacts of the Civil War
  2. Expanding world markets
  3. Developing labor needs
	Factors of
	  Production
		- In what ways did the North benefit economically from the Civil War?

C. The New South
  1. Agriculture: land and labor (sharecropping and tenant farming)
  2. Status of freedmen
    a. The economic, political, social, and educational experiences of formerly enslaved African-Americans
    b. From exclusion to segregation
  3. Struggle for political control in the New South
	Places and
	  Regions
	
	Change
		Students should understand what economic changes were brought about in the South in the years after the Civil War.
		- What new forms of economic and political discrimination developed in the years following the Civil War?
		- In what ways did the Freedmen's Bureau benefit freed slaves?
		- What were the successes and failures of Reconstruction?

I. THE RECONSTRUCTED NATION, continued

Content	Concepts/Themes	Connections
4. Supreme Court interpretations of the 13th and 14th amendments (*Civil Rights Cases*, 1883) 5. The emerging debate over "proper" role of African-Americans		- How did the Supreme Court rulings in the *Civil Rights Cases* narrow the meaning of the 14th Amendment? - Students might use excerpts from speeches and writings of Booker T. Washington and W. E. B. DuBois to compare and contrast the strategies of each to achieve equal rights. Ask students to evaluate the effectiveness of each strategy. - How did the Compromise of 1877 contribute to segregation? - Why did the Northern Republicans and Congressional leaders abandon African-Americans in the 1870s? - Use excerpts from the Supreme Court's ruling in *Plessy* v. *Ferguson* to demonstrate that the Court's interpretation of the 14th Amendment established a legal basis for segregation.

D. End of Reconstruction
  1. Disputed election of 1876
  2. End of military occupation
  3. Restoration of white control in the South (1870s and 1880s) and abridgment of rights of freed African-Americans
  4. *Plessy* v. *Ferguson*, 1896: "separate but equal"		

E. The Impact of the Civil War and Reconstruction: Summary
  1. On political alignments
  2. On the nature of citizenship
  3. On federal-state relations
  4. On the development of the North as an industrial power
  5. On American society
	Citizenship
	
	Environment
		- How successful were the Radical Republicans in achieving their Reconstruction goals?
		- How and why did the "Solid South" emerge?
		- What issues became the primary concerns of the Republican Party after 1877?
		- What major civil rights issues remained unresolved?
		- How were economic development and expansion of the United States affected by the Civil War and Reconstruction?
		- Did the Compromise of 1877 make the end of the Civil War a "draw" rather than a "victory" for the North?

Content	Concepts/Themes	Connections

A. Economic transformation and the "search for order"
  1. Business response to change: organize and rationalize
  2. Organizational responses
    a. From proprietorships and partnerships to the rise of monopolies
    b. Incorporation
    c. Capital concentration; consolidation
    d. Expanding markets: national and international
    e. Merchandising changes, department stores, mail order catalogs
	Factors of Production
	
	Factors of Production
	Human Systems
		Students should understand the elements and implications of the expansion and consolidation of American business following the Civil War.
		- What are the advantages of corporations over proprietorships and partnerships?
		- What methods did business leaders use to maximize profits, reduce costs, and/or eliminate competition?

B. Major areas of growth in business and industry
  1. Transportation: railroads and automobiles; urban transportation
  2. Building materials: steel
  3. Energy sources: coal, oil, electricity
  4. Communications: telegraph, telephone
	Science and Technology
	
	Physical Systems
		Students should understand the geographic effects of the railroads on the United States.

C. Representative entrepreneurs: Case studies in concentrated wealth and effort (other personalities may be substituted; local examples of enterprise should also be used)
  1. John D. Rockefeller: oil; Andrew Carnegie: steel; Ford: auto
  2. Work ethic: Cotton Mather to Horatio Alger
  3. Conflict between public good and private gain, e.g., use of resources
		- For the various business leaders studied, what benefits did each individual's success bring to American society? How did these "captains of industry" build great fortunes? How did they use their wealth? What effects did the practices employed by these business leaders have upon competition? Were these business leaders "captains of industry" or "robber barons"?
		- How do the prominent business leaders of the late-19th century compare with prominent contemporary business leaders?
		- What examples of philanthropic contributions exist in your community?

D. New business and government practices: Popular and government responses
  1. Laissez-faire and government support; interpretation of 14th Amendment by Supreme Court
  2. Railroad "pooling"; rate inequities (*Wabash, St. Louis, and Pacific Railway* v. *Illinois*, 1886); railroad regulation: state and national ICC.
  3. Competition and absorption; mergers and trusts; Sherman Antitrust Act, 1890 (*United States* v. *E.C. Knight*, 1895)
	Economic Systems	Students should note that while the government basically pursued a policy of laissez-faire, there were many government policies that encouraged business development at this time.
		- What is meant by "laissez-faire"?
		- How did land grants, subsidies to railroads, tariff and monetary policies, military interventions to break strikes, injunctions, and immigration policies

Content	Concepts/Themes	Connections
		aid the development of business and industry?
		- How did Supreme Court rulings affect efforts to regulate business?
		- To what extent was the Sherman Antitrust Act effective in protecting competition?
		- How did groups such as farmers, consumers, workers, and company stockholders react to railroad practices during this time period?
		- How effective was government regulation of railroads at the state level? national level?

E. Labor's response to economic change: Organize
 1. Efforts at national labor unions: Knights of Labor (1869); AF of L (1881-1886); ILGWU (1900)
  a. "Bread and butter" objectives
  b. Unions and social issues (education)
  c. Attitudes toward immigrants, African-Americans, women
  d. Union leadership (Gompers, Debs)
 2. Struggle and conflict
  a. Major strikes: gains and losses— Homestead, Pullman (*In Re Debs*, 1895), Lawrence
  b. Management's position
  c. Weapons or tactics employed in disputes between labor and management
  d. Attitude and role of government
	Factors of Production Human Systems
	
	Diversity
		Students should understand that poor working conditions led to the formation of labor unions.
		 - How did the AF of L and Knights of Labor differ in terms of types of workers organized; their views of immigrants, African-Americans, Chinese and women workers; union leadership; their positions on strikes and reform agendas?
		 - How do the goals of labor unions in the late-19th century compare with goals today?
		 - For the following three strikes, chart (a) conditions that led to the strike, (b) tactics used by both sides, (c) union leadership, (d) role of state or federal government, and (e) outcome of the strike:
		  (1) Homestead
		  (2) Pullman
		  (3) Lawrence

F. Agrarian response to economic change: Organize and protest
  a. The Grange movement as agrarian protest
  b. Populism: a political response—William Jennings Bryan and the election of 1896
   (1) Case study: The Populists as a grassroots political party
  c. National government response: Interstate Commerce Act, 1887
	Government	Students should understand the problems faced by farmers in an expanding industrial economy and assess various efforts to resolve these problems.
		 - What were the problems experienced by small farmers?
		 - Compare the problems of farmers in the 1890s, 1920s, 1950s, 1980s.
		 - What economic solutions were proposed by the Grangers?
		 - To what extent was the Populist party successful in resolving the problems of farmers? What aspects of the Populist agenda were eventually legislated?
		 - Was the Populist party a "typical" third party?

III. ADJUSTING SOCIETY TO INDUSTRIALISM: AMERICAN PEOPLE AND PLACES

Content	Concepts/Themes	Connections
A. Impact of industrialization	Culture and Intellectual Life	Students should understand the economic, social, and political implications of rapid industrial growth and the shift from a rural to an urban way of life.
1. Urban growth		
a. Attractions: jobs, education, culture, public education system		
b. Problems (slums, increased crime, inadequate water and sanitation services)		- What transformations did your own community undergo during this time period?
c. Skyscrapers and elevators; tenements and walk-ups		
d. Social Darwinism, increased class division, conspicuous consumption, social conscience, philanthropy		Students should contrast the views of Social Darwinists like Carnegie, Russell Conwell, Vanderbilt, Rockefeller, and Morgan with the views of labor leaders, Populists, and Progressive reformers.
2. Work and workers		
a. Factories and people—immigrant patterns of settlement	Factors of Production	- Use political cartoons to illustrate the images of big business and the call for reforms.
b. Geographic, economic, social, and political considerations		
c. Working conditions: "wage slavery"		- How were the lives of working-class women and children affected by industrialization? How did this reality compare with the Victorian view of traditional roles in society?
d. Living conditions: company towns and urban slums		
e. The Great Migration: The migration of African-Americans to the North	Diversity	
3. Women, families, and work		
a. Traditional roles—Victorian ideal and reality		- What insights about the nature of child labor can be drawn from John Spargo's *The Bitter Cry of the Children*?
b. Outside and inside their homes: double drudgery		
c. Jobs for domestics, laundresses, and textile workers; technology brought jobs as telephone operators and typists		
d. Emerging family patterns: two wage earners, broken homes		Describe the effects of internal migration on different regions of the United States.
e. Problems of child labor, elderly, disabled, and African-American women		- How was the class structure altered by industrialization?
(1) Case study: child labor	Culture and Intellectual Life	
f. Role of religion in a pluralistic society		
(1) Religious tolerance develops slowly		
(2) Puritan beliefs and values influenced our historical development		
(3) Religion and party politics to 1896		
4. The growing middle class (consumerism and its material benefits and effects)		
5. Art and literature (Mark Twain and penny dailies)		
B. Immigration, 1850-1924	Diversity	Students should understand the characteristics that distinguished the new immigrants (1850-1924) from the earlier immigrant groups. What difficulties did they face? In what specific ways did they contribute to the shaping of American society?
1. New sources: eastern/southern Europe; Asia—the "new ethnicity"		
a. Case studies: Italian immigration, Chinese immigration (1850-1924, West to East migration), Russian/Jewish immigration		
2. The impulses abroad	Change	
3. The attractions here: labor shortages, liberty,		

Content	Concepts/Themes	Connections

and freedoms
4. Urbanization: ghettos
5. "Americanization" process
6. Impacts on family, religion, education, and politics
7. Contributions to American society
  a. Diversity of the United States population
C. Reactions to the "new" immigration
1. Cultural pluralism: assimilation (Americanization), acculturation ("melting pot" or cultural pluralism), or both
2. Nativist reactions: stereotyping and prejudice
  (1) Case study: Irish immigration
3. Impact on African-Americans and other established minorities
4. "Yellow Peril," West Coast restrictions
5. Literacy testing, 1917
6. The Red Scare
7. Quota acts of 1921 and 1924
D. The frontier (1850-1890)
1. Land west of the Mississippi
  a. Rolling plains and the Great American Desert
  b. Native American Indian nations; concept of oneness with the environment
  c. The Homestead Act, 1862, and the settlement of the West
2. The impact of industrialization
  a. Improved transportation facilitated shipping of foodstuffs and migration of population
  b. Western migration of immigrants
  c. Potential for investment: development of key urban centers
 	
3. Native American Indians
  a. Pressures of advancing white settlement: differing views of land use and ownership
  b. Treaties and legal status
  c. The Indian wars: 1850-1900
  d. Legislating Indian life: reservations; Dawes Act (1887)
  e. Indian civil rights laws—legal status of Native American Indians, 1887-1970: citizenship, 1924; self-government, 1934; self-determination, 1970
	Culture and Intellectual Life
	
	Citizenship
	
	Environment
	
	Human Systems
	
	Science and Technology
	
	Diversity
	
	Human Systems Citizenship
		- Use cartoons from Thomas Nast to illustrate the negative reactions to these new immigrants.
		- Compare and contrast the following:
		  - nativist movement of 1850s
		  - Ku Klux Klan of 1860s and 1870s
		  - Ku Klux Klan of 1920s
		- What conflicts between American ideals and reality are illustrated in a study of immigration laws such as (1) Chinese Exclusion Act, (2) Gentlemen's Agreement, (3) Literacy Test (1917), (4) Emergency Quota Act (1921), (5) Immigration Restriction Act (1924), (6) the McCarran-Walter Act (1952), and (7) immigration legislation of 1965, 1986, and the 1990s?
		- Locate the concentrations of different ethnic groups in the United States at the turn of the 20th century.
		
		- Use an excerpt from Frederick Jackson Turner's frontier thesis and an excerpt from one of his critics to illustrate conflicting views about the role of the frontier in the making of American democracy.
		- What are the geographic differences between the Great Plains, the Southwest, and the Rocky Mountains regions of the West?
		- What role did government policies play in the settling of the West? Have students consider the Homestead Act, land grants and subsidies to transcontinental railroads, and liberal immigration policy.
		- How did the Industrial Revolution contribute to the economic development of the Great Plains? Students should understand the clash that occurred between Native American Indians and advancing white settlers.
		- How did the Native American Indians' concepts of land ownership and respect for the natural environment compare with that of the white settlers?
		- Were the Indian wars a case study of genocide?
		- Evaluate the federal government's attempts to address Native American Indian rights from 1887 to the present.

UNIT FOUR: THE PROGRESSIVE MOVEMENT: RESPONSES TO THE CHALLENGES BROUGHT ABOUT BY INDUSTRIALIZATION AND URBANIZATION

I. REFORM IN AMERICA

Content	Concepts/Themes	Connections

A. Pressures for reform
  1. Progressives supported the use of government power for different reform purposes
  2. Effects of developing technologies and their social, ethical, and moral impacts
  3. Struggle for fair standards of business operation and working conditions (*Lochner* v. *New York*, 1905; *Muller* v. *Oregon*, 1908)
  4. Increasing inequities between wealth and poverty
  5. Rising power and influence of the middle class
	Science and Technology	- What specific political, economic, and social problems in late-19th-century America led to the call for reform?

B. Progress: Social and economic reform and consumer protection
  1. The "Muckrakers" and reform
    a. Magazine writers (Steffens, Tarbell)
    b. Novelists (Norris, Sinclair)
    c. Legislation (Pure Food and Drug Act, 1906, Meat Inspection Act, 1906)
  2. Other areas of concern
    a. Social settlement movement and the problems of poverty (Jacob Riis, Jane Addams)
    b. Women's rights and efforts for peace
      (1) The suffrage movement (Elizabeth Cady Stanton, Susan B. Anthony); Seneca Falls
      (2) Beginnings of fight for birth control (Margaret Sanger)
      (3) Peace movement
    c. The black movement and reform (Booker T. Washington and W.E.B. DuBois)
      (1) Formation of NAACP (1912)
      (2) Ida Wells (anti-lynching)
      (3) Marcus Garvey
    d. Temperance/prohibition
    e. Formation of Anti-Defamation League (1913)
	Culture and Intellectual Life
	
	Diversity
		- Have students define the concept of "muckraker" by compiling newspaper articles, editorials, and political cartoons in which the media is currently exposing some evil in business, government, or society.
		- Have students complete two charts illustrating specific examples of Progressive reforms. One chart should deal with the goals of Progressive reform; the other should deal with the means by which these Progressive reforms were achieved. Possible *means* might include (1) Presidential actions, (2) Congressional legislation, (3) Supreme Court rulings, (4) constitutional amendments, (5) state government actions, (6) local government actions, and (7) actions of individuals and groups outside the government.
		- Students could compare developments of the Progressive period with those of the New Deal and the Great Society. Topics could include goals, leadership, and the accomplishments of various groups. Groups could include farmers, women, labor, African-Americans, and Native American Indians.

I. REFORM IN AMERICA, continued

Content	Concepts/Themes	Connections

C.   Progressivism and government action
   1. Emerging Progressive movement: political reform
      (1) Influence of America's urban middle class
      a. Municipal and state reform
      (1) Municipal reform: response to urban problems
      (2) Sudden growth and needed services
      b. Progressive state reform: e.g., Wisconsin (Robert LaFollette); New York (Theodore Roosevelt); Massachusetts (initiative, referendum, recall); economic, social, environmental reforms
   2. Theodore Roosevelt and the Square Deal
      a. The stewardship theory of the Presidency
      b. Legislation strengthening railroad regulation and consumer protection
      c. "Trust-busting" court cases (*Northern Securities Co.* v. *United States*, 1904); rule of reason: Standard Oil
   3. Conservation
      a. Theodore Roosevelt's concern for nature, land, and resources
      b. Federal legislation and projects: effects on states' limits
      c. Roles of Gifford Pinchot and John Muir
   4. Woodrow Wilson and the New Freedom
      a. Progressivism at its zenith; the 1912 election: Taft, Roosevelt, Wilson
      b. The Underwood Tariff and the graduated income tax
      c. Clayton Antitrust Act and the Federal Trade Commission
      d. The Federal Reserve System (monetary controls)
      e. Women's suffrage amendment
   5. World War I: effect on domestic reform
	Government
	
	Civic Values
	
	Government
	
	Environment
	
	Civic Values
		- How were the powers of the Presidency influenced by the reforming role played by Theodore Roosevelt and Woodrow Wilson?
		- How did the Supreme Court both aid and retard Progressive reform at this time?

II. THE RISE OF AMERICAN POWER

Content	Concepts/Themes	Connections

A. An emerging global involvement
  1. From old diplomacy to new, 1865-1900
    a. Role of increased American power
      (1) Communications technology
      (2) American attitudes toward international role
      (3) Growth of naval power
    b. Perry and the "opening" of Japan (1854)
  2. Other Pacific overtures
    a. United States and China; the Chinese perspective (Boxer Rebellion)
    b. The Open-Door policy
    c. Acquisition of Hawaii
    d. Naval bases: Samoa
  3. Imperialism: the Spanish-American War
    a. Causes for war
    b. United States empire—Puerto Rico; Cuban protectorate (the Platt Amendment)
      (1) Acquisition of the Philippines: "the great debate"
      (2) Disposition of territories
      (3) Constitutional issues
  4. Latin American affairs
    a. Monroe Doctrine update (Roosevelt corollary): the view from Latin America
    b. West Indies protectorates ("the big stick")
    c. Panama Canal: acquisition and construction; Canal retrocession treaty
    d. Taft and dollar diplomacy
B. Restraint and involvement: 1914-1920
  1. United States involvement
    a. Efforts at neutrality and "preparedness"
    b. Causes of United States entry into World War I
    c. United States role in the war
    d. United States reaction to the Russian Revolution
C. Wartime constitutional issues
  1. War opposition and patriotism: the draft issue
  2. Espionage and Sedition acts
  3. *Schenck* v. *United States,* 1919; clear and present danger doctrine
  4. Red Scare, 1918-1919
D. The search for peace and arms control: 1914-
	Places and Regions
	
	Change
	
	Independence
	
	Change
		Students should understand that United States imperialist designs in Asia and Latin America represent the second phase of Manifest Destiny.
		- Compare and contrast the motives and policies of the period 1890-1914 with those of the 1840s.
		- How was Social Darwinism reflected in United States foreign policy from 1890 to 1914?
		
		- Students should analyze headlines in Pulitzer and Hearst newspapers from 1897 to 1898 to illustrate Social Darwinism and the role of the press in shaping public opinion.
		- To help students understand the opposing arguments of the imperialists and anti-imperialists regarding annexation of the Philippines, conduct a simulated Senate Foreign Relations Committee hearing on the proposed 1898 Treaty of Paris.
		- Were United States actions in Latin America during this period a continuation of or a departure from previous American policy?
		- In what ways did United States policy from 1914 to 1917 violate Wilson's promise of neutrality in thought and actions? How did this action lead the United States into war?
		
		Students should understand how the rights of citizens are limited during wartime.
		- How did World War I restrictions on civil liberties compare with those imposed during the Civil War? World War II? (see *Schenck* v. *United States,* 1919 and *Debs* v. *United States*, 1919)

II. THE RISE OF AMERICAN POWER, continued

Content	Concepts/Themes	Connections
1930 1. The peace movement: Women's International League for Peace and Freedom 2. War aims: The Fourteen Points 3. Treaty of Versailles: Wilson's role 4. League of Nations: Henry Cabot Lodge and the United States Senate rejection 5. Washington Naval Disarmament Conference (1920s) 6. Reparations and war debts (United States as a world banker) 7. Kellogg-Briand Pact (1928) 8. Establishment of the World Court	Government Citizenship Human Rights Civic Values	- Why weren't the provisions of the Treaty of Versailles based more fully on Wilson's Fourteen Points? - What factors contributed to the Senate's failure to ratify the Treaty of Versailles? - To what extent did the Treaty of Versailles and subsequent diplomacy from 1920 to 1933 reflect Wilsonian principles? - Ask students to nominate individuals for the Nobel Peace Prize for actions taken during the period 1914-1930. More recently?

UNIT FIVE: AT HOME AND ABROAD: PROSPERITY AND DEPRESSION, 1917 - 1940

I. WAR AND PROSPERITY: 1917 - 1929

Content	Concepts/Themes	Connections

A. Impact of war
  1. War's effects on gender roles, on African-Americans, and other minority groups
  2. Case study: Movement of African-Americans from the South to northern cities
  3. Return to "normalcy": 1918-1921
 	
B. The twenties: Business boom or false prosperity?
  1. Post-World War I recession
  2. Avarice and scandal: Teapot Dome
  3. Coolidge prosperity; not for everyone
  4. Problems on the farm
    a. Expansion, mortgages, and advancing technology
    b. Farmers and minorities fail to share in economic benefit
  5. Speculative boom: the "big bull market"
	Diversity
	
	Factors of Production
		- What important social changes took place both during and after World War I?
		- What did the American public perceive "normalcy" to mean? (Apply the concept to both foreign and domestic affairs.)
		- Investigate the causes and effects of the South-to-North migration during this time period.
		- How did the economic policies of the 1920s contribute to the Great Depression?
		- What scandals arose during the Harding administration? What scandals have plagued subsequent administrations?

I. WAR AND PROSPERITY: 1917 - 1929, continued

Content	Concepts/Themes	Connections

C. Mass consumption and the clash of cultural values
  1. Mass consumption
    a. The automobile: new industries, products, and services
    b. Installment buying: consumer durable goods (appliances)
    c. Real estate boom and suburban development; its economic and geographic implications: decline of trolleys and trains, improvement of roads
      (1) The emergence of new regional, political, and economic units
    d. Entertainment: radio; motion pictures; advertising and cultural homogenization
  2. Constitutional and legal issues
    a. Threats to civil liberties: Red Scare, Ku Klux Klan, and Sacco and Vanzetti
    b. Prohibition (18th Amendment) and the Volstead Act: stimulus to crime, public attitudes, repeal (21st Amendment)
    c. Science, religion, and education: the Scopes trial (1925)
    d. Restrictions on immigration: closing the "golden door"
  3. Shifting cultural values
    a. Revolution in morals and manners: fads, flappers, and Freud
    b. Women's changing roles
      (1) Effect of World War I
      (2) Involvement in the political process: the 19th Amendment
      (3) Health and working conditions
      (4) Women in the workforce
      (5) Emerging role: emphasis on wife rather than mother
    c. The literary scene
      (1) Sinclair Lewis, Ernest Hemingway, Edith Wharton, Willa Cather, and F. Scott Fitzgerald
      (2) The Harlem Renaissance: Duke Ellington, Langston Hughes, Bessie Smith
	Culture and Intellectual Life
	Factors of Production
	
	Science and Technology
	
	Citizenship
	
	Culture and Intellectual Life
	Diversity
		- How did the growth of the automobile industry stimulate the growth of other industries? How did it influence United States politics and lifestyles?
		
		Have students compare the attitudes of the 1920s with those of the 1950s relative to: (1) restrictions on immigration, (2) anti-communist hysteria, (3) religion and morality, (4) role of women, (5) civil rights, (6) new forms of entertainment, (7) growth of suburbia, (8) transportation improvements, and (9) consumer attitudes.

II. THE GREAT DEPRESSION

Content	Concepts/Themes	Connections

A. Onset of the Depression
  1. Weakness in the economy
    a. Overproduction/underconsumption (maldistribution of wealth)
    b. Overexpansion of credit (e.g., buying stock on margin)
  2. The stock market crash
    a. Worldwide nature—Growing financial interdependence
    b. Interdependent banking systems
    c. International trade
    d. Political repercussions
  3. The Hoover response
    a. Rugged individualism; "trickle down" economics
    b. Reconstruction Finance Corporation
  4. Unemployment, the Bonus Army, Hoovervilles; impact on women and minorities
	Factors of Production
	
	Economic Systems
	
	Diversity
		Students should understand that the basic weaknesses in the economy contributed to both the stock market crash and the general economic collapse that became known as the Great Depression.
		- Compare and contrast the responses of Presidents Herbert Hoover and Franklin Delano Roosevelt to the Depression.

B. Franklin D. Roosevelt and the New Deal: Relief, recovery, and reform programs
  1. Relief of human suffering
    a. Bank "holiday"; Emergency Banking Act
    b. Federal Emergency Relief Act
    c. Unemployment: WPA, PWA, CCC; troubling equity issues
  2. Recovery of the United States economy
    a. NRA: "codes of fair competition"
    b. Mortgage relief: HOLC, FHA
    c. First and second AAA, scarcity and parity
  3. Search for effective reform (program examples)
    a. Banking: Glass-Steagall Act (FDIC)
    b. Stock market: SEC
    c. Social Security
    d. Labor
      (1) Wagner Act (NLRB)
      (2) Labor Standards Act
  4. Labor's response: Formation of CIO
  5. Controversial aspects of the New Deal
    a. Constitutional issues
      (1) Supreme Court and the NRA (*Schechter Poultry Corp. v. United States*, 1935)
      (2) Supreme Court and the AAA
      (3) TVA: model yardstick or creeping socialism
	Government
	
	Economic Systems
	
	Government
		Students should compare and contrast the New Deal with the Progressive and Great Society reform movements in terms of goals, leadership, and accomplishments.
		
		Students should understand that even though the New Deal did much to alleviate the effects of the Depression, the New Deal raised controversy. Some felt that it was leading to socialism, destroying checks and balances, and violating the two-term Presidential tradition. (see *United States v. Butler*, 1936)

II. THE GREAT DEPRESSION, continued

Content	Concepts/Themes	Connections

b. 1936 election "mandate"
c. Roosevelt's "Court-packing" proposal: failure and success
d. 1940: third-term controversy (the unwritten constitution)
e. Passage of the 22nd Amendment (1951)
6. The human factor
  a. FDR as communicator and his efforts to restore public confidence; press conferences, "fireside chats," and effective use of the radio
  b. Eleanor Roosevelt as the President's eyes and ears
  c. The Dust Bowl and the Okies
  d. The New Deal and women (Frances Perkins)
  e. The New Deal and minorities (shift in African-American vote): discriminatory results
  f. Indian Reorganization Act (1934)
	Culture and Intellectual Life
	
	Diversity
		- Have students analyze the political impact of the "Court packing" proposal by comparing the anti-New Deal decision in *United States* v. *Butler*, 1936 with the pro-New Deal decision in *National Labor Relations Board* v. *Jones & Laughlin Steel Corp.*, 1937.
		- Why did Eleanor Roosevelt play such a substantive role as First Lady? How do her actions as First Lady compare with the actions of more recent First Ladies?
		- Why did African-American voters increasingly change political allegiance from the Republican Party to the Democratic Party after 1934?
		- How did the Depression and New Deal programs affect women and the nuclear family?
		- What geographic/environmental conditions contributed to the migration from the Dust Bowl to the West?
		- How do the problems of farmers in the 1920s and 1930s compare with those of the 1880s, 1950s, and 1980s?
		- How did the Indian Reorganization Act of 1934 compare with the Dawes Act of 1887 in terms of (1) goals and (2) Native American Indian reactions?

7. Culture of the Depression
  a. Literature: John Steinbeck and Langston Hughes
  b. Music: jazz, swing (big bands)
  c. Art: WPA, fine arts, Hollywood, comic books
8. Opposition to the New Deal: Al Smith, Norman Thomas, Huey Long, Father Coughlin, Dr. Townsend
	Culture and Intellectual Life	- How did the New Deal support the fine arts?
		- Why did "escapist" movies become popular at this time?
		- What New Deal projects were completed in your own community?
		- What are the themes of the literature of John Steinbeck and the photographs of Margaret Bourke-White?

UNIT SIX: THE UNITED STATES IN AN AGE OF GLOBAL CRISIS: RESPONSIBILITY AND COOPERATION

I. PEACE IN PERIL: 1933 - 1950

Content	Concepts/Themes	Connections

A. Isolation and neutrality
  1. Causes of disillusion and pacifism
  2. Neutrality Acts of 1935-37
  3. Spanish Civil War: testing war technology and ideology
  4. FDR's "quarantine" speech (1937)
B. Failure of peace; triumph of aggression
  1. Aggressions of Japan, Germany, Italy: 1932-1940
  2. Appeasement: The Munich Conference (1938)
  3. German attack on Poland; start of World War II in Europe
  4. Gradual United States involvement
    a. Neutrality Act of 1939 ("cash and carry")
    b. Lend-Lease Act and 50 overage destroyers deal
    c. The moral dimension: The Atlantic Charter (August 1941)
C. The United States in World War II
  1. Pearl Harbor
  2. The human dimensions of the war
    a. The "arsenal of democracy" (feats of productivity)
    b. Role of women: WACs; Rosie the Riveter; return of the retired
    c. Mobilization: the draft; minority issues
    d. Financing the war: war bond drives; Hollywood goes to war
    e. Rationing
    f. Experiences of men and women in military service
  3. Allied strategy and leadership
    a. Assistance to Soviet Union
    b. Europe first
    c. A two-front war
 	
  4. The atomic bomb
    a. The Manhattan Project (role of refugees)
    b. Truman's decision to use the atomic bomb against Japan: Hiroshima and Nagasaki
    c. United States occupation of Japan; the "MacArthur constitution"
    d. Japanese war crime trials
  5. The war's impact on minorities
	Interdependence
	
	Places and Regions
	Interdependence
	
	Culture and Intellectual Life
	
	Science and Technology
	
	Diversity
		- To what extent did the isolationist policies of the 1930s reflect a desire to avoid a repeat of the conditions that drew us into World War I?
		
		- In what sense was the United States "involved" in World War II before the Pearl Harbor attack and the Congressional declaration of war in December 1941?
		
		- How did the need to wage "total war" alter the nature of American society?
		- How did United States domestic policies during World War II compare with those of World War I?
		
		Students should compare the role of the United States in World War I and World War II in terms of (1) the arsenal of democracy, (2) United States military leadership and strategy, and (3) role of the President in planning the peace.
		Students should understand that there were several moral issues that grew out of the war experience. These include (1) rights of Japanese-Americans, (2) integration of African-Americans, (3) United States reactions to the Nazi Holocaust, (4) morality of nuclear warfare, and (5) treatment of war criminals.
		- Students should study the origins of these concerns and the ways in which

I. PEACE IN PERIL: 1933 - 1950, continued

Content	Concepts/Themes	Connections
a. Incarceration of West Coast Japanese-Americans; Executive Order 9066; *Korematsu* v. *United States* (1944) b. Extent of racially integrated units in the military c. The Nazi Holocaust: United States and world reactions d. The Nuremberg war crimes trials; later trials of other Nazi criminals, e.g., Eichmann, Barbie	Civic Values Constitutional Principles	they have been addressed in the post-war period. - The Nuremberg trials established the concept of "crimes against humanity." What are some more current examples?
6. Demobilization a. Inflation and strikes b. The G.I. Bill; impact on education and housing c. Truman's Fair Deal d. Partisan problems with Congress e. Minorities continued to find it difficult to obtain fair practices in housing, employment, education f. Upset election of 1948; Truman versus Dewey g. Truman and civil rights	Change Diversity	- How did the economic, social, and political problems of adjusting to the end of World War II compare with those after World War I? Consider inflation, strikes, Presidential policies, political control of Congress, ways of dealing with communist threats, immigration policies, and opportunities for veterans. - How did Truman enhance the civil rights of African-Americans? Why did he use executive power rather than Congressional legislation?

II. PEACE WITH PROBLEMS: 1945 - 1960

Content	Concepts/Themes	Connections
A. International peace efforts 1. Formation of the United Nations 2. United Nations Universal Declaration of Human Rights a. Eleanor Roosevelt's role b. Senate response 3. Displaced persons: refugee efforts	Civic Values	Students should understand the role played by the United States in securing peace: (1) formation of the United Nations, (2) relief and refugee efforts, and (3) economic assistance to war-torn economies and societies.
B. Expansion and containment: Europe 1. Summitry: Yalta and Potsdam, establishing "spheres of influence" 2. The Iron Curtain: Winston Churchill 3. Postwar uses for United States power a. The Truman Doctrine: Greece and Turkey b. The Marshall Plan (1) Aid for Europe (2) The Common Market (3) European Parliament c. Berlin airlift d. Formation of NATO alliance	Places and Regions Interdependence	- How did the United States respond to the expansion of communism in Europe? in Asia? - Compare and contrast the international role of the United States following World War II and World War I. - How might the situation in Europe be different today if the United States had not applied the Truman Doctrine? extended Marshall Plan aid? conducted the Berlin airlift? formed NATO?
C. Containment in Asia, Africa, and Latin America 1. The United States and Japan	Foreign Policy	Suggested Documents: The United Nation Charter (1945); The Truman Doctrine (1947)

II. PEACE WITH PROBLEMS: 1945 - 1960, continued

Content	Concepts/Themes	Connections

a. Separate peace treaty (1951)
b. Reconstruction of Japan
2. The United States and China
  a. Rise to power of Mao Zedong and the People's Republic of China
  b. Chiang Kai-shek to Taiwan (1949)
3. USSR tests an A-bomb (1949)
4. The "hot war" in Asia: Korean War
  a. The Yalu River: China enters the war
  b. United Nations efforts: MacArthur, Truman, and "limited war"
  c. Stalemate and truce (1953)
5. Point four aid: Africa, Asia, Latin America
	Interdependence	

D. The Cold War at home
1. Truman and government loyalty checks
  Case studies: The Smith Act and the House Un-American Activities Committee (*Watkins v. United States*, 1957); the Alger Hiss case (1950); the Rosenberg trial (1950)
2. Loyalty and dissent: the case of Robert Oppenheimer
3. McCarthyism
4. Politics of the Cold War
  a. Loss of China
  b. Stalemate in Korea
  c. Truman's falling popularity
	Citizenship
	Civic Values
		- Was the Cold War inevitable? How did United States support for "self-determination" conflict with the Soviet Union's desire for security in Eastern Europe at the end of the war?
		- How did the United States respond to the communist threat at home?
		- What constitutional values were sacrificed in responding to the communist threat?
		- How did the second Red Scare compare with the first Red Scare?
		- What has "McCarthyism" come to mean?
		- How has the term "McCarthyism" been applied in more recent history?

UNIT SEVEN: WORLD IN UNCERTAIN TIMES: 1950 - PRESENT

I. TOWARD A POSTINDUSTRIAL WORLD: LIVING IN A GLOBAL AGE

Content	Concepts/Themes	Connections
A. Changes within the United States 1. Energy sources (nuclear power) 2. Materials (plastics, light metals) 3. Technology (computers) 4. Corporate structures (multinational corporations) 5. Nature of employment (agriculture to industry to service) 6. Problems (waste disposal, air/water pollution, growing energy usage, depleting resources, e.g., domestic oil supply)	Science and Technology Environment	

II. CONTAINMENT AND CONSENSUS: 1945 - 1960

Content	Concepts/Themes	Connections
A. Review postwar events 1. Emerging power relationships: East/West; North/South; (haves/have-nots; developed/developing nations)	Places and Regions	

B. Eisenhower foreign policies
  1. The end of the Korean War
  2. John Foster Dulles, the domino theory and massive retaliation; brinkmanship posture
  3. The H-bomb; atoms for peace
  4. Summits and U-2s
  5. Establishment of SEATO
  6. Controversy: Aswan Dam and Suez Canal
  7. Polish and Hungarian uprisings
  8. Eisenhower Doctrine: intervention in Lebanon
  9. Sputnik: initiating the space race
	Interdependence
	
	Places and Regions
		- How did each of the post-World War II Presidents build on and extend the policy of containment?
		- How did Truman, Eisenhower, Kennedy, and Johnson carry forth the programs of the New Deal?
		- How did Presidents Eisenhower, Kennedy, and Johnson further the civil rights initiatives begun by Truman?

C. Domestic politics and constitutional issues
  1. The Eisenhower peace
    a. Returning the United States to a peacetime economy
    b. Interstate Highway Act (1956)
    c. Suburbanization
    d. The Warren Court
  2. Civil rights
    a. Jackie Robinson breaks the color barrier
    b. *Brown* v. *Board of Education of Topeka*, 1954
    c. Beginnings of modern civil rights movement
      (1) Rosa Parks and the Montgomery bus boycott
      (2) Little Rock: school desegregation
      (3) Segregation in public transportation ruled unconstitutional
      (4) Sit-ins: nonviolent tactic
      (5) Civil Rights Act of 1957
	Civic Values
	
	Citizenship
	Civic Values
		Students should understand that in spite of the victory of the forces of integration in the *Brown* v. *Board of Education of Topeka* decision, there was much resistance to a broader application of the principle of integration. Students should study various specific events in the civil rights movement from 1955 to 1965.

D. The people
  1. Prosperity and conservatism
    a. Postwar consumption: homes, autos, and television
    b. New educational opportunities: G.I. Bill
    c. The baby boom and its effects
  2. Migration and immigration
    a. Suburbanization: Levittowns
    b. Cities: declining
    c. New immigration patterns: Caribbean focus
	Change
	
	Environment
	Diversity
	Immigration and Migration
		- Compare the attitudes, values, and social changes of the 1950s (post-World War II) with those of the 1920s (post-World War I).
		- What significant demographic changes became evident in the 1950s?
		- Explain how increased use of the automobile changed urban areas. Consider how the automobile contributed to the growth of suburbs and changed the demographic composition of the center city.

III. DECADE OF CHANGE: 1960s

Content	Concepts/Themes	Connections

A. The Kennedy years
  1. The New Frontier: dreams and promises
    a. Civil rights actions
      (1) James Meredith at the University of Mississippi
      (2) Public career of Dr. Martin Luther King, Jr., Birmingham protest ("Letter from Birmingham Jail")
      (3) Assassination of Medgar Evers
      (4) March on Washington
  2. Foreign policy and Cold War crises
    a. Bay of Pigs invasion
    b. Vienna Summit/Berlin Wall
    c. Cuban missile crisis
    d. Laos and Vietnam
    e. Latin America and the Alliance for Progress
    f. Peace Corps
    g. Launching the race to the Moon
    h. Nuclear Test Ban Treaty 1963, 1967; Hot Line established
  3. Movement for rights of disabled citizens
    a. Background
      (1) Historic attitude that disabled were defective
      (2) Emergence of humanitarian view in 19th century, development of large institutions
      (3) Development of the concept of normalization; early-20th-century programs of education and training
    b. Kennedy administration, 1961-1963; beginning awareness, changing attitudes
      (1) President's Council on Mental Retardation
      (2) Special Olympics
    c. Litigation and legislation; 1960 - present
      (1) Education of the Handicapped Act, 1966
      (2) Education for All Handicapped Children Act, 1971
      (3) Rehabilitation Act of 1973, Section 504
      (4) Americans with Disabilities Act, 1990
    d. Dependence to independence
      (1) Activism by disabled veterans
      (2) Deinstitutionalization
      (3) Mainstreaming
  4. Assassination in Dallas
	Civic Values
	
	Interdependence
	
	Places and Regions
	
	Citizenship
	
	Diversity
		- Is the "New Frontier" label for the Kennedy administration justified in terms of both foreign and domestic policies?
		- Although President Kennedy's charismatic style enhanced his public image, what practical effect did it have on his working relationship with Congress? Apply this question to the following areas: (1) civil rights legislation, (2) immigration reform, (3) federal aid to education, and (4) foreign policy initiatives.
		<u>Suggested Document:</u> John F. Kennedy's Inaugural Address
		
		- In what ways were your school district facilities and programs changed as a result of State and federal programs regarding the handicapped and disabled?

III. DECADE OF CHANGE: 1960s, continued

Content	Concepts/Themes	Connections

B. Johnson and the Great Society
  1. Expanding on the Kennedy social programs
    a. War on poverty; VISTA
    b. Medicare
    c. Federal aid to education
    d. Environmental issues and concerns
  2. The Moon landing: the challenge of space exploration
	Presidential Decisions and Actions	- In what ways did Johnson's social programs build upon the Kennedy legacy?
		- Why was Johnson more successful than Kennedy in translating social programs into legislation?

3. Continued demands for equality: civil rights movement
    a. Black protest, pride, and power
      (1) NAACP (National Association for the Advancement of Colored People): legal judicial leadership, Urban League
    b. Case studies
      (1) SNCC (Student Nonviolent Coordinating Committee): sit-in movement among college students
      (2) SCLC (Southern Christian Leader-ship Conference): promote nonviolent resis-tance, sit-ins, boycotts
      (3) CORE (Congress of Racial Equality): "Freedom Riders"
      (4) Testing of segregation laws
      (5) Others: Black Muslims; prominence of Malcolm X: advocating separation of races, separate state in the United States
      (6) Civil unrest: Watts riot, 1965, as example; Kerner Commission
      (7) Assassination of Malcolm X (February 1965)
    c. Legislative impact
      (1) Civil Rights Act of 1964 (*Heart of Atlanta Motel*, Inc. v. *United States*, 1964), modifications since 1964
      (2) 24th Amendment (eliminating poll tax)
      (3) Voting Rights Act, 1965
      (4) Court decisions since 1948 upholding or modifying preferential treatment in employment; equal access to housing; travel and accommodations; voting rights; educational equity
      (5) Fair Housing Act, 1968
  4. Demands for equality: women
    a. The modern women's movement
      (1) Kennedy Commission and the Civil Rights Act, 1963-1964
	Civic Values
	
	Diversity
	
	Civic Values
	
	Civic Values
	
	Citizenship
	
	Diversity
		- Students should understand that the 1960s witnessed protest movements of peoples of diverse backgrounds (African-Americans, women, Hispanic-Americans, Native American Indians).
		- Compare and contrast the civil rights movement after 1965 with the earlier phase (1955-1965) in terms of (1) goals, (2) leadership, (3) strategies, and (4) achievements.
		- Compare the feminist movement of the 1960s with the suffragist move-ment in terms of (1) goals, (2) leader-ship, (3) strategies, and (4) achieve-ments.
		- To what extent did the civil rights movement influence the demands for equality on the part of Hispanic-Americans and Native American Indians? How successful were their efforts?

III. DECADE OF CHANGE: 1960s, continued

Content	Concepts/Themes	Connections

(2) NOW (1966) to present
b. Issues
  (1) Shifting roles and images
  (2) Equal Rights Amendment (failure to ratify)
  (3) *Roe* v. *Wade,* 1973
  (4) Equality in the workplace: compensation, the glass ceiling
  (5) Increased focus on domestic abuse
5. Rising consciousness of Hispanic-Americans
  a. "Brown power" movement
  b. Organizing farm labor (Cesar Chavez)
  c. Cuban and Haitian immigration
  d. Increasing presence in American politics
6. Demands for equality: American Indian Movement (AIM) and other protests
  a. Occupation of Alcatraz
  b. The "long march"
  c. Wounded Knee, 1973
7. Rights of the accused
  a. *Mapp* v. *Ohio,* 1961
  b. *Gideon* v. *Wainwright,* 1963
  c. *Miranda* v. *Arizona,* 1966
8. Legislative reapportionment: *Baker* v. *Carr,* 1962
	Diversity
	
	Civic Values
		- Students should understand the tension involved in balancing the protection of the rights of the accused with the need to protect society.
		- Examine the content of the *Baker* v. *Carr* ruling to discuss how legislative reapportionment has expanded the concept of democratic representation.

IV. THE LIMITS OF POWER: TURMOIL AT HOME AND ABROAD, 1965 - 1972

Content	Concepts/Themes	Connections

A. Vietnam: sacrifice and turmoil
1. The French-Indochinese War: early United States involvement; Truman, Eisenhower, and Kennedy policies (review how foreign policy is formulated)
2. United States and the spread of communism; domino theory; credibility of other United States commitments
3. Civil war in South Vietnam; concept of guerrilla warfare
4. LBJ and the Americanization of the war
  a. Fear of "losing" Vietnam
  b. Escalation and United States assumptions; Tet offensive
5. Student protests at home
  a. Draft protesters
  b. Political radicals: protests, Students for a Democratic Society (SDS), antiwar
	Places and Regions
	
	Culture and Intellectual Life
		Students should (1) trace the history of United States involvement in Vietnam in the context of containment policy in Southeast Asia, (2) examine its domestic impact, and (3) evaluate both its short-term and long-term effects.

IV. THE LIMITS OF POWER: TURMOIL AT HOME AND ABROAD, 1965 - 1972, continued

Content	Concepts/Themes	Connections

c. Cultural radicals: hippies and communalists
  6. 1968: A year of turmoil
    a. President Johnson's decision not to seek reelection
    b. Assassinations of Dr. Martin Luther King, Jr. (April 1968) and Robert Kennedy (June 1968)
    c. The Democratic Convention; war protesters disrupt proceedings
    d. Impact of the Vietnam War on society
	Change	

V. THE TREND TOWARD CONSERVATISM, 1972 - 1985

Content	Concepts/Themes	Connections

A. Nixon as President, 1969-1974
  1. Domestic policies and events
    a. Modifications to Great Society programs (OSHA, Federal Energy Office, DEA, Clean Air Act, food stamps, revenue sharing)
    b. The Moon landing
    c. Environmental Protection Agency (1970)
    d. Self-determination for American Indians (1970)
    e. Ratification of the 26th Amendment (1971)
    f. Title IX - equal education access (1972)
  2. Nixon's internationalism
    a. Henry Kissinger and realpolitik
      (1) Withdrawal from Vietnam and Cambodia; peace talks and signing of Paris Peace Accords (Pentagon papers, *New York Times* v. *United States*, 1971)
      (2) Nixon Doctrine
      (3) Opening to China
      (4) Detente: SALT and grain
  3. The Presidency in crisis
    a. Resignation of Spiro Agnew
    b. Watergate affair and its constitutional implications
    c. *United States* v. *Nixon*, 1974
    d. The impeachment process and resignation
	Change
	Presidential Decisions and Actions
	
	Choice
		- In what specific ways did Nixon depart from Johnson's Great Society?
		- Identify and evaluate Nixon's foreign policy initiatives.
		- What factors contributed to the weakening of the "Imperial Presidency" under Nixon, Ford, and Carter?

V. THE TREND TOWARD CONSERVATISM, 1972 - 1985, continued

Content	Concepts/Themes	Connections

B. The Ford and Carter Presidencies
  1. The appointive Presidency: Ford and Rockefeller (the constitutional aspects)
  2. Domestic policy issues
    a. Pardon for Nixon and amnesty for draft evaders
    b. Oil crisis: shifting energy priorities
    c. Environmental concerns
      (1) Three Mile Island
      (2) Acid rain
      (3) Toxic waste
	Environment	

3. Foreign policy issues: the United States after Vietnam
    a. Fall of South Vietnam, 1975
    b. Oil crisis: Middle East in turmoil
    c. Middle East mediation: Camp David Accordss
    d. The Afghanistan invasion: Olympics and grain—diplomatic weapons
    e. Iranian hostage crisis: 1979-1981
	Interdependence	Assess the appropriateness of Carter's emphasis upon human rights considerations in the conduct of United States foreign policy.
		TEACHER'S NOTE: This core curriculum has been developed to place emphasis on content and understanding prior to 1980. Study of events of the post-1980 period should, therefore, focus on drawing parallels to and/or distinctions from specific events and trends prior to 1980.

C. Reagan and Bush, the "new" federalism and growth of conservatism
  1. Supply-side economics
  2. Tax policy and deficits
  3. Environmental and civil rights policies
  4. Effects on minorities
  5. The Supreme Court and the schools
    a. *Engle* v. *Vitale*, 1962
    b. *Tinker* v. *Des Moines School District*, 1969
    c. *New Jersey* v. *TLO*, 1985
    d. *Vernonia School District* v. *Acton*, 1995
D. New approaches to old problems
  1. Feast and famine: the farmer's dilemma
  2. The problems of poverty in an affluent society—"the underclass"
  3. The "new" immigrants; (Immigration Reform and Control Act of 1986)
  4. Changing demographic patterns (growing numbers of elderly)
	Economic Systems	- To what extent and in what ways did the "Reagan Revolution" constitute a challenge to the elements of the New Deal and Great Society?
		- Why didn't all socioeconomic groups benefit equally from the Reagan Revolution?
		According to Supreme Court rulings in these cases, how does the Bill of Rights apply to students in a school context?
		
		- How effectively did the Immigration Reform and Control Act of 1986 deal with the problems of illegal aliens in our nation?
		- What were the sources of immigration after 1975? How have these new immigrant groups affected American society? How do the experiences of recent immigrant groups compare with those of earlier immigrant groups?
		- What are the political, economic, and social implications of an increasingly elderly population?
		- To what extent did Reagan's foreign

V. THE TREND TOWARD CONSERVATISM, 1972 - 1985, continued

Content	Concepts/Themes	Connections

E. Renewed United States power image
  1. Central America and the Caribbean: debt and stability; Sandinistas, Contras, El Salvadorians
  2. Middle East: war and hostages
	Human systems	policy represent a return to traditional themes of Cold War and power politics?

F. Trade imbalance and divesting
  1. Japan: trade imbalance
  2. United States and South Africa
	Interdependence	

G. United States—Soviet relations
  1. Gorbachev and Soviet relations
  2. "Star Wars" and arms limitation efforts
  3. Cuts in defense spending and the fall of the Soviet Union
	Foreign Policy	

VI. APPROACHING THE NEXT CENTURY 1986 - 1999

Content	Concepts/Themes	Connections

A. The Bush Presidency
  1. Case study: The election of 1988
    a. Effects of demographics
    b. Rise of a third party (H. Ross Perot)
    c. Increasing influence of political action committees
	Presidential Decisions and Actions	Students should study these elections to deepen their understanding of prior developments in United States history. Some examples are (1) third-party candidacy of Perot in 1992 compared to Theodore Roosevelt in 1912, (2) change in party control of Congress in midterm elections (1994 compared with 1918, 1930, 1946) and its impact on the working relationship between the President and Congress.

2. Domestic issues
    a. Environmental concerns
    b. Immigration issues
    c. Savings and loan scandal
    d. Social concerns (*Cruzan* v. *Director, Missouri Department of Health*, 1990 and *Planned Parenthood of Southeastern Pennsylvania, et.al.* v. *Casey*, 1992)
	Environment	

3. Foreign policy issues
    a. Dissolution of the Soviet Union
    b. Fall of the Berlin Wall and German reunification (1990)
    c. Crisis in Bosnia
    d. Persian Gulf crisis
	Interdependence Foreign Policy	Evaluate the effectiveness of the foreign policies of Presidents Reagan and Bush.

B. The Clinton Presidency 1. Domestic issues	Presidential Decisions and Actions	
	Economic Systems	

Content	Concepts/Themes	Connections

a. Social concerns
  (1) Health care
  (2) Education
  (3) Welfare reform
  (4) Stability of the Social Security system
b. Economic concerns
  (1) Role of technologies
  (2) Impact of the baby boom generation
  (3) Balanced budget amendment (debate)
  (4) Market trends: The bull market of the 1990s
c. Political concerns
  (1) Senate Whitewater investigations
  (2) Gun control
  (3) Campaign finance reform (debate)
d. Impeachment and acquittal
2. Foreign policy issues
a. United States—Middle East relations: Israeli—PLO agreement (Rabin—Arafat)
b. United States in the global economy
  (1) NAFTA
  (2) GATT
  (3) Economic aid to Russia
  (4) United States trade with China, Japan, and Latin America
c. Intervention in Somalia, Haiti, Bosnia, and Yugoslavia
d. United States—Russian relations; 1990 to the present
e. United States—European relations: European Union (EU), NATO
	
	Foreign Policy
	
	Places and
	Regions
	
	Foreign Policy
	
	Interdependence
		Suggested Document: *Reno* v. *American Civil Liberties Union*, 1997
		
		Students should examine the foreign policies of Bush and Clinton to understand the complexities of post-Cold War issues and realities.

Grade 12 Social Studies

The curriculum for grade 12 social studies continues to focus on two major areas:

1) **Participation in Government**

2) **Economics and Economic Decision Making**

Since the content outlines have not changed in these subjects, the syllabi have not been reprinted in this document. Brief descriptions of each of these courses follow.

Grade 12 Social Studies: Participation in Government

Students studying participation in government in grade 12 should experience a culminating course that relates the content and skills component of the K-11 social studies curriculum, as well as the total educational experience, to the individual student's need to act as a responsible citizen.

Course content will:

- be interdisciplinary, for it will be drawn from areas beyond the defined social studies curriculum; will include life experience beyond classroom and school

- be related to problems or issues addressed by students, i.e., content in the form of data, facts, or knowledge may vary from school to school, but real and substantive issues at the local, State, national, and global levels should be integrated into the program

- be in the form of intellectual processes or operations necessary to deal with data generated by problems or issues addressed, i.e., the substance of the course.

In addition, the term "participation" must be interpreted in the broad sense to include actual community service programs or out-of-school internships, and in-class, in-school activities that involve students in the analysis of public issues chosen because of some unique relevance to the student involved. Defining, analyzing, monitoring, and discussing issues and policies is the fundamental participatory activity in a classroom.

Grade 12 Social Studies: Economics and Economic Decision Making

The study of economics in grade 12 should provide students with the economic knowledge and skills that enable them to function as informed and economically literate citizens in our society and in the world. The course is designed to be used with all students, emphasizes rational decision making, and encourages students to become wiser consumers as well as better citizens. Teachers will provide for different student needs by selecting appropriate instructional materials and learning strategies.

Social Studies

Learning Experiences

Reading, 'Riting, 'Rithmetic

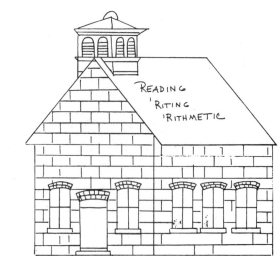

Ellen Laudermilk, Nancy Murinka

Port Byron Central School

A. A. Gates Elementary School

30 Maple Avenue

Port Byron, NY 13140

(315) 776-5731

btomassocny.tds.net

Grade 4

Standards & Performance Indicators

SS 1
▲ roots of American culture
▲ information about traditions
▲ how traditions were passed
▲ view historic events through eyes of those who were there

SS 2
▲ read historical narratives
▲ distinguish between past/present/future
▲ explore lifestyles/beliefs/traditions

SS 5
▲ what it means to be a good citizen
▲ identify/describe rules/responsibilities
▲ participate in activities

Reading, 'Riting, 'Rithmetic is a reenactment program used in the 4th Grade as an integral part of the local history study. The children prepare for, and actually participate in a pioneer school day. The children will develop an appreciation for the child of the 19th century by actually "walking in their shoes." The children will begin to view history not as a text of famous events and people, but a story of ordinary people like themselves.

Children will need enthusiasm for learning, copies of preparation lessons, spelling lists, and a poem to memorize. Costumes from home such as long skirts and bonnets for the girls, and jeans or overalls for the boys add to the authenticity.

Because this unit is activity-oriented, and is based on the lives of 4th grade students, nothing is needed except an enthusiasm for learning. Background for understanding is provided in activities, literature, and documents from the past.

The teacher's role in this unit is to familiarize the students with the classrooms and learning of the 19th century. This is introduced by reading from children's literature. These will include chapters from Laura Ingalls Wilder's stories, *Caddie Woodlawn*, and the *American Girl Learns A Lesson* series by Pleasant Company. The teacher then provides opportunities for the class to experience reading, writing, and arithmetic lessons from the past. These will involve reading from McGuffey readers, practicing writing with a quill pen and ink, and solving arithmetic problems from the past. The teacher also provides a spelling list to study for a future spelling bee, and poetry to memorize and recite on pioneer school day.

The teacher runs the reenactment day following the schedule used at a one-room schoolhouse in the 19th century. There is a series of morning lessons in reading, writing, and arithmetic, along with recess. Activities such as poetry recitation, spelldown, geography memory game, oral math contest, and singing are included in the school day.

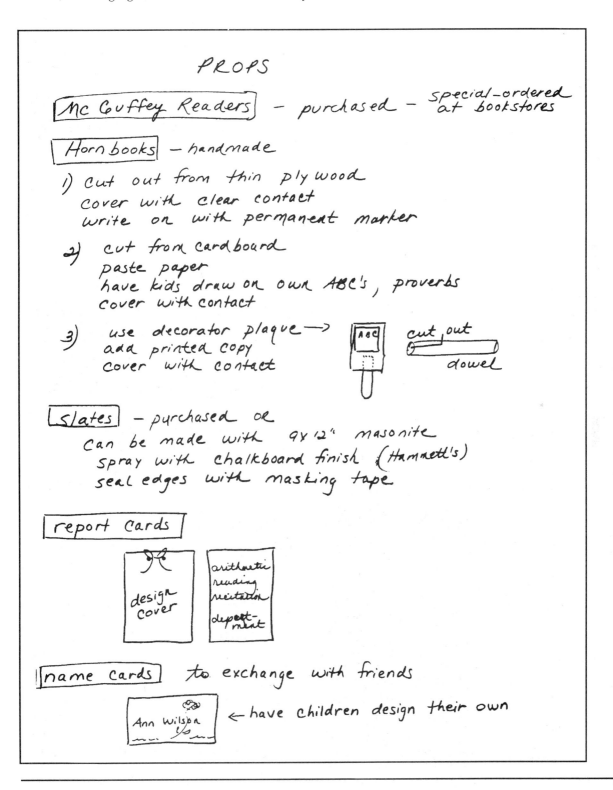

PROPS

| McGuffey Readers | — purchased — special-ordered at bookstores

| Horn books | — handmade

1) cut out from thin plywood
   cover with clear contact
   write on with permanent marker

2) cut from cardboard
   paste paper
   have kids draw on own ABC's, proverbs
   cover with contact

3) use decorator plaque →
   add printed copy
   cover with contact
   cut out   dowel

| Slates | — purchased or
   can be made with 9 x 12" masonite
   spray with chalkboard finish (Hammett's)
   seal edges with masking tape

| report cards |

design cover

arithmetic
reading
recitation
deport-
ment

| name cards | to exchange with friends

Ann Wilson   ← have children design their own

| autograph books | design cover / a recess activity – sew pages / gathering signatures |

Steve Caneys' *Kids America* is a great resource for old autograph book sayings

| Copy Book |

design + print cover on card stock (use old x table pictures from ABC books)
hand sew old paper to inside.

| Quill Pens |

best made from turkey feathers
cut nib – will last for years!

| Ink |

purchased easily
great if you use home made recipe!
(included in packet)

| Battle dore |

purchased or
can be made easily in class
similar to hornbook but on paper and folded

| Table Book |

a first general textbook
Contains reading grammar and arithmetic lesson.
available at Coopestown bookstore
can make your own class version

The children may do a variety of activities with children's literature. These may involve writing story summaries, creating comparison charts or Venn diagrams, or writing fictional school diaries. Working in learning centers, the children practice writing with proper quill penmanship, look at primers and hornbooks, and solve difficult word problems from the past. They study proposed spelling lists, and learn a poem to recite.

The focus of these lessons is to familiarize the students with the schooling of the past. Most activities are done in cooperative work groups, with a range of ability in each group. Often the activities are done at learning centers with the children helping each other. The range of reading abilities can be addressed by incorporating a range of grade-level materials, and by reading difficult materials to the class.

The reenactment can be done at an actual one-room schoolhouse, or arranged in your own classroom. Modern desks and chairs are removed from the room, and replaced with benches (usually obtained from school gym). Cardboard boxes or shelves can be used to block off "pioneer school" from the rest of the classroom.

Materials and Supplies

- copies of children's literature relating to one-room schoolhouse experiences
- McGuffey readers (reprints ordered from bookstores)
- quill pens, ink
- worksheets
- copies of poems
- spelling list (teacher-generated)
- schedule for school day
- access to one-room school (optional)

PRAIRIE SCHOOL by Lois Lenski

SCHOOLHOUSE IN THE WOODS by Rebecca Caudill

MYSTERY AT THE LITTLE RED SCHOOLHOUSE by Helen Fuller Orton

THE LITTLE RED SCHOOLHOUSE by Carolyn Sherwin Bailey

SUGGESTIONS FOR DOCUMENTS

School Office:
School board minutes
Teacher contracts
Graduation class lists
Graduation requirements
Report cards

Town, Village Offices, County Clerk, County Historian
Census records
Information on the formation of local school districts

Proficiency Report for Process Writing
Grade ___ 19___ - 19___ Teacher ___
Student Name ___

4	3	2	1	
independently writes in paragraphs with introductory sentences, main ideas, and supporting detail	**independently** creates a logical plan that includes a beginning, middle, and end	**with teacher-directed plan** follows a logical sequence with beginning, middle, and end	**with teacher-directed plan** ideas jump all over	ORGANIZATION 10 20 30 40
independently supports topic very clear, detailed many examples given to support main idea clearly shows purpose for writing creative or clever	**independently supports topic** very clear examples and details used to support main idea	**teacher-directed topic and plan** clear, but simple main ideas only few details or examples	**teacher-directed topic and plan** not sure of topic, wanders, vague	SUPPORTING TOPIC 10 20 30 40
very descriptive sentences include adjectives, adverbs, descriptive phrases, similes, and personification	**descriptive** sentences include adjectives, adverbs, descriptive phrases	**beginning to describe** sentences with nouns verbs and adjectives	**little description** basic sentences of nouns and verbs	WORD CHOICE 10 20 30 40
varied use of expanded sentences structure includes phrases, compound sentences, and unique sentence beginnings	**expanded sentences** that vary in length and include phrases	**simple sentences** that begin in a similar way	**sentence fragments and run-ons**	SENTENCES 10 20 30 40
no errors	**mostly correct**	**some error**	**serious error**	SPELLING / CAPITALIZATION 10 20 30 40
correct use of " " , in phrasing	**correct in basic** . , ? !	**many errors in punctuation**	**punctuation mostly ignored**	PUNCTUATION 10 20 30 40

General Scoring Rubric
(Abbreviated Version)

	3	2	1
Degree of Understanding	Excellent	Fairly good	Minimal
Selection of Information	Relevant	Generally relevant	Parts may be irrelevant
Accuracy of Information	Accurate	Moderately accurate	Inaccurate; misunderstood
WRITING	**3**	**2**	**1**
Accomplishment of Task	Successful	Reasonably successful	Not successful
Organization	Logical, focused, clear	Minor flaws; may lack focus	Confusing; no direction
Development	Well developed, explained, supported	Fairly well developed and explained	Minimally developed
Sentence Structure	Correct; varied	Some errors; limited variety	Many errors; lacks variety
Vocabulary	Clear, precise, expressive	Appropriate; not vivid, precise, or expressive	Limited; unsuitable
Mechanics	Few significant errors	Several errors	Many significant errors

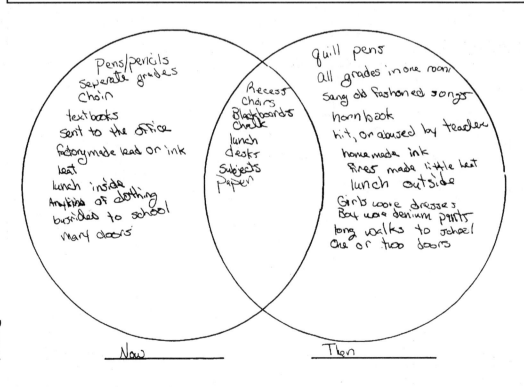

ASSESSMENT

The personal reflection essay is the best insight for the teacher. The children are asked to tell about their experience at the schoolhouse, and to decide which type of learning they prefer. The supporting statements for their choice can be a basis for assessment, or for group debate and discussion.

Another evaluative piece is the Venn diagram, comparing 19th century learning with today's schooling. The paper, "You Be The Teacher," from the Laura Wilder's activity guide gives the children the opportunity to view the school from the other side of the classroom.

There are also ample opportunities to discuss the literature read, to write story summaries, and to make dioramas of the schoolroom. Most of the activities used to prepare for the reenactment can also be used as assessment tools. All of the activities can be gathered together and used as part of a portfolio, if the teacher wishes.

Rearrangement of Classroom if Cato 1-Room Schoolhouse is unavailable to you.

other classroom furniture or all "modern" stuff

door | Room Dividers (shelves or refrigerator box

Pretend store

(bench)

(bench)

(bench)

gym (benches)

X
(tape for recitation)

Teacher Desk

water bucket wi: dipper

Student Work

The pre- and post-activities give students ownership of the schoolhouse experience. All of the pre-activities build an understanding of 19th century school life, which will enrich the actual experience. The literature sharing is especially good for making the connection for children of today to children of tomorrow.

The on-site activities help build the realism. They add the feeling of actually being there for the class.

The post-activities allow the children to reflect on their experience. They are able to express what impressed them, to know how they connect to children of the past, and to make a judgment using support from actual experience.

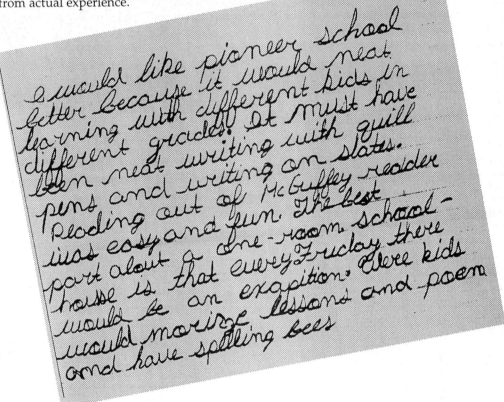

I would like pioneer school better because it would neat. learning with different kids in different grades. It must have been neat writing with quill pens and writing on slates. Reading out of McGuffey reader was easy and fun. The best part about a one-room school house is that every Friday there would be an exapition. there kids would marize lessons and poem and have spelling bees

REFLECTION

This unit connects all levels of learning for the student. It is a study of history without texts and dates. The children experience pioneer living on their level, with the common experience of schooling as the connection. The writing and literature lessons fit naturally into the unit, as do math and geography. This unit can be as extensive or as limited as the teacher desires, and can be adapted to fit all learning styles.

I have used this reenactment unit for 12 years, and find it the most successful activity I do with children. The enthusiasm and interest for the history of schools is very positive. I have recently included primary documents to this unit, bringing in school board notes, report cards, and graduation programs for the children to compare to the present. It is such a natural connection. I feel this type of learning experience may take more planning time, but the benefits are worth the effort.

Cookie Factory

Standards & Performance Indicators

SS 4

▲ individuals/groups satisfy needs/wants

▲ scarcity requires individuals to make choices

▲ societies organize their economies

▲ investigate economic decisions

▲ locate economic information

SS 5

▲ willingness to consider other viewpoints

▲ participate in activities

▲ suggest alternative solutions

▲ evaluate consequence

▲ prioritize solutions

▲ propose action plan

This interdisciplinary project allows students to work together to make decisions, solve problems, and learn about the world of work and economics. They will produce, promote, "sell", and evaluate a product —cookies.

Valerie Jodoin, Billie VanCour

Beekmantown Central School

West Chazy Elementary School

P.O. Box 223, 44 Academy Street

West Chazy, New York 12992

(518) 493-3761

FAX (518)493-4194

 Grade 2

I ntroduce concepts and terms (factory, product, produce, employee, supervisor, survey, customer, production).

Students sign up for the team of their choice:

Accounting
- figure out cost of cookie, collect and count money

Research
- research prices of cookie dough, frosting, and sprinkles
- find out how many cookies we would need (take orders with or without frosting)
- graph results later

Management
- decide sequence in making cookies
- define jobs needed and write job descriptions
- collect feedback from workers
- write a note to workers about how to change jobs (if they want to)
- create a time card to use

Design
- design cookie cutter size and shape
- decide on frosting, color, and sprinkles

Customer Service
- design a survey for customers
- compile results

Advertising
- talk to classes about sale of cookies
- decide on factory name
- make advertising signs and write notes to classes
- collect feedback in regards to advertising

1. Did you like our cookies?

    yes   no

2. Circle what you liked the best.

    spinkles

    frosting

    taste

    shape

3. Do you have any suggestions?

A. Meet in small groups to accomplish team goals. (Teacher facilitator)

B. Meet as a whole group to brainstorm ingredients and utensils needed to make sugar cookies. (Teacher facilitator) For homework, research a sugar cookie recipe to find out what the ingredients are and compare it to the prepared dough we will be using.

C. Sign up for jobs:
    roller
    cutter
    mover
    remover
    froster
    sprinkler
    janitor
    deliverer
    (Teacher is baker)

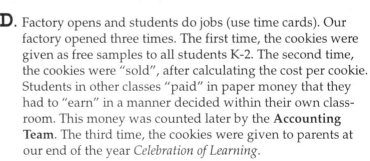

D. Factory opens and students do jobs (use time cards). Our factory opened three times. The first time, the cookies were given as free samples to all students K-2. The second time, the cookies were "sold", after calculating the cost per cookie. Students in other classes "paid" in paper money that they had to "earn" in a manner decided within their own classroom. This money was counted later by the **Accounting Team**. The third time, the cookies were given to parents at our end of the year *Celebration of Learning*.

Cookies Ordered

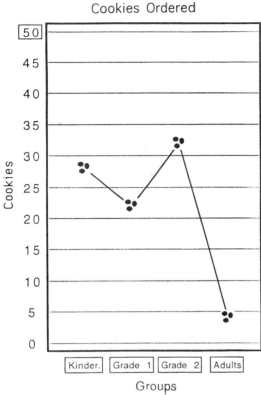

Numbers of Cookies Ordered

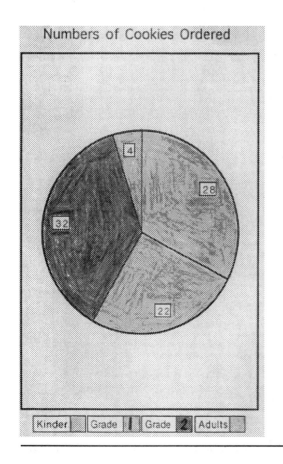

E. Have an employee meeting(s) to evaluate the factory. (Use **Robert's Rules of Order**). This may lead to smaller team meetings and eventual oral reports to group. (Teacher facilitator)

F. Students write a description of their jobs.

G. Possible extension activities: graphing (computer), design and have technology department make their own cookie cutter, visit a bakery in the community to compare, counting money, and letter writing, as needed.

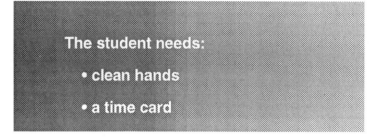

The student needs:
- clean hands
- a time card

The Cookies Ordered

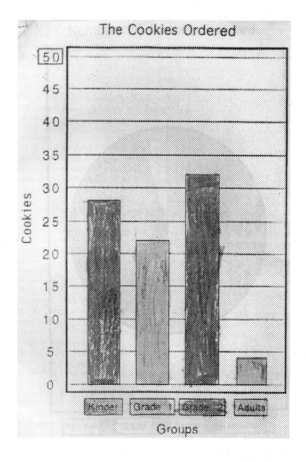

ASSESSMENT

Assessment

1) observation of students during teamwork and cookie factory

2) photographs of teams and students performing cookie factory jobs

3) performance of tasks and completion of product (team planning and factory operation)

4) writing about the job they had and illustrating

5) drawing conclusions about their work and reporting at employee meetings

6) student-made surveys and graphs

The photographs indicate the level of involvement the students had with their jobs.

The survey informed us that the factory was a success.

The completed research showed that the students could gather and compile information.

The writing demonstrated how the team solved problems and that they understood their roles in the production process.

REFLECTION

We work in a small primary building (K-2). Our project involved the whole student body and staff. The project was expanded further into the school community when the technology department constructed the students' design for a new cookie shape. Finally, the project was carried outside the school into the local community when we visited a real bakery.

Possible problems might develop if your school has any policies about giving away food or does not celebrate holidays, which two of our factory openings centered around. However, the project could be easily adapted to any activity that has a sequence. Some examples might include other foods, such as pizza, crafts, or growing plants to sell.

Team Self-Evaluation Questions

Accounting
> How much did each cookie cost?
> Total cookie cost?
> How much should we charge next time?

Research
> Some teachers did not get any cookies. How can we solve that problem next time?
> Do we need the same amount of ingredients next?
> How do you know?

Management
> Do we need any more jobs?
> Did we have enough employees on each job?
> How did the employees feel about their jobs?

Design
> Was the design successful? How can you tell?
> What will next time's design be?

Customer Service
> What were the results of the survey?
> Can you figure out how to compile the results to share with all employees?
> What should we do differently?

Advertising
> Where are your signs?
> What should we do with them?
> Do you think people noticed them?
> How can we make sure that they do notice them?
> Did we have enough advertising?

Geography Booklet

Standards & Performance Indicators

SS 3

▲ gather geographic information

▲ present geographic information

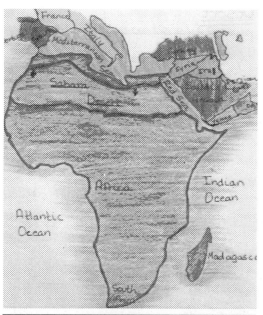

As a culminating activity for a heterogeneously mixed sixth grade class, this activity introduces a unit on world geography.

Teacher

Valentina B. Schatoff

City School District of

New Rochelle

Isaac E. Young Middle School

270 Centre Avenue

New Rochelle, New York 10805

(914) 576-4360

WATOB@aol.com

Grade 6

The materials, supplies, and equipment needed to successfully complete this assignment are:
- old maps, discarded social studies textbooks
- old magazines (*National Geographic*, *Travel and Leisure*, etc.)
- Appropriate software (*Encarta*, etc.)

This unit of study connects to the standards in that it allows students to use geography as a tool to learn more about the world around them. This unit of study lends itself quite well to interdisciplinary study.

Teacher

Social Studies/Schatoff   Name _____
Period _____   Date _____

GEOGRAPHY BOOKLET PROJECT

Dear Student:

Congratulations! You have just been assigned your first long-term project. In this project you will use your knowledge and understanding of the definitions of common land and water terms to identify real examples of these forms on maps.

You will create a 10 term geography booklet using real world examples for each term. Your geography booklet can be a paper booklet or it can take the form of a video "booklet". The assignment sheet on the following page will detail all the requirements for this assignment.

Shown below are illustrations of two possible layout styles that can be used. If you can think of any others, please share them with me.

This unit could work well at every grade level, K-12, but is particularly suited for students at the Intermediate level. The assignment can be modified for those needing academic intervention or enriched for those students who need enrichment.

Teacher

DIRECTIONS

1. Read all pages of this assignment handout.
2. Choose at least 10 terms from the attached "Geography Terms and Definitions" list.
3. Using resources such as the encyclopedia, dictionary or atlas, find a real example of the landform somewhere in the world. Draw a map showing where the landform exists. You must label the surrounding features, countries and states. The labeling is very important because it will identify where the exact location is. Do not assume that I will know of the place you have chosen.
4. You may use a map as your drawing if it appropriately shows the landform, as would drawing a bay. If ,however, the map shows only the location of the landform, then an illustration must be included. For example, a map showing the location of a desert does not show what a desert looks like. You might draw a sun shining on a sandy landscape with cactus growing.
5. Use each geography term in a sentence. The sentence will show that you understand the meaning of the word. General sentences in which any term could be inserted are not acceptable.

GEOGRAPHY TERMS BOOKLET INFORMATION SHEET

You will create a booklet with a minimum of 10 geographic terms. Below is a checklist of the five items that must be included on each page.

CHECKLIST

_____	1. A geography term
_____	2. The definition of the geography term
_____	3. A drawing (picture, magazine clippping, etc.) that illustrates the geography term chosen
_____	4. A map section showing where one of these landforms exists. You must show the name of the ocean, continent, country, etc., where it can be found
_____	5. A sentence using the word correctly.

Definitions

archipelago	a group of many islands
atoll	a ring-shaped coral island or string of islands, surrounding a lagoon
basin	an area of low-lying land surrounded by higher land
bay	part of an ocean, sea, or lake, that extends into the land
beach	the gently sloping shore of an ocean or other body of water, especially that part covered by sand or pebbles
butte	a small, flat-topped hill
canal	a waterway built to carry water for navigation or irrigation, usually connecting two other bodies of water
canyon	a deep, narrow valley with steep sides
cape	a point of land extending into a body of water
channel	a narrow, deep waterway connecting two bodies of water
cliff	a high, steep overhang of rock or earth
coast	land along an ocean or sea
dam	a wall built across a river to hold back the flowing water
delta	a triangular deposit of sand and soil that collects at the mouth of some rivers
desert	a very dry area where few plants grow
dune	a mound, hill or ridge of sand that is heaped up by the wind
fjord	a deep, narrow inlet of the sea between high, steep cliffs
foothills	a hilly area at the base of a mountain range
glacier	a huge mass of ice that moves slowly down a mountain
gulf	part of an ocean extending into land, usually larger than a bay
harbor	a sheltered area of water where ships can anchor safely
hill	a rounded, raised landform, not as high as a mountain
island	an area of land completely surrounded by water
isthmus	a narrow strip of land, bordered by water that connects two larger bodies of land
lagoon	a shallow body of water partly or completely enclosed within an atoll; shallow body of sea water partly cut off from the sea by a narrow strip of land
lake	a large body of water surrounded by land on all sides

Assessment

ASSESSMENT

Your grade will be based on many criteria. The project will be graded not only on the content but on the quality of your work.

- The booklet was colorful.
- The text and pictures were arranged attractively.
- There was detail in the drawings and pictures.
- The cover was eye-catching and colorful.

Four points will be deducted from your total score for every day that your project is late.

Geography Terms
Booklet Rubric

	0	1	2	3	4	5
Content						
at least 10 terms						
correct spelling						
appropriate sentence						
correct definition						
map location for each term						
maps labeled correctly						
appropriate picture						
Visual						
done neatly						
print.clearly/wordprocessed						
colorful						
detailed						
artistic						
appropriate cover						

Students progress was evaluated through ongoing observations and individual conferencing. The final product was presented to the teacher and the class. Each project was viewed, critiqued and discussed. Final evaluation was made using a scoring rubric.

Evidence that the students have mastered the objectives of this unit include the following measurable criteria:

They have:

- included a correct definition of a geographic term.

- indicated on an existing map or on a map of their own creation a real world location for their geographic term.

- written a sentence using the geographic term correctly.

- made a drawing showing that they understand what the specific land or water term looks like.

REFLECTION:

The study of social studies, and especially of geography, is an integral part of educating students for the burgeoning global economy and for the coming millennium. That is why this unit is so well suited for the intermediate students. It allows them to make a connection between their classroom assignment and the world at large. It allows them to have a "final product" that is within the grasp of the vast majority of students.

The unit would better meet the needs of all students if the work were done exclusively in the classroom, rather than in the way I have assigned it in the past. This is because there can be a huge discrepancy in the quality of work between those who have access to parental intervention and a ready access to supplies and those who are left to finish the product left to their own devices. Otherwise, the unit is easy to implement and gives the students important skills while, at the same time, instilling a sense of accomplishment.

INTERMEDIATE

Standards & Performance Indicators

Study of Gender Equity— Age of Homespun

Witness – Stephen Tappen of Lysander
Proven – 5 March 1818

Bod... ...Bi... ... ...n of
Marcellus and county of Onondaga ...Unto wife, Asenath
Lawrence, one-third pa... ...ll... ...
horse, one side saddl... ...di... ... ...
the late husband of my daughter, Susanna, deceased, the sum
of twenty-five dollars to be paid in six months after my
... ...e Farmer Society in Marcellus an annuity of...

SS 1

▲ meaning of American culture

▲ how ordinary people/historic figures advanced democratic values

▲ sources of historic documents

▲ understand how different experiences lead to different interpretations of events

William J. Neer

Liverpool Central Schools

Soule Road Middle School

8340 Soule Road

Liverpool, New York 13090

(315) 453-1283

FAX (315) 453-1286

Grade 7

...much as either of my sons, ...sons, Bigelow Lawrence, Joab
Lawrence, Peter Lawrence, Ru...
Clavin Lawrence, Jeptha Lawre...

Prior Learning necessary for completion of this exercise

- an awareness of the time period, or era, of American history in which these wills were written,

- previous teaching of the letter writing unit in Language Arts, both friendly and business letter formats.

shall be considered as advanc...
be made to said son, Calvin, ...
vested in him until he shall ...
at home at least three years ...
his family and unless he shal...
above stated within ten years...
dividend is to go to his thre...
Executors – Sons, Bigelow Law...
Written – 1 March 1811
Witnesses – Dan Bradley, Nanc...
Proven – 11 March 1818

1. What is the purpose, objective or focus?

Students will analyze actual wills from the Homespun Era. From this analysis, students will be able to document:

1. how females were treated differently than males

2. how morality played a key role in an inheritance

3. the importance of religion in Homespun society

4. the extent of an upper middle class estate during this era

Students will, after this analysis, make evaluative comments to the authors of the wills.

You need readable copies of the wills. If one wishes to look for wills from a specific time and place, a couple of hours at the county clerk's office is all that is necessary.

THE LAST WILL OF JOHN MATHEWS

I, John Mathews, now of the village of Liverpool in the county of Onondaga and State of New York do hereby make and publish this to be my last will and Testament. To my daughters, Mary Case, wife of William Case 2nd of Gloversville in the County of Fulton and Lois Ann Johnson, wife of James Johnson of the City of Syracuse, I give and bequeath to each of them the sum of Two thousand Dollars to be paid unto them by any Executors within one year after my decease. The balance and residue of my estate real and personal of every kind and description I give and bequeath to my son Daniel Mathews of Gloversville in the County of Fulton aforesaid. And I hereby nominate and approve my said son Daniel Mathews my sole Executor without bail or other surety of any kind for the faithful performance of his duties as such. I having full faith that he will perform his duty and represent one in all respects according to his best ability. In witness Whereof, I do herewith set my hand and seal at Liverpool aforesaid the first day of January one thousand eight hundred and sixty two, John Mathews. The above instrument consisting of one fourth of a sheet was now here subscribed by John Mathews the testator in the presence of each of us, and it was at the same time declared by him to be his last will and testament and we at his request sign our names as hereto as attesting witnesses, D.A.Oreutt of the City of Syracuse, Onondaga Co., N.Y.

> *The Lawrence will was found in a typewritten format, but it is interesting for students to work with the handwritten Mathews will. It is a good idea to provide the typed transcription as well...it is fun for students try to read the original Mathews will with the aid of hand held plastic magnifiers which are readily available at most office supply stores very inexpensively.*
>
> Teacher

The Last Will of John Mathews — I John Mathews now of the Village of Liverpool in the County of Onondaga and State of New York do hereby make and publish this to be my last will and Testament. To my daughters, Mary Case wife of William Case 2 of Gloversville in the County of Fulton and Lois Ann Johnson, wife of James Johnson of the City of Syracuse, I give and be-

Brandon
Period 10

Dear Bigelow Lawrence,
    I think your will is very unfair. You only gave your daughters one half of everything. If you plan to do it over, try to include your daughters. In today's society women are treated just like men, equally. Women can own businesses, receive high wages, and are head of households.

Sincerely,
Brandon

Dear John Mathews,
    I liked to see the value that you placed on your family when writing your will. You tried to give your daughters and son large amounts of money, thus allowing them to meet their personal needs, as well as family needs. When recieving large amounts of money today, it helps to purchase goods with prices rising everyday. However, it appears that you treated your daughters in a manner that was unfair in comparison to that which you left for your son. Women have just as many needs and responsibilities as men in this day and age.

Sincerely,
Kristin

2. The students demonstrate their level of understanding of gender inequities. At the middle school (intermediate) level, fairness, consistency, and equal treatment are of paramount importance. The students easily see the inequity shown by these two wills. It is very interesting to note how they interpret these inequities by reading their letters. The worksheet readily gives insight concerning the students' recognition of the values of the work ethic, marriage, religion, and gender equity.

Dear John Mathews,
    I believe you did a great job on your will. You divided your belongings among your children equally. I wouldn't have changed a thing. In your will, your daughters are given about the same amount of your belongings as your son. Your will is very well constructed.

Yours truly,
Brandon

177

USING THE ATTACHED TWO WILLS, ANSWER THE FOLLOWING:

BIGELOW LAWRENCE'S WILL:

List what was left to the following:

a. Asenath, his wife, – one third of all personal property, one horse, one side saddle and one bridle. She can use ½ of the farm & orchard.

b. Ebenezer Pierce – $25.00 six months after the death

c. Eastern Society – $15.00 every year as long as the Rev'd Levi Parsons continued as minister, $100 to support the gospel, finish the meeting house or ___

___ters treated in the will in ___sons? The girls were treated poorly.

___ne half as much as the boys.

___ated differently than his brothers.
___t his share of the estate. Calvin must
___in ten years of his dad's death
___at least three years to get the estate.

___ about Mr. Lawrence's "family
___Lawrence favored his sons over his
___vide for his sons because his daughters would
___vided for.

___eave to his two daughters? He
___2000 each.

___ son, Daniel? He left the balance
and residue of his estate real and personal.

c. Nothing is left to Mrs. Mathews, John's wife. What conclusion can you make from this fact. The conclusion I can make from this is maybe his wife is dead.

Now that you have read both wills, write a "letter" to these two men explaining what you like or dislike about their wills. Include why their ideas are either appropriate or inappropriate in relation to our more modern values.

Such a lesson would be appropriate when studying Homespun roles of men and women.

- In what ways are men and women treated differently?

- Is birth order a factor to consider?

- How have these ideas changed since our study of the colonial period?

- What would the Iroquois say about a will?

- How would they respond to treating men and women (or sons and daughters) differently?

- How do people today react to such situations?

- How are women's roles different today?

3. The second day, students could read letters aloud. (I did this and it was fun). Such readings help to stimulate class discussion and can be a source of peer evaluation. It's just a simple assignment. Let's not make much more of it. It was a big hit with the kids!

ASSESSMENT

Evaluation and assessment of this lesson are accomplished in two ways:
a. class discussion during and after the assignment is completed, and
b. letters written by the students to the two men.

DOCUMENTS STUDY   NAME_____
 - WILLLS-
                                             PER._____

USING THE ATTACHED TWO WILLS, ANSWER THE FOLLOWING:

BIGELOW LAWRENCE'S WILL
1. (30 points) List what was left to the following:

    a. Asenath, his wife, _____

_____

    b. Ebenezer Pierce - _____

_____

    c.   Eastern Society - _____

_____

    d.   How are his two daughters treated in the will in comparison to his eight sons?_____

_____

_____

    e. Calvin, son # 9, is treated differently than his brothers. Tell what he must do to get his share of the estate._____

_____

_____

    f. What does this tell you about Mr. Lawrence's "family values?"_____

_____

2. (20 Points) JOHN MATHEW'S WILL:

    a. What does John Mathews leave to his two daughters?_____

_____

    b. What does he leave to his son, Daniel?

_____

    c. Nothing is left to Mrs. Mathews, John's wife. What conclusion can you make from this fact? _____

_____

3. (50 points) Now that you have read both wills, write a 'letter" to these two men explaining what you like or dislike about their wills. Include why their ideas are either appropriate or inappropriate in relation to our more modern values.

REFLECTION

This lesson provides a concrete example to students for evaluating historical documents, analysis of values and customs and reinforces reading and writing skills.

Law and Life in
Two Ancient
Societies

Standards & Performance Indicators

SS 2
- ▲ define culture/civilization
- ▲ norms and values of Western/other cultures
- ▲ interpret/analyze documents/artifacts

SS 5
- ▲ values of nation/international organizations affect human rights

Students are introduced to document-based questions in the first month or two of the school year. They are also introduced to charting information and analyzing its impact.

While this learning experience is done with grade 10 students, it would be part of the grade nine course under the new Global History scope and sequence.

Francine Mazza

Ramapo Central School District

Ramapo High School

400 Viola road

Spring Valley, New York 10977

(914) 577-6446

 Grade 10

This is a two-day classroom activity within a series of lessons in a unit. The students may have an introduction to ancient civilizations or the lesson may be used to introduce the unit. The teacher rotates from group to group guiding students, when necessary, with questioning. Each group is instructed to select a guide and a recorder. Students compare/contrast Mesopotamian Law to Hebrew Law as it relates to how each society values women, social responsibility, negligence, and equality under law. They chart their findings on the outlined chart so it will be a natural progression to answering questions about values in these two societies. The class moves from charted information to critical conclusions/evaluations. Finally, the class discusses the values of those societies and how American law/values is related.

1. Compare / Contrast the values of these two ancient societies.

Women in Hebrew society were almost are equal as men. They could remarry after being divorce. Women in Mesopotamia were 2nd class citizens, they were like object or property of men. Men gave their wife or children it pay off their debts. Women were drowned for being disreet but they did have alimony if the man was to divorce his wife.

Laws were different for different social classes in Mesopotamia society. Plebeian would get the eye for eye, tooth for tooth treatment. When patrician did wrong they got the eye for money and hand for money treatment. In Hebrew society If a man hurt his servant or maid, they shall only be set free for the sake of whatever was hurt.

Negligence in Hebrew society was if an ox kills a man or a women the ox shall die. owners of an ox was to keep an eye on them and if someone got hurt the ox was always killed and sometimes the owner. In Mesopotamia society it was like an ox for an ox.

Social responsibility in mesopotamia socity was if food didn't grow on land you rented you are still responible. Hebrew socity they are considerable with food, leaving some for strangers and the poor.

Materials:

■ Copies of *Code of Hammurabi*

■ Copies of parts of *Old Testament* for each student

2. What is the origin of Hebrew Law? Mesopotamian Law?

The origin of Hebrew Laws came from Moses who was a prophet, and lawgiver of Jews. It says in the Bible, Moses saw G*d face to face. From G*d he recieved the Ten Commandments for his people. These were the laws which became the foundation for the Jewish religion. The Commandments are recorded in full in Exodus, XX, 2-7, and in Deuteronomy, V, 6-21.

The origin of Mesopotamian Laws came from King Hammurabi, who wrote the Code of Hammurabi. The code was inscribed on a stele. At the top of the stele, Hammurabi was pictured receiving the laws from a g*d although most of the laws were already old and had long been in writing.

3. Compare / Contrast the ancient Egyptians to the Mesopotamians and
   Hebrews.

The ancient Egyptians and Mesopotamians were polytheistic while Hebrews were monotheistic.

The Hebrews and Egyptians were very considerable with there food when farming.

Egyptians were farmers and craftsmen while Hebrews and Mesopotamians were farmers.

Egyptians had pharaohs and nobles who were rich The rest of the people lived simple lives. Mesopotami had different social classes, plebeians who were the poor people and the patricians who were the rich people.

Women in ancient Egypt and Hebrew women were almost as equal as men. Women in Mesopotamia were 2nd class citizens, although they did have some rights such as alimony but were drowned when they cheated.

Critical Conclusions/Evaluations Questions

182

Claudeen

Comparing Law and Values in two ancient societies

Compare	Mesopotamians	Hebrews
Equality Law: Exodus, Ch. 21 #26 and 27 vs. Hammurabi's #196, 197,198 & 199	If a plebeian commit a crime they get the eye for an eye treatment, but when patrician commits a crime they pay a certain amount of money.	If man hurts any body part of his servants or maids, they shall go free for the sake of this part.
Negligence: Exodus, Ch. 21 #28, 29 & 32 vs. Hammurabi's #245 & 251	If a man loans his ox to another man, and has caused the death of the ox he will repay with an ox. If an ox is a killer and its owner doesn't silence the ox, and the ox kills a free man the owner will pay	If an ox kills a man or a woman the ox shall be killed. If the owner had been warned about his ox and did nothing, the owner and ox shall die. If a servant was killed the owner will pay the master and the ox will die.
Social Resp: Leviticus, Ch. 19 #9 & 10 Hammurabi's #42	If a man rents land for farming and no crops grow, he shall still be responsible for no food being grown and pay an average rent.	Don't think of yourself only when your taking up food from your feild, but leave some for the poor and strangers.
Women: Deuteronomy, Ch. 24 #1 & 2 vs. Hammurabi's # 138, 143, 117 & 128	Women and children were 2nd class citizens.	If a man had married his wife but then finds out he doesn't love her. He can divorce her and send her out of his house. She may them go be another man's wife. Women were almost as equal as man.

REFLECTION

I enjoy the lesson because it requires higher order thinking skills and uses the content to impress values on students. The lesson should be expanded to include other ancient civilizations that will be part of the new world history course.

REFLECTION:

Assessment

Student self-grading sheet. All other team members must sign it. Signatures equal approval of self-grade. Six categories are worth up to four points each for a total of 24 points of grade.

Member of a Team Scoring Guide (Rubric)

School Year: _____

Student: _____

Grade/Course: _____

STUDENT PERFORMANCE

SCORING CRITERIA	*4. Excellent	*3. Good *STANDARD	2. Needs some Improvement	1. Needs much Improvement	NA
Group Participation Participated in group discussion without prompting. Did fair share of the work.					
Staying on Topic Paid attention, listened to what was being said and done. Made comments aimed at getting the group back to the topic.					
Offering Useful Ideas Gave ideas and suggestions that helped the group. Offered helpful criticism and comments.					
Consideration Made positive, encouraging remarks about group members and their ideas. Gave recognition and credit to others for their ideas.					
Involving Others Got others involved by asking questions, requesting input or challenging others. Tried to get the group together to reach group agreements.					
Communicating Spoke clearly. Was easy to hear and understand. Expressed ideas clearly and effectively.					

NOTE: NA represents a response to the performance which is "not appropriate."

This scoring guide may be used by a student for the purpose of self-assessment, to score the work of an individual student, and to obtain a composite profile on the performance of the class.

COMMENTS:

LAW AND LIFE IN TWO ANCIENT SOCIETIES
GRADING RUBRIC

Chart	students draw logical, specific conclusions in all 8 boxes of the chart **19 points**	students draw logical specific conclusions in most of the boxes in the chart **16 points**
	students draw logical specific conclusion in half of the boxes **13 points**	students reword the statements as they are given in the readings **9 points**
Question Number 1	students cite 4 values of Mesop. and 4 values of Hebrews as they relate to each of the four categories (equality, women, etc.) with reference to similarities and differences **19 points**	students cite most of the values of Mesop. and Hebrews and make some reference to similarities and differences **16 points**
	students cite some of the values of each society but do not make any reference to similarity or differences **13 points**	students do not make any value judgements. Students repeat the laws as they are given in the readings and make no comparisons **9 points**
Question Number 2	students cite the origin of Hebrew Law(god) and Mesop. Law(Hammurabi) and comment on the spiritual vs. Earthly difference **19 points**	students cite the origin of Hebrew Law and Mesop. Law **16 points**
	students cite the origin of only one of the laws (either Hebrew or Mesop.)	the origins are incorrect for both Mesop. and Hebrews
Question Number 3	students cite at least three specific societal similarities for their decision and effectively draw the connection between the two societies **19 points**	students cite 3 specific reasons for their decision but fail to draw the connection between the two societies **16 points**
	students use 1-2 specific similarities for their decision **13 points**	students use incorrect facts (9 points)* or did not attempt to answer the question **0 points***

*Please note that there are two grading options in this one section! ! ! !

185

COMMENCEMENT

Standards & Performance Indicators

Student Investigation of a Key Public Policy Issue
in Participation in

GOVERNMENT AND ECONOMICS

SS

4

▲ identify/locate/evaluate economic information

▲ apply problem-solving model to economic problems

SS

5

▲ analyze issues

▲ take/defend/evaluate positions on attitudes

Joseph Corr, John DeGuardi

Diane Hobdan, Donald Mion

Thomas Pallas

North Colonie Central Schools

Shaker High School

445 Waterliet-Shaker Road

Latham, New York 12110

(518) 785-5511, FAX (518) 783-5905

Grade 12

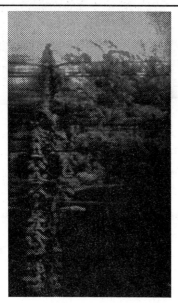

The ability to analyze a public policy issue is critical to good citizenship. To be truly informed on an issue and to make knowledgeable decisions about it requires knowledge of multiple viewpoints, individuals, and past and proposed legislation. Furthermore, electronically accessing information allows for expansion of knowledge to include databases, information retrieval systems, and other library and museum resources throughout the world.

What Students Do:

- Select and analyze a public policy issue.

- Create a hot list of web sites that have been explored and investigated as a result of a web search on the Internet. The list must include the accurate web address, a brief description of each web site explaining why it is useful and/or for what it is used, a list of email addresses, and at least one contact.

- Access two different viewpoints on the issue via CD ROM. Submit a hard copy of these sources with a brief description of why the source was or was not useful.

- Locate information through traditional/print methods including textbook searching, magazine articles, first-person interviews, television reports, newspapers, microfilm, or other sources. Obtain two viewpoints from the above sources, one in favor of the topic position and one opposed to the topic/position.

- Create a journal in which students reflect upon the search process citing searches and resources they found useful and productive and those they found to be frustrating and difficult. The journal must indicate the reasons for success or failure of a particular search and offer evidence of substantial time on task.

- Produce a group *Hot Issue Newsletter* containing the following:

  ○ a list of useful web sties and e-mail addresses

  ○ a summary of positions on all sides of the issue

  ○ a list of key individuals involved in the issue

  ○ two visuals, one of which is a political cartoon, the other a student created graphic representation

  ○ information incorporated from previous stations.

- Individually produce a position letter following the format of the National Issues Forum and send it via e-mail to one or more of the following:

  ○ elected public officials

  ○ editors of news periodicals

  ○ corporate leaders.

- Function effectively as a cooperative work group.

Dewey or Truman 1948, Environmental Bond Act Pass or not 1996

Albany - In 1948, Truman went to bed thinking he was the loser. In the morning he was the President. Forty eight years later, when New Yorkers looked at the election results one last time Tuesday night before going to bed, they thought the bond act was defeated. The reason was, with 73% of the polls reporting, the bond measure was losing by 8 points. The next morning many New Yorkers awoke to surprising news, the bond won with 56% of the vote.

How could this dramatic change happen? On Tuesday night most of the precinct reporting were from upstate New York. When the New York city precincts finally tallied their votes, the upstate landslide in defeat changed to a downstate landslide in approval.

It wasn't surprising that New York city voters wanted this passed, while upstate New Yorkers wanted it defeated. It has been suggested that 1.3 billion, or 77 percent, of the money conceivably could go to New York City projects.

Actually, specific projects aren't detailed in the bond act legislation. Now that New York voters approved the borrowing, eligible projects will have to compete for funding, and they'll be reviewed by technical experts in state environmental and park agencies.

Editorial

It is about time that the voters got a chance to decided if they want to fund an environmental project or not. New York does need to spend more money on the environment. If not, the future of this state will be grim.

The Bond Act will provide funding for much needed clean water, clean air, land conservation and waste site cleanup activities. It will improve drinking water facilities, solid wastes areas, and encourage environmentally sound technologies.

The money New Yorkers pay for this act will be used for the enjoyment and future of all. Most money that is paid in taxes aren+t always paid back directly to the taxpayer, but this act is different. Every person will be paid back Whenever they walk through a cleaner park, drink water, fish, swim, or breath.

The people who are complaining about this Bond act should think about how much they enjoy the environmental before they open their mouths.

Tony

The Editor Speaks

The time has come to determine what is more important: the obese funding of the defense industry, which swallows massive amounts of capital with no visible product or additional funding for environmental preservation and protection, currently undefended and undersurpported by those who stand in a position to lend their support.

Whi

le it is possible to ignore any political issue for an extended period of time, until it becomes a rallying cry for an unknown group, the environment must cease to be a political issue and become strictly a matter of common sense.

It is uncomprehendable to imagine that anyone would not favor increased funding for a cause so benevolent as the environment, and while the Clean Water, Clean Air Bond Act recently proposed in New York State passed by a fair margin, it was still widely protested by groups of mostly middle and upper class citizens, who have children whom will reap the harvest of their parent's greed. The bond act means an additional $3.25 per tax payer, per year for the next 20 years. For the price of a cup of coffee and a donut the citizens of NYS could improve their environment on a grand scale.

As a member of the Nature Conservancy I heartily believe in increased funding of the environment. I find it hard to believe that a general apathy for the environment can be the universal feeling of the public majority. Unless the current level of funding is increased the environment is in most certain danger of destruction by industrial landfills, suburban sprall and the American tendency toward disposable goods. We must act now or it will soon be to late.

Learner Outcomes:

- to recognize key issues in public policy debates, examine all sides, and defend positions on the issues

- to become knowledgeable and competent in the tools of the electronic work place, including electronic mail, CD ROM, and on-line services

- to enhance skills relative to data collection through the use of online resources, CD ROM, e-mail, print resources, interviews, and speakers

- to organize, analyze, and interpret data collected into a newsletter informing classmates about the multiple aspects of an issue

- to work effectively as a cooperative group.

- to take action on an issue by writing a letter to involved individuals and agencies explaining one's position and, where appropriate, prescribing a specific response.

Groups will be created to study a public policy issue. Each group will be required to use a variety of sources, both electronic and traditional print, to analyze a public policy issue. Class time and time after school will be utilized to collect information on the issue through the use of online services, e-mail, CD ROM information banks, print resources, interviews, and speakers. Each individual student will be required to keep a journal that reflects upon their successes and difficulties when engaged in electronic searching. The following represent the objectives for each search section:

Online Objectives

1. Create a Hot List that pertains to your issue. This Hot List is a list of web sites that you have explored and investigated as a result of your web search on the Internet.

2. Each Hot List must contain:

   a list of web sites' accurate addresses

   a brief description of each web site explaining why it is useful and/or what it is used for, a list of e-mail addresses, and at least one contact.

CD ROM Objectives

1. Using CD ROM sources, locate information on your project. Obtain two different viewpoints on your issue.

2. Submit a hard copy of any information you accessed via CD-ROM with a brief description of whether the source was useful or not and reasons why it was or was not useful.

Speaker Presentation Group Objectives

1. Choose an issue or topic. Find resource persons or organizations related to the issue. Include name, address, and phone number.

2. Group must find speakers who represent views on a particular side of an issue. Two such speakers must be contacted in order to present their viewpoint to the class at large. Speakers may be contacted via letter, phone, or email.

3. All issues and speakers must meet the approval of instructor prior to any arrangements being made. A speaker request form must be approved by the social studies supervisor, Mr. Corr.

4. A directory must be kept by group of persons or organizations contacted.

5. An outline of topics or subtopics must be prepared to address points of interest the group wants speakers to address. This should be typed in standard form and presented to class for discussion.

6. Compile a list of e-mail addresses of speakers on both sides of the issue.

Traditional/Print Objectives

1. Locate information on your project by using the following methods: textbook searches, magazine articles, first-person interviews, television reports, newspapers, microfilm, etc.

2. From TWO of the above sources, obtain TWO viewpoints, ONE in favor of your topic/position and ONE in opposition to your topic/position.

3. Then, submit from your group to your teacher for inspection the hard copy of the item(s) that have been researched using traditional search methods.

Groups will then be required to produce a *Hot Issue Newsletter* containing the:
- a hot list of useful web sites and e-mail addresses
- a summary of positions on all sides of the issue
- a list of key individuals involved in the issue
- two visuals, one of which is a political cartoon, the other a student created graphic representation
- information incorporated from previous stations.

After the newsletter has been completed, each individual student is to produce a position letter. This letter should follow the format of the National Issues Forum and should be sent via e-mail to one or more of the following:
- elected public officials
- editors of news periodicals
- corporate leaders

Assessment

ASSESSMENT

The completed project will be evaluated using a rubric (scoring guide) to measure four components in varying amounts. You must complete all four components of the project for it to be accepted. The following is a list of the project components and their grading value:

REFLECTIVE JOURNAL RUBRIC

EXEMPLARY	PROFICIENT	SATISFACTORY	NEEDS IMPROVEMENT	UNACCEPTABLE
•A thorough and complete listing of resources is given using proper citation as specified in the <u>Shaker High School Guide to Research</u>.	•A thorough and complete listing of resources is given using proper citation as specified in the <u>Shaker High School Guide to Research</u>.	•Listing of most resources is given with few errors in citation.	•Listing of resources is incomplete and/or contains significant errors in citation.	•Fails to list the resources used in the search.
•Reflective commentary includes an evaluation of all resources with specific reasons offered as to the usefulness or lack of usefulness of each specific resource.	•Reflective commentary includes an evaluation of resources with specific reasons offered as to the usefulness or lack of usefulness of most specific resources.	•Reflective commentary includes some evaluation of resources with some specifics offered as to usefulness or lack of usefulness of resources.	•Reflective commentary merely summarizes content of resources. Little or no evaluation offered.	Little or no reflective commentary.
•Evidence of outstanding effort and time on task.	•Evidence of substantial effort and time on task.	•Evidence of satisfactory effort and time on task.	•Evidence of inconsistent effort and time on task.	•Evidence of minimal or no effort. Attention to task is infrequent or nonexistent.

POINT BREAKDOWNS

Reflective Journal
20%

Exemplary	18-20 points
Proficient	16-17 points
Satisfactory	14-15 points
Needs Improvement	12-13 points
Unsatisfactory	Below 11 points

TOTAL:

Letter
10%

Exemplary	9-10 points
Proficient	8 points
Satisfactory	7 points
Needs Improvement	6 points
Unsatisfactory	Below 6 points

TOTAL:

Group Process
20%

Exemplary	18-20 points
Proficient	16-17 points
Satisfactory	14-15 points
Needs Improvement	12-13 points
Satisfactory	Below 11 points

TOTAL:

Newsletter
50%

Exemplary	47-50 points
Proficient	42-44 points
Satisfactory	37-39 points
Needs Improvement	33-35 points
Unsatisfactory	Below 32

TOTAL:

FINAL MARK: _____

Letter Rubric

	OUTSTANDING	COMMENDABLE	COMPETENT	NEEDS IMPROVEMENT	UNACCEPTABLE
QUALITY OF INFORMATION	*Accurate information *Uses 2 or more specific examples *demonstrates a clear understanding of the issue	*Accurate information **Uses at least 2 specific examples *Demonstrates an understanding of the issue	*Generally accurate information *Uses 1 example *Demonstrates a general understanding of the issue	*Generally inaccurate information *Uses no example *Has a vague understanding of the issue	*Inaccurate information *No example *Has little or no understanding of the issue
ORGANIZATION AND STYLE	*Letter is clear and concise yet thoughtfully presented *Writer makes his/her point while remaining polite and complimentary	*Letter is clear and concise *Point is made in a polite manner	*Letter is generally to the point *Tone of the letter is generally polite	*Letter is unclear and poorly put together *Letter is neither polite nor impolite	*Letter is wordy and/or vague and poorly put together *Letter is not courteous
ACCURACY	*Grammatically perfect *No spelling errors *Format is followed perfectly	*Few, if any, grammatical errors *Few, if any, spelling errors *Format is followed perfectly	*No serious errors in grammar *No serious errors in spelling *Format is generally followed	*Basic grammar needs improvement *Basic spelling needs improvement *Format is partially followed	*Many grammatical errors *Many spelling errors *Format is disregarded

GROUP PROCESS RUBRIC

EXEMPLARY	PROFICIENT	SATISFACTORY	NEEDS IMPROVEMENT	UNACCEPTABLE
•all students enthusiastically participate	•almost all students actively participate	•some ability to participate	•strong reliance on one or two spokespersons	•exclusive reliance on one spokesperson
•students reflect awareness of others' views and opinions	•students reflect awareness of others' views and opinions	•students generally reflect awareness of others' views and opinions	•students reflect some effort to reflect others' views and opinions	•students reflect little or no effort to reflect others' views and opinions
•consistent preparedness of notes, discussion, and evidence of planning	•consistent preparedness of notes, discussion, and evidence of planning	•generally prepared	•inconsistent preparedness	•consistently unprepared

NEWSLETTER RUBRIC

EXEMPLARY	PROFICIENT	SATISFACTORY	NEEDS IMPROVEMENT	UNACCEPTABLE
•All for components are present.	•All four components are present.	•All four components are present.	•Missing one of the four project components.	•Missing more than one component of the project.
•"Hot List" clearly and concisely provides useful and accurate information.	•"Hot List" provides useful and accurate information.	•"Hot List" provides useful and accurate information.	•"Hot List" provides some useful information. May contain errors.	"Hot List" fails to provide useful information.
•Summary thoroughly, specifically and accurately discusses both sides of the issue and identifies the key individuals involved in the issue.	•Summary includes mostly specific information. Both sides of the issue are clearly discussed. However, one side may not be discussed as thoroughly, specifically or clearly as the other.	•Summary is a general discussion of the issues and individuals involved. May lack specifics on one or both sides of the issue.	•Fails to address one side of the issue.	•Summary fails to discuss the issue in any meaningful manner.
•Graphics are clear and enhance the reader's understanding of the issue. Attention to presentation is evident.	•Graphics are related to the topic. Attention to presentation evident.	•Graphics are generally related to the topic. Some attention to presentation.	•Graphics are remotely reflective of the issue. Little attention to presentation.	•Graphics fail to reflect the issue. No attention to presentation.

REFLECTION

As a group product, there existed opportunities to demonstrate multiple intelligences. For example, students were required to search and arrange for speakers as an effective group. (interpersonal). The requirement of producing a graphic appealed to the visual/motor domain. Students were accorded the opportunity to demonstrate what they can do and know in an arena other than "on demand" traditional pencil and paper exam.

Social Studies

Appendix

Resources

The use of primary sources and other documents should be an integral part of a social studies program. Students should learn how to analyze historical documents and prepare essays and reports that describe different perspectives on various historical issues, events, and questions. An important resource for teachers to use as they incorporate documents into their instructional programs is *Consider the Source: Historical Records in the Classroom* (State Archives and Records Administration), available from the Publications Sales Desk (518-474-3806).

Additional documents can be found on a number of websites including the following:*

American Historical Association . .http://www.theaha.org
American Presidents . . . . .http://www.americanpresidents.org
Amnesty International . . . . .http://www.amnesty.org.uk/fastindex.html
The Armonk Institute . . . . .http://www.armonkinstitute.org/
Asia Society: Ask Asia . . . . .http://www.askasia.org/for_educators/fe_frame.htm
BBC Online Network . . . . .http://news.bbc.co.uk/
British Library . . . . .http://www.bl.uk/welcome.html
British Maps Home Page . . . . .http://www1.pitt.edu/~medart/menuengl/mainmaps.html
Capital District Council for the
    Social Studies . . . . .http://home.nycap.rr.com/cdcss/
Central New York Council for the
    Social Studies http://www.lm.liverpool.k12.ny.us/cnycss2/cnycss.html
CNN World News . . . . .http://cnn.com/WORLD/
Economic Education Web . . . . . . .http://ecedweb.unomaha.edu/home.htm
Edsitement . . . . .http://www.edsitement.neh.gov/
Federal Resources for Educational
    Excellence-Social Studies . . . . .http://www.ed.gov/free/s-social.html
Gilder Lehrman Collection . . . . . . .http://www.gilderlehrman.com
Internet History Sourcebook
    Project .http://www.fordham.edu/halsall/
Historical Atlas of the
    20th Century http://users.erols.com/mwhite28/20centry.htm
History: Central VCatalogue . . . . .http://www.ukans.edu/history/VL/
The History Net . . . . .http://www.thehistorynet.com/THNarchives/WorldHistory/
Law, Youth, and Citizenship . . . . . .http://www.nysba.org/lyc/LYC.html
The Library of Congress . . . . .http://www.loc.gov/
The Library of Congress
    Country Studies http://lcweb2.loc.gov/frd/cs/cshome.html
Lower East Side Tenement
    Museum . . . . .http://www.wnet.org/tenement
Map Collections: 1544-1996 . . . . . .http://memory.loc.gov/ammem/gmdhtml/gmdhome.html

National Archives . . . . .http://nara.gov (future site http://www.nationalarchives.com/)
National Archives and
   Record Administration:
   The Constitution Community . .http://www.nara.gov/education/cc/main.html
National Archives and
   Record Administration:
   The Digital Classroom . . . . .http://www.nara.gov/education/classrm.html
National Archives and
   Record Administration:
   Presidential Libraries . . . . .http://www.nara.gov/nara/president/address.html
National Council for the
   Social Studies . . . . .http://www.ncss.org/
National Council on Economic
   Education . . . . .http://www.nationalcouncil.org
National Gallery of Art . . . . .http://www.nga.gov/
National Geographic Society . . . . .http://www.nationalgeographic.com
The National Park Service . . . . .http://www.nps.gov
National Register of Historic
   Places . . . . .http://www.cr.nps.gov/nr/twhp/home.html
NATO 50th Anniversary http://ac.acusd.edu/history/20th/nato50.html
New York State Archives and
   Records Administration . . . . . . .http://www.sara.nysed.gov/
New York State Council for the
   Social Studies . . . . .http://www.nyscss.org/
PBS Online .http://www.pbs.org/
Perry Castañeda Library . . . . .http://www.lib.utexas.edu/Libs/PCL/Map_collection/Map_collection.html
Project WhistleStop . . . . .http://www.whistlestop.org/
SUNY New Paltz Department of
   Geography . . . . .http://www.newpaltz.edu/geography/links.html
US State Department . . . . .http://www.state.gov/
University of Cambridge http://www.classics.cam.ac.uk/Faculty/links1c.html
University of Texas at Austin . . . . .http://www.utexas.edu/index.html
Virtual Library History Index . . . . .http://www.msu.edu/~georgem1/history/medieval.htm
Women Watch . . . . .http://www.un.org/womenwatch/
Women's History Sourcebook . . . .http://www.fordham.edu/halsall/women/womensbook.html
Yale University Library . . . . .http://www.library.yale.edu/humanities/history/index.html